BODY LANGUAGE

and
Behavioral Profiling

M A R K H. F O R D, JD

authorHOUSE®

AuthorHouse™
1663 Liberty Drive
Bloomington, IN 47403
www.authorhouse.com
Phone: 1-800-839-8640

First published by AuthorHouse 10/27/2010

ISBN: 978-1-4520-4943-4 (e)
ISBN: 978-1-4520-4942-7 (sc)

Library of Congress Control Number: 2010910710

Printed in the United States of America

This book is printed on acid-free paper.

Dedication

To the loyal believers in the
the power of body language.

Contents

Introduction

Human development occurred in different parts of the world at different times, yet people have remained linked to each other throughout the ages. The 16th century English metaphysical poet, John Donne, expressed it best in *Meditation XVII:* "No man is an island, entire of itself; every man is a piece of the continent, a part of the main; ...therefore never send to know for whom the bell tolls; it tolls for thee". Indeed, nobody is isolated and no one is alone as long as people communicate with each other.

Intercommunications are absolutely essential to survival and reproduction in a hostile world of limited resources. As a result, early-day humans learned to communicate with each other in numerous ways. They developed verbal expressions into languages that conveyed the facts of their reality in the world around them, and most importantly, effective nonverbal communications that conveyed such things as heartfelt attitudes, social status, and strong emotions like compassion and love.

At ground zero, life depends upon communications organized and understood within basic social structures created and put in place by the members of all the different races. People naturally developed speech because verbal communication is the basic mechanism for expressing the brain's objective response to external stimuli. For example, people use words to describe their reality, and the verbal feedback they obtain tells them who, where, and what they are.

Nonverbal communications, on the other hand, express feelings, attitudes and thoughts that are arguably the most important dimension of the intercommunication equation. They are more personal and subjective than the objectivity of verbal speech. Effective intercommunications evolved from the adaptive cooperation of both forms of communicating.

In the new millennium, digitizing verbal speech and curtailing nonverbal language through powerful new technologies threaten to scuttle the beauty and effectiveness of human intercommunications, unless people will increasingly recognize and appreciate the bonding value of nonverbal communications in daily life, as well as the role it plays in revealing the inner purposes of human activity.

Social science research has unleashed new marketing tools that utilize number crunching, data evaluating, and information grinding, among others to profile consumers. Geographical purchasing patterns, *data mining,* and the *revealed purposes* approaches are new ways of interpreting and predicting the future behavior of customers and their buying patterns. Businesses are able to form better relationships with customers by using these tools in lieu of relying on what customers say about themselves in more or less objective surveys and questionnaires. The underlying principal is: actions speak louder than words.

Adaptive psychology is an updated discipline of great interest to jurisprudence, since it focuses on how and why people's brains function in situations that require instant judgments and quick decision-making. How we perceive others and how they perceive us has been a factor in legal court cases since the beginning of lawsuits in courtrooms. For just one example out of thousands, Harvard professor Joseph Beale's *Selection of Cases and Other Authorities upon Criminal Law* published over a hundred years ago in 1907, reports a Connecticut Supreme Court case, that said in pertinent part, "That he (i.e. the defendant) is considerably below par in intellect is apparent to us all. This is indicated by his countenance and general appearance".

Every trial has two important elements: the verbal or what people hear and the nonverbal or what people see. Jurors make their minds up early and then look for evidence to support their initial conclusions. They filter out evidence that is non supportive. As it a result, complicated trials are often won or lost in the first few hours.

Plaintiffs in tort cases automatically get a big advantage by employing body language that makes a good first impression, because jurors initially want to give injured people money. Little "slices" of information gained from first impressions lead to quick evaluations that are difficult to change. On the other side, defendants also want sympathetic jurors, but persuading them takes longer because many jurors have already put on their subjective blinders.

A good example of what can happen in a trial is the O. J. Simpson murder trial. In a survey for *U. S. News & World Report* after the acquittal of football and movie star O. J. Simpson for the murder of Nicole Brown Simpson, forty-eight per cent of the respondents agreed with the statement: "Jury decisions will always be based largely on personal prejudices".

The Simpson case received world-wide attention due to the sensational evidence of the domestic violence in the Simpson marriage. Astonishingly, the evidence revealed that Nicole Simpson had called the police eight times alleging that she had been beaten, and O. J. had pleaded "no contest" to hitting and threatening to kill her in 1989, for which he paid a $700 dollar fine. Moreover, in the murder investigation, the police found traces of her blood on his car, and in his bedroom. Even so, one juror in O. J. Simpson's murder trial said afterwards that she thought he was innocent from the very first day. The mountain of forensic evidence against him, and the months of trial, apparently had little impact on defendant Simpson's hand-picked jury. He was later found guilty in a civil trial.

Jury nullification of the facts and law is nothing new however. In my opinion, nearly all trials are eighty percent over after the opening statements. As I said earlier, a majority of typical jurors make up their minds quickly, and changing their conclusions is an uphill battle.

Putting lawsuits aside, ponder the fact that there are over six billion people in the world, and all told they speak some nine thousand languages and dialects. The largest number, well over a billion people speak Chinese, and English is the second most widely spoken language of over three hundred and fifty million people. Another billion and one-half people use English worldwide making it the language of over one-third of the world's population.

Next, consider that The *Oxford English Dictionary* collectively contains over a half-million words; however, ordinary Americans speak "marketplace English". That is because the everyday vocabulary of most Americans seldom consists of more than two to three thousand words which they use repeatedly. This economy of speech plus the many restrictions and limitations of widespread cultural diversity, dialect, and diction make it easy to understand why individual discourse is limited.

Humans, however, are extremely clever in devising wonderful nonverbal techniques to supplement their lack of vocabulary. Everyone, to one degree or another, has a personal array of nonverbal skills that express their innermost attitudes, feelings, and beliefs in ways that other people quickly and clearly understand.

Americans spend an increasing amount of their time texting each other. On average, Americans incredibly now send twice as many texts as phone calls. *The Week* magazine reports that American teenagers send and receive an average of 1,742 text messages per month. In my opinion, the people who ignore body language and continue thinking only of oral speech and written communications will pay a stiff price in lost communications. Although cell phones companies tout instant voice and digital text messaging, for a fee of course, as a new way of communicating, the technology fad will never be able to include everything that everyone wants, and by nature will be limited to compressed conversations and short text messages.

As far as text messaging goes, writing everything down in choppy abbreviated clips makes a poor conversation. Instant feedback is gone as well as how the writer feels about what is being written. Moreover, it takes time to compose, and is subject to volumes of grammar, syntax, style, and spelling rules. Furthermore, potential readers are usually remote in time and distance, and unintended written errors and omissions are not instantly correctible, thus giving readers the wrong idea.

One plus for written communications may be that writing something down allows extra time to reflect. Writers do not get tongue-tied and are always able to let some air in any written dialogue by taking their time. In addition, text can be preserved and analyzed repeatedly. It is well-established that everyone has a style of writing, which is a form of body language. For example, handwriting reveals traits such as whether the writer is sloppy or neat, educated or uneducated, long-winded or not, and so forth, but having made this point, that is another subject altogether.

Here is the thing. Americans live in a society that provides them with a steady flow of new technology from computers, cell phones, cable and satellite services, broadband, mobile devices, and hundreds of applications. Social networking on the Internet has absolutely exploded since the first weblog went online in 1999. Today, there are a 112 million blogs with an incredible 175 thousand new blogs created worldwide every single day.

Americans have more information pushed at them every day than anyone could have ever imagined. According to *The Week* magazine for Jan.25-Dec.08, 2010, the average American spends close to seventy percent of their waking hours in consuming information. That translates into about twelve hours a day of viewing so-called Internet "content", and absorbing nearly thirty-four "gigs" of data. Americans have so much going on that it is difficult for them to find enough time to keep up with everything new and still keep their already hard-earned communication and social skills. It is like trying to drink water from a high-pressure nozzle.

It is reductionist logic, but a blog is only as good as its content, and much of it is execrable. Quality issues and the tendency to promote "groupthink" are difficult to mitigate without the interpretive value of behavioral body language. Electronic communications lack the "human touch", the interpersonal pleasures that result in valuable social skills being "left in the lurch". Without the ability to interpret, manage, and use body language in the new millennium, people risk being socially overwhelmed. People may know how to text message each other, but not how to shake hands.

Nonverbal communications can help people get through the day, maintain their equilibrium, form identities, present themselves better, and sustain important relationships. If we have to make quick decisions with little or no information to go on, body language can help to tell us such things as whether a person's personality is structured or unstructured, passive or aggressive, social or antisocial, and in so doing provide us with a quick response that could save our money or our life.

As people find out more about each other over time, they compare themselves to their peer group through specialized body language in order to cultivate their self-image, and discover what kind of attitudes prevail in different areas of daily living, and which emotions are acceptable. This is a catalyst for opening doors to productive relationships both socially and in business. Simply put, nonverbal communications function as an indispensable part of "us".

An overlooked factor in the study of behavioral body language is its historical ties. Body language is organic and undergoes many changes over time. New body language continually comes into existence, while time tested expressions, gestures, and movements remain powerful. Often, body language originates in one context, but over time ends up expressing something else. Arcane meanings fall by the wayside, but new ones step up, because most humans loathe getting rid of anything useful.

Unfortunately, some older behavioral signs, gestures, and expressions become difficult to understand on a comprehensive basis, and traditions as immense as classical body language do not survive in a linear fashion. As a result, the significance of body language became unclear, relative, and subject to widespread cultural variants.

Despite sporadic attempts to demystify and unify the multi-ethnic adaptations of nonverbal communications in the early days of human history, it took the nineteenth century speculative work of the British naturalist Charles Darwin to revolutionize things.

Today, molecular biology, the unraveling of DNA, genetic blueprinting, and brain imaging are transforming our understanding of human behavior. Whether or not Darwin is correct in his evolutionary thesis set forth in *The Origin of Species* published in 1859 is not the point. The point is that much body language behavior is "species" specific instead of "culture specific". In a great leap forward, Darwin rejected historical and causal explanations in favor of micro targeting unique aspects of behavior in a scientific way that makes more sense than folklore and mythology.

During the latter half of the twentieth century, genuine attempts to evaluate nonverbal communications on a systematic and collective basis gained speed from largely back channel studies after WWII. In the 1970s, however, the study of nonverbal communications spectacularly emerged from its backwater status to a serious discipline. It continues unabated today in areas of genuine science such as genetics, biology, psychology, and most importantly, the social sciences.

Transcending the customary lag between emergent trends and entrenched cultural institutions, the rapid discovery of the many ways people communicate with each other is a stunning phenomenon in contemporary America. For example, successful trial lawyers know that judges and juries decide cases from the verbal and nonverbal information they accumulate and interpret according to their respective experiences and cognitive styles. The verbal part encompasses direct questioning, cross examination, and documentary evidence presentation while the nonverbal part concentrates on body language dynamics.

Practiced trial attorneys know that success often depends on the "attitudinal" and "people" aspects of trials as much as the physical evidence. For example, not long ago, an eighty-nine year old plaintiff and her grown children got an $800,000 dollar verdict in a thorny negligence case wherein they sought lifetime damages. Instead of view-ing the six plaintiffs as very old people wanting money, the plaintiff's lawyer realized the key to success was connecting with his clients, and more importantly, the jury in a personal way.

Their lawyer was inspired to get away from the ages of the victim and children, and stress a point that really hit the jury's hot button: the love between a mother and her children. He used a children's book in his closing argument that had the jurors weeping. He said afterwards, and I am paraphrasing, "It's not about sleight of hand; it's not about the letter of the law; it's about getting past being a lawyer and emphasizing the human issues in the case".

In a civil trial, plaintiffs need to look as if they could use some money and deserve it. In criminal trials, a defendant's overall appearance should be inconsistent with the crime charged. If defendants look guilty, it is best to take the jury's focus off them. In the same vein, a witnesses' appearance and demeanor should complement his courtroom role.

In a criminal case, motive and design may be fixed, opportunity established, and the means set forth in an indictment drawn up by the prosecutor's office. Case over, right! Not at all. The weightiest part of every case comes next: the presentation of the defense via nonverbal evidence such as the countenance, dress, demeanor, and expressions of a defendant, his witnesses, and attorneys. In 1992, a national poll found that twenty percent of the jurors polled said their opinion of the lawyers in a trial was a major influence.

A trial is a campaign of persuasion. Persuasion techniques attempt to create, change, or reinforce the attitudes, beliefs, and behaviors of judges and jurors. Each juror is a separate target. Consequently, astute trial lawyers are incorporating behavioral science tools and techniques into their trial practices.

Before saying one word in court, trial attorneys display a winning attitude. "Style, body language and a degree of drama are all important", says a University of Arizona trial advocacy teacher. He offered this advice to attorneys in a newspaper article: "You have to send off subliminal messages-you're good, you're well-prepared, you believe in your case and you expect to win because you have a winning case".

Known jokingly as "putting an ascot" on a client, attorneys desire their clients to be attractive. People have a bias toward viewing attractive men and women as intelligent, interesting, competent, talented, pleasant, and sensitive. Many veteran trial lawyers say that having a client that looks good to the jury is the most important factor to winning than anything else.

Mirror and matching techniques and use of space also are keys to winning in court. Horizontal space connoted degrees of "intimacy" while vertical height implies authority and power like the judge's elevated bench. Always talk to jurors from a socially acceptable horizontal distance of three to four feet.

Good trial attorneys never invade a juror's space, unless it is preplanned. Too close is too intimate, and to far is too aloof. Our territorial space is the space around us. The longer we use it, the more it becomes ours. The closer people come to our center of territorial space, the stronger is our response.

Elective and non-elective body language is more important than speeches. A popular national newscaster said the 2008 presidential candidate debates went beyond the words of the candidates. People want to observe presidential candidates in action to see who "looks" the most presidential.

In business, executives know that consumers buy products with an awareness of the message their choices signal to neighbors, family, and friends. Individual business people, marketing departments, and the advertising media, among others, now use focus groups, consumer testing, and other diagnostic tools to preview the emotional and attitudinal behavior of potential consumers.

"Bundling" is one of the newest trends in marketing. It is a one-on-one approach in lieu of mass marketing. The idea is to get a larger percentage of an individual consumer's needs by "bundling" multiple services. The bigger the slice of a consumer's total purchases the better.

Nonverbal communication studies are showing up everywhere in business settings. A recent national morning television show featured experts who conduct personality assessments based on nothing more than a worker's office or workplace. Two new 2009 television shows highlight the use of body language in their plots.

In law enforcement, Federal government and local law enforcement agencies have long used body language and the interpretation of signs and symbols as a tool to solve crimes and to protect individual citizens as well as national security interests. Several government agencies now have "profilers" on the payroll. In addition to profilers, the FBI has begun to teach new agents body language for the first time in fifty years. The United States Army and the Department of Defense definitely use the science of behavioral body language to profile America's enemies.

On the social front, people are looking for new ways to live together peacefully, conduct their business, handle social situations, and assimilate change in their fast-paced lives. The task is a daunting one because most people do not have any background or training in interactional living, which makes them ill equipped and highly vulnerable in the challenges of everyday social interplay. In addition, an endless variety of experimentation with new technologies, lifestyles, and multiple ways of doing things compound people's ability to keep up.

Working-men and women are too busy to stop what they are doing and speculate on the behavioral, attitudinal, and emotional ramifications of such things as multicultural living, making new friends, and changing jobs. Few people have the luxury of taking time off in the middle of a job interview, a significant meeting, or potentially threatening situation to analyze the motives of others.

All of us have to make split-second judgments in life, and too often, we make hasty decisions based on skimpy information that have potentially serious consequences for us and the people we love. Our existence becomes more and more compressed as we rush through the ever-increasing demands of daily living.

New books are out that stress the significance of critical "tipping points" in people's lives and "slicing techniques" to manage our daily tasks. The good news is that some experts say split-second decisions are actually better than over thinking, which gives body language a critically important role to play.

Body language is almost impossible to conceal from people who know how to read it. Good people readers are able to quickly organize information, assess intentions, and deal effectively with others because body language is more direct, honest, and memorable than the spoken word. Moreover, body language expertise has a pivotal role in discerning the difference between scripted and spontaneous performances.

The bad news is that the context in which most people live their lives today is a combination of the bump and run of the last century and the fast-paced technology of the new millennium. The post modern rate of social and technological change is so fast that many people cannot communicate as they did in the past. New technology is like watching the mythical Gods on Mt. Olympus fight. It makes you uncomfortable, but it is very powerful.

The World Wide Web, E-mail, and wireless communications enhance the speed and coverage of communications, but at the same time, people are losing important interpersonal contacts formerly gained from daily exposure to co-workers and peers. Marketplaces and traditional workplaces are disappearing, and as a result, too many people do not know the life-giving benefits of building and maintaining mutual relationships in person.

A note of caution is in order, however, because no matter how many people or agencies use body language in socializing or on the job, absolute perfection is elusive. No one has a unified theory that covers everything. Consequently, cross-cultural body language clues, signs, and symbolism are often ambiguous and unmediated. In addition, body language is not always consistent, and does not always lend itself to precise categorization, exact definition, or precise repetition every time.

In this book, I do not to follow any one system of body language interpretation. Instead of writing a detailed historical record of the development of body language, I take what I think is the best part of many different disciplines. This eclectic approach probably seems informal and adumbrated. However, since no single theoretical position is universally applicable I deem it expedient to fuse together all of the available information that is reasonably applicable to particular kinds of body language. This sometimes means taking one kind of approach in one instance and another in other situations.

Not to worry, however, because eclecticism is a healthy thing in a dynamic field like body language since human behavior is unimaginably complicated, and behavioral profiling is still immature and waiting on a unified theory to fit every occasion.

The practical result is that readers can gain useful insights into behavior by looking at the convergence, frequency, and distribution of body language signs and symbols free from the ideological baggage of a single approach. The field of behavioral profiling is growing on many fronts. As it unfolds, new theories are being developed, research continues, and new applications abound.

Chapter 1

Body Language Boot Camp

"It's not what you say, but how you say it that counts"

Body language is the fuel that makes effective communications go. Sometimes it is a matter of degree, but its presence is always there. Plainly put, it is communication horsepower. Actions speak louder than words and make up fifty-five per cent, or more, of the human communications system. The reason why we rely so heavily on nonverbal communications is that we have a need to express our feelings, attitudes, and motives along with the bare facts; a need to manage the impressions we make, and a need to assure others we mean what we say.

> Body language transcends the spoken word.

What are nonverbal communications? In the broadest sense, nonverbal communications are composed of *kinesics* that involve movements such as posturing and gesturing; *proxemics,* which is the study of territorial zones and how people use them; and *paralinguistics,* which is concerned with the aspects of oral speech that are not linguistic such as voice tones, pacing, hesitancy, sub vocalizations, and even gestures, mannerisms, and expressions.

By combining all three elements of nonverbal communication in multiple ways, people make life more particular and profound. I believe that body language is a phenomenon that even extends to inanimate objects because all things have meaning and represent something to us.

The interpretation of body language symbolism and external signs require a sizable degree of internal awareness since people cannot accurately understand someone else's body language behavior independent of their own experiences and worldview. Externally, people have no way of fully understanding their situation absent awareness of nonverbal communications in social interplay. Many experts believe that all language, including body language, co-evolves with consciousness. That is how important it is.

Origins

The origin of human behavior is a subject of public debate that began a long time ago. Although the roots of theories about human behavior can be traced back over 2,000 years to Plato and Aristotle, the study of body language has been a serious discipline for less than a 100 years. Experts to this day argue about whether human behavior is the result of heredity or environmental upbringing. An early day eugenics pioneer, Frances Galton, coined the phrase "nature vs. nurture" in an attempt to narrow down the carnival of terminology that described the relative contributions of heredity and culture to the formation of human behavior.

Although we are born according to a genetic blueprint, we know that our nurture within a particular culture and environment exerts a powerful influence on our behavior. The fact that experts disagree on what a modern human being is in the first place complicates the picture. In order to be brief, however, I believe that the available evidence to date shows that nature and nurture each contribute about fifty percent to the total makeup of human behavior, but the uncertainty that fosters debate will no doubt continue for some time.

The genetic predisposition of all living beings compels them to interact with their environment in ways that trigger conducive behavior. For instance, baby sea turtles instinctively head for the ocean from the moment of birth. They have no time to learn life saving behavior; they just unerringly take off.

Humans also have a strong territorial predisposition to take, hold, and defend certain areas as their own. The nature versus nurture argument will continue for some time; therefore, the precise origin of early body language behavior is still debatable.

Universal emotions and archetypal expressions set the patterns that persist today. It is only when something strange and unusual attracts our attention, or happens unexpectedly, or has a special consequence for us that the genesis of body language behavior clamors for explanation.

Humans are supreme in the animal kingdom. They have countless ways of expressing themselves. While animals bark, croak, whistle, and rattle their bodies around, humans are able to make thousands of different gestures.

Hundreds of emotions reside in humans, and several thousand different traits are in the human catalogue. It comes as no surprise, therefore, that nonverbal communications, often beyond any conscious intentions, take the form of countless gestures, expressions, postures, movements, vocal intonations, signals, and coded meanings in word choices.

Nonverbal Signs

Signs, in general, are things that represent something else. Practically anything is a sign as long as it has meaning for us and signifies something other than itself. The world around us is a world of signs whose job it is to represent reality.

> People organize body language signs into nonverbal codes.

Signs are one of the ways that people have to understand the reality of the world around them. Signs are also capable of having more than one meaning. They denote something as literally true or have secondary meanings that are more personal.

Pursuant to the human structuring tendency, and in order to make sense of so many ways to communicate nonverbally, people organize the world of body language signals and signs into a multitude of *nonverbal codes* that become an integral part of their social reality.

Nonverbal codes help determine social differentiation. People communicate their socio-economic identities through the way they walk and talk, the clothes and accessories they wear, their hairstyles, their work, their homes, and their possessions.

Nonverbal codes also play a huge role in the sensory world. For instance, codes of looking regulate how people look at each other. American children learn to look at their parents and not stare at strangers, or certain parts of the body. Eye contact is polite unless held too long, which is hostile and even threatening. Looking at the wrong people at the wrong time is impolite and disrespectful.

We learn to read the world around us by learning to read body language clues that give people away, give emphasis to life, and help people to convey attitudes and feelings. In short, nonverbal codes play an indispensable mediating role between people, society, and reality. Indeed, the evolution of body language follows the social history of humankind and cannot exist outside it.

Linguistic systems and usage, as opposed to nonverbal systems, are structurally different, and constitute an entirely separate field of study. but readers need not worry. For this book, I present body language in the context of everyday living instead of compli-

> We can remember what was first and what was last, but little of in between.

cated linguistic theories and nebulous social codes. Also, because there are so many possible gestures and expressions, many of which are unconscious, I only deal with the more familiar and meaningful ones normally employed in everyday behavior.

Symbolism

Symbols are signs too, but symbols are technically a class of signs that tend to reflect only one thing such as the conventional letters in a system of writing. The way people write is a sort of body language itself, but that is beyond the scope of this book.

Putting written communications aside for the moment, in terms of body language, symbols are concepts or real things that by their inherent nature represent something more profound than what they appear to be. Often, they are select material objects that help define who we are or want to be in a rapidly changing technological world that challenges our self-identity. Particular examples are our jewelry, homes, and cars.

Many symbols have arcane origins and a history of change over the centuries, while others remain constant from the earliest times. For example, the elements earth, water, wind, and fire are eternal constants in humankind's psyche. Many Native Americans still revere smoke as symbolic of the eternal connection between Heaven and earth.

The American flag is a changing symbol of national unity. As such, it represents the unification of diverse peoples, and serves as an icon for American culture. This is, however, an intentionally simplified example of a symbol. In reality symbols are complicated mechanisms with numerous applications, both consciously and unconsciously.

First Impressions

First impressions are the products of people's innate ability for rapid cognition and the use of people's outward appearance to draw inferences. Although we are taught that appearances are deceiving, studies show that people use clues such as clothing and accessories to make judgments about what others are like without much supporting evidence.

> First impressions rule the mind.

One explanation that many experts point to is the theory of *thin slicing*. Thin slicing postulates that humans make consequential decisions on narrow slices of experience. With very little to go on, people have the ability to detect patterns that predict behavior. When people need to make sense of something new or complicated, thin slicing saves the day.

One of the most enduring principles of body language is the tendency of human beings to let first impressions rule their minds. It is so important that in a sense first impressions are reality. For example, physical attractiveness plays a very important role. The configuration of a person's face affects judgments.

Researchers point out that many people do not realize that first impressions begin within seven seconds of meeting someone, and it takes about eight subsequent encounters to reverse a bad first impression. Evolutionary psychologists theorize that the impulse to locate allies quickly prompted our ancestors to use surface appearances as a clue to allegiances; consequently, first impressions have a long resume as valuable survival tools in adaptive biology.

Even today, first impressions are the easiest and quickest way to assess others in ambiguous circumstances. The moment we spot another person we look for impressions about that person's physical characteristics. However, we do not make judgments simply on physical appearances. We use people's nonverbal behavior to assess their thoughts and inner feelings. Also, we use body language indicators that accompany speech such as gestures and expressions as additional sources of information.

We use information such as personality, attitudes, state of health, and desire to connect with us as insights into the personality and character of others. Central traits help organize impressions of others and provide a framework for interpreting subsequent information. Armed with this information, we do our best to decide on the spot whether we "can or can't" interact with someone.

Social emotions such as shame and embarrassment are obvious facial expressions that appear right off the bat, and it is almost impossible to hide conditions such as being irritable, nervous, or fatigued from the face. Moreover, without saying a word, people are able to deliver many different impressions with their eyes such as a blaming effect, a diabolic effect, or a lofty effect, among others.

The first impression is huge in the courtroom. For example, wearing the wrong attire is a costly mistake. Generally, expert witnesses need all the power they can muster and therefore dress formally. Sloppy or inappropriate attire greatly reduces a litigant's or their witness's ability to possess authority and sustain credibility.

On the other hand, neat, well-dressed, and attractive defendants who make a good first impression such as O. J. Simpson and his so-called "dream team" get better treatment in court. If convicted, the illuminati get lesser sentences as in the cases of Patty Hearst, Robert Downey, Jr., Winona Ryder, and Paris Hilton. The judge in Ryder's case reduced her felony convictions to misdemeanors and allowed her to finish probation unsupervised.

> "The better you look, the better off you are in court".
>
> The Neal Boortz Show. Radio talk show. May 5, 2010.

Criminal defendants who on first impression look sad or depressed do better than those who look angry and defiant like the disruptive Chicago Seven. Defendants who first appear to be suffering or experiencing painful remorse do much better than those who appear to be sullen, impervious, or unremorseful for their actions, and have an attitude like "your funeral, my trial".

Dress attire, jewelry, cosmetics, eyewear, personal props, and other external symbols that augment first impressions are especially revealing. Normally, people can dress "down" after first meetings but not "up." Status or class position is often associated with first impressions, and people tend to retain the status from initial meetings to subsequent meetings.

If people focus on you for wearing the wrong clothes, you are probably wearing the wrong attire for the circumstances. As temperatures rise, formality diminishes. For women, the more skin they show the less influence they have; consequently, the best practice is to mix seasonal items with classics. For men, neatness and cleanliness matter. They should avoid wrinkled, stained, or faded attire.

Men should wear socks again. Button-down shirts with chinos continue to be popular for a casual "I'm at work" look. Both sexes need to eschew flip-flops outside the shower or swimming pool. They are noisy and distracting. In sum, people tend to manifest themselves in the season of the year they like the best.

External signals are elective, so they are one of the best-organized shows of body language possible inasmuch as most people put a lot of thought into their wardrobe and accessories. The bottom line: there is no second chance to make a first impression.

Single vs. Multiple Clues

Single body language clues are ambiguous, and are not weighty enough to affect the rare atmosphere of preordained conclusions. However, when signs and symbols come together in their composite patterns a total picture evolves. Like Gestalt psychology that postulates that the "whole" is different from the sum of its parts, behavior can only be understood as a unified whole, an organized totality. The best practice, therefore, is to look for multiple clues that form patterns of behavior signifying different emotions, traits, and attitudes.

Multiple clues can occur at the same time like simultaneously locking the arms and ankles, or contiguously such as walking then jogging, or sequentially such as clinching the fists, then raising a stiff arm and jerking it down in a sign of solidarity.

Increasing stress clues are moving from an open sitting position to crossing the ankles in front of a chair, to crossing the ankles underneath the chair, to crossing the ankles with hands clenched and knees closer together. Add increased preening and the cumulative effect is a case of severe stress.

Multiple displays of body language information converging on a common conclusion give it weight, reliability, and validation. In other words, despite the fact that we often base our impressions on outward surface features, the better practice is to combine every available clue and sign to form an overall impression or central theme that includes both the visual and the verbal. If there is a consensus that a waterfowl walks, quacks, looks, and acts like a duck then it is probably a duck.

A comprehensive understanding of gestural behavior is extremely difficult if non-sequent elements are not put in context. For instance, it is tough to understand a pothole if it is separated from the street. All gestures, movements, and expressions, therefore, are part of the context in which they occur including any oral communications at the same time.

Focusing on single, isolated clues is not reliable, because body language usually includes combined, sequential, and contiguous clues that form bright lines and gestural clusters that underlie behavior.

Order Effects

The methods that people use to form judgments of each other is not a simple process. People employ more than one cognitive approach, and none are one hundred percent accurate in an imperfect world. Known as the *primacy* and *recency* effect, the order in which impression information is received influences people perception. As a result, cautious people place the greatest emphasis on the latest information available, whereas early primary information resonates with goal-oriented people.

The front page of the newspaper is typically the most important. Likewise, initial impressions are the strongest ones to many people. In fact, first impressions are such powerful influences that most people seek reinforcement for them while simultaneously rejecting all inconsistent data. Most people take the path of least resistance, and few will search for information contrary to their first impressions.

Think about meeting someone for the first time that has dark colored hair that is not particularly attractive. Later, you meet this person again with lighter colored hair that is more attractive. Which impression is the dominant one? The answer lies in the order effects of receiving impression information and individual taste.

The *primacy effect* is giving the first information received more impact than subsequent information. On the other hand, some people want to know what a person has done lately. This is the *recency effect,* which treats the last available information as more powerful than early information because it is up to date and overrides older, stale information. Other things being equal, recent impressions ought to be the strongest. For instance, most diagnosticians want the last information available for their diagnosis, and adversaries contend for the last word.

In general, competitors who perform last have an advantage and usually rate higher than people who are first in line, due to the *serial position* effect. Instead of rushing to the front of the line, it might be better if you go last; therefore, try to be at the end of the line when competing for something important such as a job.

Fundamental Attribution Errors

Since there is no single approach to people perception, and the two views in the nature vs. nurture debate continue to be less than full proof, people look for other ways to explain the causes of behavior. In a perfect world, all behavior is due to situational causes when external reasons are responsible and to dispositional causes when internal reasons are at work. Realistically, however, circumstances often eclipse character and overwhelm individuality. Consequently, when we make someone the focus of our attention, we often overlook the situational causes that influence their behavior. This inclination to over-attribute the behavior of others to their disposition is a *fundamental attribution error.*

One more thing, we know that certain motivational biases influence impression management. That is, people strive to look good in front of their peers and maintain their self-esteem even at the cost of accuracy. For example, according to a study done in 1991, prospective jurors often conceal socially undesirable tenden-

> People's faces can be in neutral while their minds are in high gear.

cies and erroneously state to the court that they would not be influenced by potential bias.

People are highly reluctant to reveal their potential flaws, and will go to great lengths to cover up their imperfections in front of peers. However after jurors have "settled in", clusters of body language in the way they sit, stand, move, and talk reveals what kind of persons they really are and what their attitude to specific aspects of life are. Then, you can adjust your presentation to establish complementary body language rhythm and gain rapport.

Studies show that people's cultural view of the world influences their susceptibility to the fundamental attribution error. For instance, people fail to judge the correct causes underlying behavior due to their tendency to view negative outcomes as something some people deserve. Often, their intolerance is the result of blind ideological enthusiasm that has infected people with a meanness of spirit that is difficult to overcome.

Display Regulators

The most informative and revealing body language displays are spontaneous and unplanned. However, body language is subject to cultural display rules that transcend knee jerk reactions. Allowing people to behave any way they wish in a shared world is unthinkable and civilized people govern themselves accordingly. Likewise, every culture has display grounds where people go to display themselves such as bars, festivals, and dances.

Civilized society requires suitable behavior; hence, its members must manage the impressions they make by masking, intensifying, de-intensifying, and neutralizing their thoughts and feelings in public. "Boys don't cry" is a cultural masking rule.

Another example of a masking display rule is the way people handle off-the-wall, ugly, and unusable gifts on their birthday and other occasions. Despite their real feelings of "ugh", they somehow manage to display a toothy grin and make the best of it, because we are taught that polite people show appreciation when given gifts.

In order to intensify experiences, people will exaggerate, speak louder, smile, or do whatever they think of to bestow a greater degree of importance on events than is really called for under the circumstances. Most of us think we are special and deserve the good things we get in life.

The reverse of intensifying is minimizing the display of a strong emotion by de-intensifying it. For example, when we get upset we still manage to put on a happy face. Nothing makes people happier than beating their competition, yet wise winners know not to show their true feelings at such times so the losers can save face.

We neutralize emotions when we show no expression whatsoever. This strategy involves the intentional effort to downplay attitudes and emotions with a neutral expression. We learn to remain calm in situations of great emotional distress, and to adopt a neutral expression when it pays a dividend. For example, card players cannot bluff or finesse without having a good neutral or contrived poker face that suppresses inner reactions.

If body language is subject to masking strategies, how are we able to read a person's true intentions in dicey psychological territory? The best way is to look for clusters of body language signs that point to a certain behavior. Even if the real self does not get fully expressed, small portions of it come through, and not many people are able to fake every single clue, sign, and signal that they unconsciously give out over a protracted period.

We must also be alert to whether or not someone's conduct and appearance are appropriate under the circumstances, since our perceptions of other people are so context dependent. At times, we will make attribution errors, and even though no formulaic movements and expressions fit every situation, body language is unquestionably one of the best meaning-makers there is in the forest of interpersonal relationships.

People build huge buildings, skyscrapers, and vertical monuments to express their greatness and strength, but when they put a fence around their house, they put one around themselves as well. Despite this, in the new millennium, a better understanding of people's body language will help supply the answers to whether or not we should interact with them. In actuality, there are many visible differences between honest and meretricious behavior.

Practical pointers

Language is the ultimate horizon of intelligibility. Language transforms experiences into internal models that serve as guides to future action; therefore, people desire a dialogue of concrete signs and symbols, which have meaning for them instead of a thin soup of words.

People develop powerful appearance biases based on body type, posture, and other prominent physical features. From such observations, they construct long-lasting impressions of the motives, credibility, status, trustworthiness, and goals of others.

Unfortunately, people often make attribution errors because single body language hints and clues do not adequately describe an independent reality.

Chapter 2

The Influence of Personality

"Personality influences everything we do"

Personality and body language are interwoven parts in the sumptuous tapestry of human behavior; consequently, it is helpful to look at some of the countless personality theories on parade today. A brief review of the many personality variables will facilitate an understanding of the integral role played by body language.

Historically, the term "personality" derives from the Latin word "persona", which had to do with the mask that people present to the external world. Naturally, most of us wish to present the socially acceptable side of our inner nature, but life is much more complicated than that.

> Personality theory helps predict behavior from an individual's trait matrix.

For example, research has shown that a person's personality has an important effect on their health as well as the health of those around them.

In this vein, consider just for a moment the saying, "The observer affects the observed", which is a tenet of *Postmodern Relativism* that postulates the notion that all knowledge is subjective, individual, or socially constructed. By extension, this includes personality, but whether we agree or not, is unimportant. It is sufficient to say that the human personality includes the diverse body language postures, expressions, gestures, and movements that make up the total person.

Perfect indicators of personality do not exist. There are only signs, markers, clues, and hints, which can be subtle and uncertain. The reality of personality is that it is the result of many cumulative factors not just our social charm or charisma. A convenient starting point for our analysis of personality is a tripartite one that includes emotional, behavioral, and cognitive aspects, good and bad, that are consistent across time and different situations. Even the time span and historical era in which we live affects our learning and thinking; therefore, we will never be like anyone who has ever lived, or ever will live, and that is a good thing. Different theories go toe-to toe in claiming the rationale behind human behavior, including several psychometric ways of measuring people's personality.

Major theoretical approaches to personality developed during the last century are the subjective *Psychoanalytic* theories that view personality as integrated with underlying motivations that are measurable, while the *Behaviorism* theories are objective approaches that look to the only two things that are amenable to observation-behavior and environment. The *Social* learning theories treat the notion of personality as those aspects of behavior acquired in a social context, whereas the *Interactions* theories postulate personality to be the result of complex patterns of interaction between a person's predispositions and particular situations.

Philosophers, psychiatrists, psychologists, scientists, and many others have sought a single all encompassing theory of personality for a very long time, but with little success. Researchers often point to this or that theory; however, it seems clear that there is no single unified theory of personality that picks up all the marbles. The Internet, for example, has millions of matches for the term "personality assessment".

Two popular personality theories are the *Type* and *Trait* approaches. For simplicity, *Type* theories emphasize how people that are consistently alike represent certain universal types, and *Trait* theories emphasize how various behavioral characteristics account for people's consistencies and differences.

Personality Typing

Personality typing has a long history that is wider than deep. Ancient ideas called the "constitutional theories" of personality are classic examples of the correlation between body shapes and behavior. In the Third Century B.C., Aristotle, believed that large foreheads indicated a sluggish person, small foreheads meant a fickle person, broad foreheads meant a person was excitable, bulging foreheads demonstrated a person of quick temper, low foreheads signaled stupidity and lack of feeling, and a high forehead indicated a brainy and very sensitive person.

In the Fifth century B.C., the Greek physician Hippocrates proposed a link between body language and motivation. He believed that four basic human temperaments came from four basic biological humors. Although his ideas gradually disappeared over time, his pioneering efforts helped pave the way for several other constitutional theories of personality with the focus on a direct relationship between a person's physiology and their inner nature.

The best known of the "body typing" theories to emerge from folklore is Sheldon's mid-nineteenth century work on three fundamental body types. The short, fat, soft, rounded, plump, and poorly developed *Endomorph* was supposed to be social, relaxed, loving, talkative, and sybaritic. The hard, square, big-boned, strong, and well-developed *Mesomorph* was vigorous, physical, energetic, assertive, and courageous. The tall, thin *Ectomorph* was a person who demonstrated restraint, shyness, introversion, inhibition, lack of sociability, and self-consciousness. The work of Sheldon is worthy of some praise, but despite all of his efforts he failed to make out a comprehensive case for a reliable theory of constitutional body types and personality.

A couple of theories worth mentioning is the First century A.D. works of Galen linking four types of so-called body humors he called, *sanguine, melancholic, phlegmatic,* and *choleric* with behavior. In the early twentieth century, a theory that connected various mental problems with three body types called *pyknic* (stocky), *asthenic* (slender), *athletic* (muscular) and one mixed type was formulated by a man named Kretschmer.

Two other classic examples of personality typing are the so-called "Type A" and "Type B" personalities. Type A has excessive energy and competitiveness. Everything has a time urgency, so they tend to be impatient, accelerated (i.e. they walk, talk and eat hurriedly), and competitive. They value quantity over quality and hate delays and waiting in line. They have a controlling temperament and are constantly struggling for power. Body language indicators are overworking, nervous energy, excessive animation, food binges, smoking , drinking, and lack of self-care.

Type B personalities have a much slower cognitive tempo. They are passive, relaxed, easy going, and take one day at a time. They are less ambitious, prefer self-reflection, and are not competitive. They focus on quality over quantity, and their body language is thoughtful and deliberate with less irritability.

Many other body type theories of personality have been put forth, but they generally are little more than derivatives of the Swiss psychologist, Carl Gustav Jung's, acclaimed work on personality classifications such as *extroverts* who tend to be outgoing and *introverts* who tend to be withdrawn. These two polar opposites form by the interplay of opposing natural tendencies toward assertiveness and passivity, as well as by the conflict between individual behavior, which derives from a general *life urge*, and the deepest level of the personality he called the *collective unconscious* (i.e. the archetypes, concepts, myths, and symbols passed down from earlier generations). Since these expanded theories are something I do not need to cover extensively in this book, a brief mention will do.

Extroverts have an outgoing attitude about life, and believe that external forces govern what happens to them. They direct their energy outwards and derive satisfaction from the physical and social environment. Extroverts are animated and outgoing in dress, manner, and behavior. They seldom need "assertiveness training," since they stand up for themselves. They think aloud, talk back, and change the subject often to keep a conversation going, so ask for their thoughts, listen carefully, and do not interrupt them.

Active in local community, school, and church activities, extroverts score high in social integration. They want to keep their community safe, and are willing to get in the face of anyone who creates a health or safety hazard to the environment. People who are high on external forces attribute success to fate, luck, and the actions of others. Extroverts do not feel strongly about their failure or successes in life due to generalized expectancies.

Introverts have an inward attitude towards life, and feel that what happens to them is a result of their own efforts and skills. They believe their own intelligence and hard work pays off. They are reflective and think before they speak. Introverts are less likely to feel for people in need of help since they believe people bring trouble on themselves. They feel pride when they succeed, but shame and guilt when they fail. Introverts know more about themselves and their problems. They tend to be shy and ask more questions than extroverts. With them, discuss one thing at a time, give them time to reflect, and get things in writing. Some people joke about how to spot an introvert. If he is looking at his own shoes instead of yours, he is an introvert.

Jungian theory further sub-divides all personalities into four types: Intuitors, Thinkers, Feelers, and Sensors. Each type has its own unique body language for the most part. Up to date examples of spin-offs from Jung's theories are the popular Meyer-Briggs Personality Type Indicator, which is primarily concerned with the "information-gathering function" and the "decision-making function" of a person's personality and the personality assessment test called the Motivational Appraisal of Personal Potential or "MAPP".

Another useful way of looking at opposing personality types is the well known structured versus the unstructured types. The structured person is likely religious, organized, and has a job in a strong hierarchy with pressure to conform to a collective goal. The structured type is an institutional person who works for a bank, "C" corporation, school system, or the military, and respects rules, schedules, and authority.

The unstructured person's credo is "Don't organize yourself out of business". This person is a free spirit who has not fully bought into mainstream society and does not mind bending the rules, or tinkering under the hood of a car. Unstructured persons are highly individualistic and independent people working in jobs such as farmers, artists, independent contractors, and self-employed professionals.

In a broad sense, the ways people mentally perceive themselves and others, make attributions, decide on courses of action, and construct their worlds becomes less opaque and a little bit more predictable through personality typing. However, trying to organize personality into tidy categories with neat labels is problematical.

Each category assumes that there is an underlying pattern of behavior that meets its parameters. This formulaic approach fails to address the disconcerting tendency of most humans to exhibit behavior that overlaps several different categories. We are never quite sure everyone is singing the same tune.

Personality Traits

Certain behavioral traits define particular personalities by emphasizing how people are different from one another. How are personality traits and the body language that goes along with them used to ascertain behavior? There are three different approaches to defining personality by traits: the *central trait* approach, the *multiple trait* approach, and the *essential trait* approach.

> The old believe everything; the middle-aged suspect everything; and the young know everything.
> Oscar Wilde

The central trait approach is the notion that some people's personality is so dominated by a single, overwhelming trait that it influences everything they think and do. The best example of the central trait approach is the authoritarian personality, which is the subject of another chapter in this book. The trouble with this approach is that it more apt to apply to social issues since it has political ramifications.

The *multiple trait* approach utilizes a laundry list of traits that reveal behavior by filling out a personality questionnaire. Typically, these are long lists of adjectives, some painstakingly devised by legitimate psychologists, and some dreadfully amateurish such as those seen in tabloid magazines that when combined somehow constitute different personalities.

However devised, they all operate from the notion that personality is a basket full of traits that deal with ways of reacting, feeling, and behaving. They are the underlying matrix that experts use to predict behavior. The trouble with this theory is its inherent overlaps and the tedium of filling out long questionnaires truthfully.

The *essential traits* approach to personality is one of the most useful paradigms for predicting behavior. The development of the so-called *Five-Factor Model* is the middle ground between the other two approaches set out above. Many psychologists feel that the "Big Five" is the most appealing approach because it postulates that five essential traits with pertinent body language are all we need to know about someone in practically all situations. The "Big Five" are *extroversion, neuroticism, agreeableness, conscientiousness,* and *openness.* The general idea is that out of all the thousands of possible human traits, the Big Five are elemental in understanding all of the others.

The Big Five, according to recent research, continue to evolve throughout the lifetime of the average person. Although controversial and sometimes criticized as being vague and overbroad, the utility in summarizing personality traits into five broad categories is to bring a degree of useful organization to the complex and confusing array of traits that play a role in personality.

Each of the five traits has its own set of body language indicators that helps us identify, understand, and predict human behavior. For example, use the "Big Five" framework to ask the following basic questions about another person:

1. Does this person's body language seem controlling?
2. Does this person act sane or crazy?
3. Does this person seem to agree or disagree with me?

4. Is this person acting like someone reliable?

5. Is this person open or closed?

The efficacy of this kind of simplified personality assessment transcends its potential to precisely comprehend and predict human behavior; however, in a pinch it is all we need to make reasonably informed judgments about why people do the things they do.

In particular situations, extroversion is the active search for social acceptance and support. Neuroticism is a kind of anxiety and instability. Agreeableness is associated with happiness, warmth, and generosity. Conscientiousness is about discipline and organization, and openness is about trying new experiences. Being open-minded does not translate into vacant mindlessness, indifference, or a magnanimous mood. It is more of a genuine constant in one's life.

When using a trait assessment approach, we need to remember that we care about what others think, so at times, we do not behave in accordance with our genuine traits. Moreover, to complicate matters, in large societies such as America, different people are liable to interpret the traits of others in different ways, which creates ambiguity in the true meanings of some body language expressions. With this in mind, I believe the best thing to do is to stick to the core of the Big Five personality approach without worrying too much about superficial overlays.

To complete the picture, I hasten to mention the existence of many other personality theories based on such things as birth order, chronological age, outlook, and a host of other variables. For instance, some experts say the first-born child receives more attention and is more outgoing and prone to leadership traits, while the middle born child demonstrates more attention-seeking traits.

As they grow older, elderly people become more conservative and concerned with law and order. They tend to develop generalized roles as their models of behavior rather than specific roles. They have more understanding of human frailties and adopt easier, safer, and more convenient body movements.

On the other hand, young people are more competitive and naïve about life. Between the ages of twenty-one and thirty, they tend to reflect their parent's values. Out of their lifestyles, characteristics emerge that reflect the things that are important to them: getting attention, acquiring status, and accumulating material possessions.

In connection with social differences based on definitions of masculinity and femininity, numerous personality variables come into play from genetics and gender specific styles of speech, dress, body language behavior, and so on. One of the most significant codes for constructing gender meanings is the appearance code. Clothes usually distinguish men and women, and help to broadcast what it means to be a man or woman from a specific social group. Typical meanings deal with power and solidarity. From these, more complex and individualistic personality variables take shape.

Personality variables, however, are more reliable when they become long-term trends with similarities in different times. It has been said that, "One is an accident, and two is a trend." At any rate, it is safe to say that every individual is like everyone else in some ways, but is unique in other ways depending upon the circumstances of time and place.

What really makes the observation of different personalities interesting is the long-standing challenge of pinning down what is and what is not truly characteristic of someone's personality. Remember Dr. Sigmund Freud wryly observed that much of human behavior is motivated by unconscious drives that are exactly opposite of the ones expressed outwardly.

Practical Pointers

People develop a personality predisposition early in life and stick to it. For example, some people are outgoing and extroverted and others are passive and introverted. Some people are egoverts who care only about themselves. A huge factor in family and workplace strife is the failure to understand that different personalities tackle problems, conflict, and success in different ways.

Neither the *trait* or *type* theories of personality are perfect; however, they both have mass appeal and are popular ways of determining such things as people's likes and dislikes, if a person makes decisions slowly or quickly, and if a person prefers facts and evidence or depends on intuition. Either theory does a decent job of revealing whether people are most likely to react emotionally or rationally to problems.

No matter which theory is under consideration, the reason that a thorough knowledge of body language is so important is because most personality theories tend to assign extreme values to certain characteristics of the theory, which in my opinion dilutes its power and credulity. On the other hand, the new art of body language is a skill that parts the curtain around the true attitudes, motives, and emotions embedded in people's psyche.

Chapter 3

Interpersonal Attraction

"Opposites don't always attract".

What are the dynamics of people liking one another? What turns complete strangers into friends? Do opposites really attract? Interpersonal attraction, or the degree of liking between people, originates from two closely related human needs: the need for affiliation and the need to be in the company of others.

When people meet each other, the main components of attraction are proximity, familiarity, and social comparison. If people have ample time, they assess their situation, and the people in it by dispassionate analysis. If people are short of time, situational influences such as how close they are to others geographically count, as well as how similar they are to others, how accustomed they have become to others, and if they share the same attitudes and outlooks with others.

Afterwards, most people go out of their way to engage themselves in social interplay, both in mannerisms and dress, and except for a few people who want to be anonymous, many become initially attracted to each other since no one wants the loneliness of isolation.

Humans, by design, easily connect with others for the simple reason that social relationships are essential to life. No one makes complete sense by himself or herself so people make comparisons. It is only through our changing social relationships with others that we are able to identify ourselves.

People spend most of their time cultivating and maintaining interpersonal relationships. Interactive contact is a large part of day-to-day existence, since it promotes reproduction and survival. As born interreactors, we innately reach out for others as a matter of course, and the relationships we form shape and mold us to become who we are in the context of our relational systems.

Interpersonal attraction and our innate sense of territory go hand in hand. We permit only those we approve of into our territory, oft times with little more to go on than first impressions.

Mutual attraction permits social comparison by allowing us to evaluate our own abilities and opinions against those of others. It also fulfills a vital need for affiliation by helping us to establish and maintain relationships that prevent isolation, angst, and despair, and thereby reduce the anxiety of being "out there" all alone. Mutual nurturing attractions or lack thereof, affect childhood brain "imprinting" and play an important role in determining whether a child is resilient or vulnerable in later life.

The Twin Towers: Similarity and Proximity

What kinds of persons initially attract us? On a very basic level, some personality researchers are learning that genes are somehow involved in shaping our social preferences, but more research is necessary in this area. The strong affect of nurturing, especially during childhood, is powerful evidence that not everything is rooted in biology. A purely biological approach does not adequately explain the heavy influence that the environment, culture, and adaptive learning experiences have upon our relationship choices.

> Communication is most complete between equals.

As a rule of thumb, the more similar we are the more we like each other. We have a natural bias in favor of people who look and act like us; consequently, the body language behavior of people similar to us is a natural attraction. That is why astute lawyers neither preach to nor lecture a judge or jury, but talk to them about a case as if they are a neighbor. In your best intimate voice, experts on juries say, "Tell them what you are going to tell them. Tell them. Tell them what you told them". Prearranged redundancy sounds nutty, but it is a key to effective communication.

We unilaterally behold each other with a special awareness of each other's clothes, speech patterns, expressions, and deportment in an effort to find some way to relate. Similarities in dress, age, sex, race, status, education, attitude, and values are easier to organize in our minds, are more reinforcing, and more appealing to us than disparate, non-reinforcing attributes.

We all take different journeys in life, but no matter where we go, we take a little of each other with us. Our common bias for similar physical and cultural traits is most notable at initial encounters when there is precious little other information to go on. Consequently, at the moment of attraction the tiniest similarities lay the foundation for building new relationships.

In addition to similarities, being in the right place at the right time is a powerful influence on nascent relationships. The most common situational factor is little more than a proximity to others that naturally leads to the development of relationships with people nearby. The power of proximity lies in the low cost, but high return in social integration and cooperation.

Propinquity, repeated contact, and increased exposure enhance the chances of drawing people together, and allow people to test the waters of a potential relationship, seek reinforcement from multiple contacts, and obtain valuable feedback.

The Magnetism of Attractiveness

American culture is a visual one and attractiveness is a form of cultural currency, especially in screenland. For example, network executives prefer to hire news people that are young, sexy, and attractive. They know physically attractive people are more magnetic, and that the majority of television viewers favor a good visual person over heavy intellectual hitters or phony nice people.

People will try anything to "improve" their attractiveness. They strive to enhance their finer points, play down their imperfections, and look younger as well. One motivation is to level the playing field in a highly competitive society. Another is the fact that attractiveness and goodness have become almost synonymous in America.

Attractive people are more knowledgeable and trustworthy in people's minds. In addition, the perception of many is that attractive people have superior qualities such as the ability to achieve great things, live longer, and have more relationships, which psychologists call the *positive halo effect,* although there is little scientific evidence to support such beliefs.

The magnetism of attractive people is not limited to their physical beauty. True attractiveness is multidimensional and only limited by people's creativity. In some cases, a man's financial security and social power enhance his overall attractiveness. Opposites attract, and women that are interested in romance need to polish the body language skills that make them interesting, mysterious, and opposite from men.

In the new millennium, both men and women will need more than an attractive persona, since no one seriously contends that attractiveness correlates with well-being. With the possible exception of the movies and politics, in the future attractive people will need complimentary job skills as well as being aesthetically appealing.

Practical pointers

Mutual attraction inevitably leads to social interaction, which leads to concern over each other's safety and welfare. Out of welfare concerns many other attachments emerged, which caused our ancestors to organize social infrastructures that not only provided safety and a sense of well-being, but also encompassed economic and cultural matters.

Chapter 4

Forming Relationships

"We were meant for each other."

After being attracted to one another, how do people form lasting relationships, and vice versa, how do they keep from forming relationships with everyone they come into contact with? The answer is that interpersonal relationships are either *primary* or *secondary* with each type having unique components. According to many scholars, the first recorded primary relationship was Adam and Eve in the Garden of Eden. Since they were unable to replace each other with a third person, their relationship was long lasting, basic, and primary.

Today, most interpersonal relationships are short lasting, limited, and secondary, and the members are easily replaceable. Another difference between then and now is that Adam and Eve did not have the option of picking each other, whereas most interpersonal relationships today are a matter of choice based on various circumstances.

> The only way to have a close friend is to be one.

Primary Relationships

A primary relationship is a close, long-term relationship characterized by intense commitment and intimacy. Primary relationships exist in varying strengths, degrees of closeness, and commitment under a variety of behaviors and circumstances.

The three building blocks of primary relationships are the fulfillment of needs, emotional attachment, and a strong sense of interdependence. Need fulfillment is the most important building block. For example, we form close relationships out of a need to have a safe harbor during bad times, or from a need to love and be the object of love.

Emotional attachment fulfills our desire to be accepted, and strict norms help preserve our sense of interdependence. Although the people involved do not have to be head-over-heels in love with each other, they do have to know each other very well, and have a mutual need for a close relationship.

Secondary Relationships

Secondary relationships are the casual and short-term associations that people enter into practically every day. They are the result of well-defined social rules, customs, and norms that dictate how civilized people act around each other. Most importantly, secondary relationships do not require long-term commitment, intimacy, and need fulfillment. Jury duty is a good example.

Typical jurors summoned to court to do their civic duty will enter into secondary relationships with special limited needs. For example, they will have a physical need to be comfortable, a mental need to be fair, and a social need to do something for their community. However, they do not feel as though they need to get personally involved with the litigants, because it is improper and they do not plan to be there very long.

Practical Pointers

Good interpersonal relationships cover more ground than just being sociable or being one of the guys with co-workers. Solid relationships require much of our time because they help define our lives in different settings. In a sense, our very existence in the world is dependent upon our interactions with others and the gradual acquisition of mutual body language signals.

Primary relationships benefit us because they influence our brains in much the same manner as spiritual development. It is a good thing when people find strength in their connections with others who believe in them.

Chapter 5

The Battle of The Sexes

"The relational identity of gender is the psychic reality."

Over the course of time, the relationships between men and women have changed in most cultures. These changes reflect the improved status and roles of women beyond child bearing. The so-called battle between the sexes is less intense as women have come a long way in their journey to absolute equality. Despite technological advancements and Constitutional protection of "adversely impacted" minorities like women, critics still point to the economic disparity and validation problems that still face modern women.

The battle of the sexes has been illustrated by a few noteworthy authors. One of the best examples of the difference between men and women's sensibilities is the poem, *Home Burial* published in 1915 by America's beloved poet, Robert Frost, who reputedly studied women and knew his subject well. His poem probes a woman's nature to the core and is a beautiful analysis of the spiritual gulf between men and women.

The sociologist Margaret Mead, in the mid-1930s, conducted a very influential study of men and women in primitive societies. Her book dropped a bomb on contemporary society's long held notion that the sexes are (i.e. biologically) different in their psychological attributes and that males are dominant both physically and cognitively. She concluded that there is no inherent psychological difference between the sexes, and what society believes to be inherent is nothing more than the social environment and customary upbringing of men and women.

"Social Darwinism" was also the mainstay of the thinking of Simone Lucie-Ernestine-Marie-Bertrand de Beauvoir (1908-1986). A French literary figure and intellectual, she wrote in her book, *The Second Sex,* that on the important level of gender instead of biological sex, women are artificial social inventions.

Ever ready to throw a wrench into masculine machinery, Mlle Beauvoir wrote that women are defined and treated as a second sex by a male-oriented society. She kicked things off by taking the position that all personal and intellectual differences were the result of social inequities, pressures, and conditioning.

Mlle. de Beauvoir was partially correct in that society configures many norms of behavior based on gender, which tend to ossify over time into conventional rituals and rigid patterns that form social constructs and artificial barriers. Missing, however, is the overwhelming advanced research in genetics, biochemistry, and the cognitive sciences that were unavailable when she wrote her book. Abundant new evidence clearly points to biological characteristics and brain functions that make women undeniable females without the sinister influence of men or society.

> Human brains are not unisex.

Socially learned female behavior might be something like the fear of insects, since it is more permissible for females to express fear. In addition, playing with dolls is a form of social training. Some female characteristics such as emotionality, timidity, and space usage may be partially learned as well.

The real explanation for gender differences has more to do with creation of elegant and complex language devices in an effort to describe reality in terms beyond mere sexual ones than it does with the "social Darwinism" of Simone Beauvoir. For example, for very young children to understand sex differences they need to have an inkling of the gender scheme. The best way to learn gender differences is to put an ideology of social roles versus biological sex identities in the local language system.

Even in the worst case, most cultural norms have room for change or deviation, especially in multi-ethnic societies of rapid change and ever-increasing technology.

The bedrock of American constitutional law is equality matching for men and women, but in the realm of body language, long-time experience teaches that there are enduring differences and neither sex wants to give up their gender prerogatives. Both sexes seek to accentuate their differences through available avenues of expression such as specialized body language that reveals the power and solidarity of sexual differences.

Gender distinctions that only deal with economic, political, and egalitarian social norms tend to attenuate with men and women squeezed together in a middle-of-the-road existence that neither sex likes.

In the world of body language, sex and gender differences are stimulating and exciting. Recent biosocial research strongly suggests that a novel stimulus arouses people. In addition, chemistry, hormones, and genetics play a much larger part in gender roles than previously suspected. For example, women have a different foreign policy philosophy, and are less likely to use military intervention. Men are more likely to be lenient in criminal cases involving violence, while women are more forgiving in child cases.

> "Men and women do not speak in the same way."
> Luce Irigaray
> quote in *TPM-2008*

Both sexes have equal rights to be individuals with a body language all their own, and the interpersonal skills, opportunities, and freedom to pursue what is best for them, but it is not necessary or productive for men and women to be absolutely equal in everything.

In some instances, men and women do share many similarities. Identical movements and expressions in both sexes often have the same meaning and differences are not readily ascertainable. This occurs in common situations where both men and women adopt identical behavior due to the expediencies of interactional living and the normative expectations of peers.

Mutual expressions such as smiling and frowning are small examples, as well as indicating initial interest by simply cocking the head at an angle to the subject of interest, or when seated, propping the chin up with the fingers while listening intently.

On the other side of the coin, men and women are as different as apples to oysters, to quote an often-heard phrase borrowed, in pertinent part, from Sir Thomas More, the patron Saint of Lawyers. In other words, both sexes behave differently even though the situation is similar. For a very well defined example, the clothes they wear distinguish men and women even in the same circumstances.

Charles Darwin believed that females make the initial choice of a mate. Not too long ago, a female experimental psychologist who agrees with Darwin came up with a catalogue of fifty-two gestures women use to signal their interest in men. Some of these are smiling, winking, licking the lips, glancing, laughing, giggling, primping, and bare neck presentation, as well as head tossing, hair flipping, and whispering. Sometimes they hike their skirts, pat their buttocks, hug, request a dance, move closer, touch a knee, or employ a variety of preening gestures such as smoothing their hair, arranging their clothes, looking at a mirror, leaning forward, making eye contact, and caressing.

Sibilant sighing is very feminine, as is putting a little sway in the hips and exposing skin. Fingering the hair and pretending to be somewhat helpless is feminine. Remarkably, at times, a simple palm up gesture is all that it takes to encourage a man's desire to protect and help females. Women are never stronger than when they show their weaknesses.

Male preening involves atavistic impulses to flex muscles, puff out their chests, and use their hands on a higher horizontal plane by adjusting their neckties to look bigger. They also play with their cuff links, unbutton their coats, and conduct subtle personal inspections of themselves. Men try to reduce stomach and shoulder sag by maintaining a stiffer posture than women maintain.

Men keep their wrists stiffer, and when sitting they prefer the stiffer figure four-position with legs slightly apart, one foot on the floor, and one ankle over the opposite knee. Due to the competitive nature of their upbringing and chemistry, men tend to be loud and dominant types, whereas being too loud or too talkative are turn-offs in women.

Getting it right is equally important to both men and women, because of the need to protect the ego and get feelings across at the same time. The more confused people are about each other, the more they hope things will work out. When opposites attract, women should be women and men should be men.

Both sexes cognitively process and express their thoughts and feelings differently. Men use fewer words, and when they talk, it is to get an advantage, while women talk to draw out feelings. Women seem to be in touch with their emotions, while men have to work at getting in touch with their feelings. Men never seem to know how to break off a relationship and women never seem to know when.

Men learn early that showing emotion is a no-no. Women will stick up for each other more than men who remain confused about how much they dare to share with each other. The most successful and widespread gender gestures in the courtship ritual are those that generally serve the image of men being strong, protective breadwinners, and women as being homemakers and child-care providers.

The biological reality is that men and women take on the world in very different ways. Some experts believe that biochemistry plays a much bigger role than previously thought even in seemingly insignificant behavior. For example, increasing levels of estrogen and progesterone induce the propensity for melodrama.

Gender Versus Sexual Differences

We have all heard the clichés: Men are from one planet and women are from another. Men seek solutions while women prefer to have someone care about them rather than solve their problems. Women ask for directions and men don't. The pundits say women love talking on a cell phone and driving to the mall to buy more shoes, whereas men only care about sex, sports, and beer. Besides such myths, what are the real differences between men and women?

Human biochemistry is vastly different in men and women, and solid ongoing research clearly convinces me that it is the biggest factor in the battle of the sexes. Nevertheless, there are many social gender differences as well.

Some intellectuals claim the differences between men and women do not have to be based in either biology or gender. According to *TPM* Magazine, Luce Irigaray, a French intellectual, writes in her latest book, *Sharing the World*, that men and women have different relational identities not just sex or gender differences. She says that the order in which men and women speak is different.

Mlle. Irigary is a controversial philosopher; however, recent research seemingly supports some of her ideas. For example, a striking difference between men and women is the way they respectively deal with emotions. It is possible to link this with brain function. The brains of men and women are essentially identical, except in the region that deals with emotional processing.

Sophisticated brain scanning shows that action-oriented emotional responses that express aggression are more active in men, while women express emotions in more refined, subtle, and symbolic ways. The bottom line is that their own biology slams the door shut on absolute equality.

The Male Profile

Robert Bly wrote *Iron John* in 1990. His book explores the thematic models of males from archetypical myths to the brothers Grim. He proposes that the perfect male is a combination of untamed impulses and thoughtful self-discipline. However, males such as *Iron John,* he says, can be whole only through a woman, or in other words, through a *relational identity.* Some experts say the reason why there cannot be unisex roles and a generic psyche for both men and women is because biological fulfillment for both sexes requires differentiation

As it happens, males are physically more powerful than females. They have deeper voices and are more aggressive, hairier, and bigger. Males have longer legs and feet, run faster, and throw farther. Men are safer from physical attacks because they have broader shoulders, larger hands, and longer arms as well as bigger chests, lungs, hearts, and stronger skulls and jaws. They have more upper body strength and are able to carry more.

The hormone testosterone and embedded biology make males taller and heavier than females. Typically, men have a stiffer stance and control their space better. Reputedly, males have a greater frequency of sexual thoughts than females do, which affects their aggressive behavior and lack of constraint.

Socially, men will not automatically open up when conversing, because they tend to convey objective facts more than their subjective feelings in a conscious effort to be unemotional, which makes for shorter and more pointed conversations.

Males adopt the body language that works best for them in areas that reveal their purpose as beings who are good at such things as bread winning, companionship, achievement, and security. Men who are "code" heroes are usually older with a certain calling and set of values by which they live.

As 9-5 jobs replaced hunting and planting, men became more aware of the bottom line and the cost saving effects of their behavior. Males transitioned into economic engines instead of simple hunters and farmers. This was not always the case, however.

Prehistoric males had to be equipped with survival qualities such as agility, good vision, strength, and stamina to be successful providers. For example, men have more red blood cells than women, and have more iron stored in their body than females, which tends to collect at the tip of the nose and responds to magnetic north This would be very handy in finding your way home after a long hunt for food. Is this tantalizing fact the reason men are better at directions?

In order to find attractive, healthy, nurturing mates, males have power moves to project the maximum fatherhood cues such as looking muscular, energetic, athletic, virile, and robust. Early day males also had to be adventurous, competitive, and resourceful to feed their families, which gave rise to other things such as the tendency to make decisions and take security precautions.

The power moves that enable men, as well as women, to survive and reproduce are the ones most likely to show up in succeeding generations. As a result, survival pressures contribute to men's total makeup along with biochemistry.

The Female Profile

Females are powerful communicators and emphatic listeners, as seen by the patented way they tilt their heads-at least in America. As said before, the biggest power move differences between males and females are rooted in biochemistry with some gender distinctions created by society.

Although increasing levels of estrogen and progesterone induce the propensity for melodrama and contribute to such things as intimacy, which can cause higher levels of oxytocin, the sight of children always brightens a woman's face.

The economic justice, perks, female equality, and body language freedoms are advanced by the prevailing ideology of gender in almost every enlightened society. On the other hand, less enlightened ideology found most notably in the middle east, considers women dangerous objects of desire and second class citizens.

Gender distinctions are apparent in middle-east dress customs which have been unchanged for hundreds of years. For example, full dresses or burquas cover the anatomy more than pants and a blouse do, while veils and shawls cover the face, all of which are visible signals of constraint.

In American culture, in general much female body language behavior focuses on finding mates that are healthy and resourceful enough to provide the sustenance necessary for their own well-being, as well as their children's survival and expansion. Thus, the most prominent needs of most females are affection, financial security, and child-rearing support. Such needs tend to make women relationship oriented rather than goal oriented.

Women have a better eye for detail as well as better peripheral vision, which helps locate their children, but they are worse at spacial visualizing like catching a high fly to right field.

Females have more verbal ability, multi-tasking abilities, and the ability to remembering lists better. They have an uncanny ability to recall trivial matters from the past that baffles and terrorizes most men They ask more questions, plan more, and follow instructions better such as jury instructions. In addition, Women are better at reading faces and detecting sadness in other women than men.

Feminine communications, as said before, tend to indicate feelings rather than baseline information, and they have adopted a wide variety of linguistic devices to soften the message and emphasize emotional content. In addition, they are adept at communicating in special coded meanings. A good example is my wife asking me at social events, "What time is it". Actually, she does not care about the exact time. This is her special code for telling me that she is ready to leave.

The meaning behind much female gesturing is largely parallel to male gesturing, except where physical considerations override convention. For instance, females take up less space, but make more head movements than men such as the head tilt to acknowledge someone, the head toss to flirt, and the head tuck to demonstrate seriousness, which is accomplished by pulling the head back, lowering the chin, and narrowing the eyes at the same time. Since women pay more attention to their hair on average than men do, stroking, twirling, and rearranging it frequently means they find a man attractive.

Just like men, the most rewarding body language for many women relates to appearance and sexuality-always two of humanity's biggest concerns. Female's skin is more sensitive than male skin. Females learn to accentuate their hips; hold objects close to their breasts, tilt their heads, keep their chins up, and glance sideways. Females who want to take things up a notch or two have the option to lift their skirts a little bit, half-close their eyes, casually bend forward, pat their buttocks, or simply touch a man's knee.

Females show displeasure by sulking, pouting, or protruding their lips. They express negative emotions such as pent-up anger differently than males do by defensive posturing, setting their jaws, crossing their arms or legs, and scowling. They avoid all contact by turning their body and eyes away from possible conflicts instead of moving into them aggressively. Disapproval is a full turn of the head and eye roll. A one-half turn is not full disapproval.

Women become more verbally combative than physically combative when they "hit the ceiling". They prefer to express their anger through short, but loud vocal outbursts, instead of physically aggressive body language, which they save for moments when no one is looking. Dr. Laura, the unforgiving women's guru wrote a book that basically advises women to stop whining and start winning.

The minute boys and girls are born they are treated differently due to a set of expectations dictated by society for men and women's behavior. The expectations are so ingrained that they often become hard differences that lead to bias and stereotyping. These prejudices take hold in well-established, predictable areas, but do not argue against real, scientifically proven differences.

Practical Pointers

Gender distinctions are important cultural configurations. Blurring the distinctions between genders does not make sense. The recognition of men and women as biologically different is universal after four million years in which men and women prospered by maximizing complementary characteristics, eons that etched different patterns on the neural networks of the two genders.

Countless cultural rules prescribe and regulate behavior along gender lines, but body language characteristics largely spring from biological sex differences. Even though gender inequities do arise out of social and cultural conventions for a variety of reasons that may be less than ideal, his-and-her towels are still all right.

Chapter 6

Behavioral Profiling

"Just another term for body language."

Behavioral profiling is in the forefront of the news. In a hostile geopolitical world it is a indispensable tool for diplomacy, business, and safeguarding the welfare of innocent people worldwide. Actually, it is the use of body language. Most of us learn to be observant in early childhood as an adaptive lifetime skill, but few of us know enough body language to profile people effectively.

Well-defined business, social, and individual profiles facilitate stronger relationships that augment our psychological power and solidarity instead of giving control to others who don't have our best interests at heart. Since most of us have at least some skill in these areas, the task is to expand upon what we have.

On the threshold, behavioral profiling is not unconstitutional since it is not inherently prejudicial. Stereotyping people solely on the basis of their membership in a certain race, group, or class is unconstitutional. The reason is that a few people, like minorities, become the victims of stereotyping because the human mind sometimes prefers the simple in lieu of the complex, and tries to generalize from a limited number of characteristics. Also, the protections of the United States Constitution are specific in that they do not apply in foreign countries.

Behavioral profiling is data dependent and requires a basic knowledge of the norms and customs of others, especially in a multicultural society like America. Armed with the data, simple cognitive powers that acquire, store, interpret, and put information to use is all that one needs.

Acquiring the core data of behavior through the observation and interpretation of body language not only advances the understanding of complex behavior in others, but also provides a platform for the enrichment of our own lives through self-discovery and self-improvement.

The best way to learn the art of behavioral profiling is to pay close attention to people's behavior, and follow these simple rules:

1. Give careful attention to initial information because we all tend to select certain kinds of information and exclude information that is inconsistent with our worldview. Making up our minds early relieves us of the cognitive dissonance of difficult decision making such as deciding "yes" or "no".

2. The more important something is to us, the less objective we are. Since we make bad decisions when we pay attention to trivial information, know what is important and what is unimportant.

3. Devote your full attention to the practice of profiling, because we do worse when our attention is unfocused or fragmented.

4. Keep it simple. Most of us are unable to handle more than two or three pieces of information at a time. We process small amounts of information automatically, but when information exceeds two or three items, then we have to handle it in series by controlled and focal point thinking.

5. Keep it simple. Do not look for things that are not there. Doing so requires more focused attention, which is more difficult.

6. A corollary to "keeping it simple" is making sure we do not become overloaded with information or we risk going into "illusory conjunctions". Avoid letting people over-share information. We do not need to know everything. Inappropriate combinations of information are the result of demands on us that are too high.

7. Since we learn early to be wary of strangers, we need to overcome treating people as non-persons. We need to give people the attention

they need and treat them with courtesy and etiquette, because these things mimic friendships.

8. Be more objective and less emotional by acquiring more data since knowledge overcomes our fear of being wrong.

9. Do not be too proud, stubborn, or afraid to use the science of behavioral profiling.

10. Most people do not like scrutiny, so it is best to keep your evaluations to yourself. In particular, people do not want to hear about their flaws.

In summary, tag for future linking people's most striking visible behavior in displaying their size, postures, mannerisms, clothing, and speech characteristics. Anything that makes them standout. Always be cognizant of the situation in which signs and clues occur. Look for extremes such as whether people are extremely big or small, intense or easy going, subtle or in your face, and pay special attention to deviations and rogue traits.

Sometimes we do not have ample time to cover every base in behavioral profiling. Don't panic, however, because some experts claim we get a quick idea, or all we really need to know about someone from *thin slicing* in three simple areas of inquiry: their *compassion, socio-economic status*, and *satisfaction in life*.

It is relatively easy to get a quick bearing on whether a person is compassionate or not by using a simplified score of one to ten on a behavioral scale ranging from unemotional, uncaring, critical, intolerant, unforgiving and harsh to warm, pleasant, smiling, open, and friendly. In a broad sense, does the person in question put humanity first? This means behaving in ways that consider the welfare of others as an essential part of human flourishing as well as a matter of personal ethics.

The second area of inquiry is the status of a person in terms of whether or not he is fulfilling his physical and emotional needs. The reason is that the fulfillment of needs affect people's worldview and socio-economic behavior. For example, people who have to scratch for a living are more hardened, insecure, unkind, stingy, and lacking in confidence because they have to fight for survival, whereas people with few needs are more confident, secure, and open.

Generally, people who are self-made exhibit behavior that manifests focus, drive, and dedication while people who had everything handed to them behave in self-indulgent ways that eventually drive them into an egocentric ditch that gets deeper and deeper because they never seem to have enough, and what they do have they don't take care of.

The third area involves people's satisfaction in life. People who achieve their goals have their feet planted firmly on a well-paved road of personal accountability and responsibility. On the other hand, people who have not met their goals adopt a victim's mentality with behavior that is bitter, angry, vengeful, and cynical of others who are achievers.

Practical Pointers

The more individual information we have about someone the better, but sometimes a small amount of essential information is quite enough, like adding sweetening to your food. In situations where we do not have enough observable information, adequate knowledge base, or free time to process all of the behavioral information normally required for accuracy, it is possible to use social science tools such as convergent validation theory, correlation theory, and inferences to supplement the available data and get a fair idea.

Chapter 7

Sense Perception

"Keep your eyes and ears open"

Seeing, feeling, hearing, tasting, and smelling are the main links to the world around us. Through our sensory channels, data is constantly streaming to our brains, which enables us to experience external reality. In extreme situations, people typically pick one and exclude the others as the most reliable and trustworthy sensory channel for gaining accurate information. This practice is acceptable since each sensory channel has its own body language correlates, and people are comfortable choosing one and excluding others as a means of reinforcement.

Sight

Sight is arguably the most important of all sensory data. Many behavioral experts think that people truly know only those things they see, and they see all they need to know. When the act of seeing conflicts with another sense, sight will always dominate, and its loss is the greatest loss of all.

Social factors that influence the way we see others, and how they see us are important to body language interpretation. Sight is how people fix their position in relation to external objects. Socially, sight is a way of questioning things. Some people will not act or attempt to act upon something, unless they can form a mental image of it in their mind.

Things that people cannot see are uncertain, and ideas that cannot be seen mentally have no solution.

Of cursory note, sight is not always one hundred percent reliable. When one's kinesthetic information does not agree with the visual information, the visual tends to dominate whether right or wrong.

Touching

People love to touch. They touch to greet each other, to flirt, to show support, to express sympathy, and to set the atmosphere, as well as a multitude of lesser things such as the tactile pleasure of turning the pages of a great book. Touching plays a pivotal role in relationships, because it not only acts as an icebreaker, but also increases exponentially as people become more intimate.

Moreover, spontaneous touching facilitates demonstrative reactions to situations that pop up and call for a response and we cannot think of anything suitable to say. Current examples are high and low-fives, knuckle touching, chest bumping, and double half back combos another form of symbolic touching that professional athletes use to celebrate personal accomplishments is the single finger gun or "the outlaw", which is the quick draw of the single finger gun on each hand.

On the other side of the coin, touching that is totally unintentional like accidently bumping into someone is a bad thing that can provoke violent reactions from sensitive strangers. Impulsively touching the opposite sex can have unintended sexual connotations.

Sometimes uninvited body contact invites aggressive behavior. For example, people using their elbows to push their way to the front of a line causes other people to respond back. In other cases, uninvited body contact only entails innocent and benign acts like guiding someone through a crowd, attempting to get people's attention, or maybe con-gratulating them.

In connection with intentional touching of a quasi-sexual nature like hugs and kisses, bear in mind who you are and where you are. Often a situational relationship exists between members of the opposite sex where one person is subordinate to the other, like a boss and his employees. In this context, what is the best approach to touching? A warm, friendly, low-key approach never hurts, and the best answer to whether a kiss on the cheek, a hug, or a handshake is sending the right message depends on the particular environment and the local norms of behavior.

Since the social rules of intentional touching vary from place to place, the best practice is to learn the local rules in advance either from observation or a mentor, because there is an apparent relationship between the human sense of territory and cultural rules involving touching.

Casual Touching

Research has shown that a majority of people greeting or saying goodbye to each other will touch in some way. For example, the greeting norm in mainstream American society today involves casual touching in the form of a firm handshake and a simple, "How's it going"? In the business world, the handshake is the most portentous method of greeting available because it sets a professional tone.

Handshaking has an uncertain destiny. Whether it is flimsy or firm, strong or weak, wet, or some other way, lies in the future. The rules are subject to change due to factors like the advent of women in the labor force and the rise of pandemic flu viruses, so just about anything is possible as long as it does not draw unwanted attention.

My generation still thinks a firm handshake and the rules of introduction play an important body language role in conveying seriousness, assurance, and good health, but such thinking is in danger of becoming a cultural anachronism.

Touch lets us know we have made contact with an object. From the sense of touch, we learn shape, firmness, and texture. Touching often occurs under circumstances such as recognizing each other, asking for a favor, giving a command, conveying information, and trying to persuade someone to do something. In this context, it adds emphasis, but in other contexts, touching has a different meaning.

Depending on variables such as when and where people touch, how long they touch, how much pressure they use, and whether others are present can completely change its meaning. In private, for example, stroking each other signals a bond or close relationship between two people, whereas in public people tend to substitute physical stroking for verbal stroking.

Some groups such as inner city teenagers and athletes have different versions of hand shaking that replace the standard style. Their personalized versions involve more ritualistic hand moves and gestures than the ordinary handshake. However, a simple handshake is usually sufficient.

Slow Hands

Intimate touching ranges from the casual to the intense in four general progressive stages. In public, intimate touching known as PDAs (i.e. public displays of affection) make others uncomfortable. This social norm is widely understood, and in countries such as Japan, PDAs are a cultural taboo. Therefore, only the bold or pretentious will dare break them; however, in private there are four kinds of intimate touching: tickling, hugging, cuddling, and kissing.

Tickling is a form of teasing that involves light touching in sensitive areas. Since tickling causes uncontrollable giggling, laughter, and twitching, it is problematic if the person on the receiving end does not want or like it, thus this form of touching depends a great deal on the intentions of the participants.

Hugging is a matter of positioning. The higher up on a vertical plane the more likely a hug is just a friendly greeting or a protective, nurturing hug, whereas lower and tighter hugs are more intimate and less acceptable in casual relationships.

Cuddling is a more intimate form of touching that borders on being a discovery encounter as a preliminary to more serious bonding. Both sexes love to cuddle because of its warmth, closeness, and protection. The problem is that males get an unintended sexual message from cuddling, and misunderstandings arise when the sexes have different intentions. Still, cuddling is an integral part of courtship and marriage.

The standard Bible advises people to greet each other with a holy kiss. The kiss also serves as a form of goodbye. More importantly, a kiss symbolizes a spiritual union and is the language of amore. Love gives meaning to life, so knowing how and when to kiss is extremely important. The dilemma is that the fundamentals of kissing are highly subjective and private, and as a rule, kissing is not an activity that anybody teaches anywhere or studies scientifically.

Realistically, kissing is a matter of preference and style and not scientific study. Experience is the greatest asset in the realm of kissing, since kissing is anything from a friendly peck on the cheek or forehead that is for greeting or departing to the deep throat kiss of intense passion that is for seduction. The experience of either one is difficult to misinterpret, which preserves the polyvalence of the kiss and the ambiguity of its countless different forms. Of course, not all kisses are the same. There is a difference in how people kiss their spouse, their siblings, their friends and parents.

Sounds

Linking certain sounds with body language creates a heightened effect. For example, audible breathing plays a prominent role in the expression of frustration and disgust, and love without its highly expressive sound effects would not be the same.

Highly excited people tend to hyperventilate, which amplifies their physical state by inhaling and exhaling air in quick, short, noisy bursts. Infuriated persons exhale air with an audible snort for added effect.

In circumstances of grief and sorrow, people often move their head from side to side in a kind of silent no, while slowly exhaling deep sonorous breaths. Early in life, children learn to tighten their abdominal muscles when throwing a temper tantrum, which enables them to become rigid and emit the loudest possible sounds.

A typical sound arising out of nervousness, apprehension, and foreboding is the throat clearing exercise, which is common in public speaking. Apprehension causes mucus to form in the throat and the natural thing to do is clear the throat followed by a drink of water.

Men engage in throat clearing more often than women do, and adults need to clear their throats more often than children do. Outside of public speaking, male throat clearing serves as a useful nonverbal admonishment to be careful or to behave.

Another common sound is a sibilant "whew" coupled with symbolically wiping beads of sweat from the forehead. An audible expulsion of air conveys a sense of relief when some obstacle or difficult task is over. Whistling usually signals the expected easing or planned termination of a difficult problem.

A sound in widespread use for a wide variety of human feelings is whistling. Whistling is most often associated with the pleasant harmonics of song birds and a sense of happiness and contentment; however, people also whistle to summon pets, to show appreciation, and to communicate surprise and astonishment at particularly useful times such as paying someone else's bill. Pragmatically speaking, whistling helps muster up courage and confidence in situations of fright and apprehension, and along with humming makes difficult tasks seem easier.

Sounds that are insulting or less than flattering are most body sounds; consequently, imitating body sounds is a popular way of expressing the sentiment "to heck with you". Placing your tongue between your lips and forcefully expelling air, which causes the lips to quiver loudly and sound something akin to flatulence is the so-called Bronx razz sound.

Some highly confident people have a simple and irrepressible clicking or clucking sound they make when they want to signal their success at doing something, and others emit a unmistakable snorting sound by inhaling great gulps of air when they prevail.

Unforgettable Smells

Smells are a powerful and useful way of remembering and describing notable events in our lives. Historically, smelling has a long history of use despite being the most primitive of our five senses. For example,

> Attraction begins in the nose.

long before humans were able to see predators in the heavy bushes, or hear a tell-tell branch snap, they were sniffing at the olfactory environment around them to discern the relative safety of their location.

Consequently, our sense of smell is second only to sight in overall importance. Although the human sense of smell is not as good as a canine's, many people are able recognize as many as ten thousand different smells.

The latest research available reveals that people handle information from their nostrils in a more unique way than previously thought. Information goes directly to those parts of the brain associated with memory and emotion instead of the analytical parts that process seeing, hearing, and touching.

The odor receptors located high in the nose theoretically trigger thousands of nerve signals that our brain interprets as separate smells, but not all of us use the same equipment. Some people remember distinctive smells for years, but for others the nose is little more than "face furniture".

Important information, especially of a gaseous nature, arrives via the olfactory receptors in the nose. No one knows for sure what happens when an odor molecule hits a nose receptor, but memories evoked by odors feel more vivid and alive than those of the other senses do because certain areas of the brain linked to emotions become much more active in response to certain odors than the other senses.

Much of our behavior depends on our sense of smell. For example, smell is unmatched in evoking emotional reactions such as fear and disgust. There is such a close connection between smell, emotions, and memory that many of our emotional experiences would be much less lively and more ambiguous without our sense of smell.

Good vs. Bad Smells

Good smells have unique effects on our behavior as therapeutical tools to help improve our mood and outlook on life. In addition, the concept of "smell" is a powerful and highly useful way of describing and remembering important events in our lives. For instance to invoke a nostalgic sense of home and happy times with the family, people use the scent of vanilla to help bring out these pleasant memories. The smell of cedar helps protect clothes against insects and the smell of certain herbs and soporific floral extracts help calm the nerves.

On the other hand, bad smells are a turn off. If a person you are conversing with has bad breath, the impression is given that he probably does not care much about personal

> Some things, like nuclear waste, are so bad, even Heaven pinches its nose.

hygiene or his social image. In any event, you will most likely form and keep a negative image of a person whose breath smells like swamp gas.

What smells good to you is a complete turn off to someone else. For example, studies show many women do not care for the smell of many male types of cologne, as well as other things like charcoal smoke. On the other hand, food smells are "in" these days, because food smells remind people of their childhood when life was simpler. This trend puts fragrance companies under a lot of pressure to create new smells in an already flooded market.

The Pleasure of Tasting

In social terms, taste means having a sense of appreciation and refinement. In this sense, taste is an acquired trait. People have a so-called taste for the good things in life, and people link good taste with sophistication and polish. For simple appreciation and discernment, some people place their fingers gently to their lips and kiss them in a sweeping outward gesture as a form of personal approval.

Taste approval plays a decisive role in keeping all living creatures from ingesting harmful substances by acting as a go-between the head and heart. Taste data goes directly to the brain via receptors in the mouth; consequently, many bad things that seem good never reach the digestive tract. One caveat is that our sense of taste is not perfect, and is sometimes misleading.

It suffices to say that sensory body language plays just as important a role in the social context as it plays in the biological context of maintaining good body equilibrium.

Practical Pointers

People acquire information about their environment through their sensory receptors at a high rate, which allows for a quick respond. However, since most of us rarely have time to thoroughly analyze all incoming sensory data, we develop reflexive body language routines that automatically deal with familiar situations without time consuming conscious analysis. Reflexive touching on the arm is a good example of a quick and easy response that helps break down artificial barriers in a tense situation.

Chapter 8

Accustomed To Your Face

"For news of the heart ask the face"

The face is the first thing we notice about people and the first thing we recall about them later. Part of the reason is that the face has multiple functions. The face is a permanent billboard for who we are and where we come from. What is more, it is the body's billboard for emotions and attitudes. Facial expressions are more personal and communicate inner feelings and thoughts faster, more subtly, and more efficiently than oral speech.

In speech, we are able to deceive, obfuscate, and cover-up how we feel and think; but facial expressions are more difficult to contrive due to their primary role as the initial source of spontaneous impression information. Faces are weapons grade. Every emotion we feel shows up in the face, which gives it an experienced look and makes it the most expressive and overworked feature of the body. On the bright side, research has shown that people who are more expressive tend to be happier and more successful.

How do faces assist people? First, faces are how we identify others and ourselves. Secondly, faces communicate emotions and attitudes faster than a proton in a particle accelerator. Thirdly, facial fashion reflects our outlook, attitude, and priorities about health. For example, glowing skin, rosy cheeks, and bright eyes are a testimony to good health. Typically, people with animated and lively faces are more popular because they tend to be more fun.

Often we can remember someone's face, but not his or her name. Because facial recognition is so important, the human brain has a separate storage area just for remembering faces. The reason for this probably lies in the ancient friend-or-foe acknowledgment that was critical to personal safety. At any rate, facial features and expressions have had thousands of years to evolve and our brains have had thousands of years to understand the meaning behind each one. Moreover, in the new millennium, facial recognition technology will proliferate as computers become faster and more advanced in the ability to match faces with digital images

Mythology

Widespread body language myths have their psychogenesis in cultural needs that help ground people. Joe Campbell writes in his book, *The Power of Myth,* that the meaning of life is the *experiencing* of life and myths help to ground us, center us, and teach us how to live. All myths everywhere call people to a deeper awareness of the act of living according to Joe Campbell.

Face mythology has a long history dating back as far as the ancient Greeks who studied and wrote about the relationship between facial structure and human character. Because of humankind's fascination with faces, and the fact that each face is unique, gave rise to the need for early-day people to seek a commonality of face themes that would help them fulfill the constant requirement of their psyche for *centering* in terms of universal principals. For example, some Greek writers thought a round face to be a jovial face, while a thin face was a stern face. Lowbrows were associated with being insipid, while high brows were a sign of intellect.

Down through the ages various people developed dicey ideas that rapscallions, whose character was difficult to easily explain, had facial features such as big pointy and hooked noses, closely set eyes, large jaws, sloping foreheads, heavy brow ridges, and handle shaped ears. The thinking was that the more animal-like a person's face, the more dangerous he or she was.

Whether or not physiognomy is scientifically valid, it has survived over the centuries. Hollywood thrives on vampires and other strange characters that fit arcane stereotypes such as seen in Harry Potter movies or *Avatar*. In addition, they proliferate in television shows like *Star Trek* and *Battleship Galactica*.

Even though facial configurations vary from culture to culture in response to genetics and environmental challenges, people everywhere have a similar sense of facial aesthetics. New research suggests that people tend to believe that typical things are the most attractive. The trick to creating an attractive face is to average many faces into one, because our brains like things that are the easy to process. For example, typical baby faces have a special kind of beauty that we instinctively love and desire to protect. They have large heads, but delicate jaws and chins, chubby cheeks, high foreheads, large captivating eyes, small mouths, and smooth skin. And, that is not all.

Baby features are what most people around the world also find attractive in adulthood, because they are associated with youth and beauty in most cultures. The closer a face is to a prototype, the faster people are able to process it mentally. Processing efficiency is slowed down by unusual features that are asymmetrical and rough-hewn from the storm and stress of a hard life.

The immensely popular Clara Bow, the movie star who starred in the 1920s era, was dubbed the "It" girl, because she just had the looks of "It", a Twenties era code word for sex appeal. At least, that's what the Hollywood fantasy factory wanted American audiences to believe. Features that contributed to her "It" look were a well-cut hairstyle dyed blond, a high forehead, doe eyes, smooth complexion, even teeth, small nose and chin, and coy smile. To cap it off, Ms. Bow epitomized the emancipated woman of her day.

We identify faces by the light and shading that provides texture and contour. Next, we note how distinctive a face is from the average. Finally, we visually measure the relationship and symmetry of the face's differ-ent features For instance, former President Clinton has an evenly spaced and symmetrical face despite a slightly bulbous nose. Face readers say he has even spacing between his eyes, between his eyes and cheekbones, and between his nose and mouth.

Men and women have different facial dynamics. Men's noses, jaws, and eyebrows are larger and wider, and they have more facial hair than women due in part to higher levels of testosterone. Women have lighter and smoother skin, smaller bone structure, but larger cheeks.

Many males like plump lips on women because it is a sign of sexual arousal. In general, males like female faces that are warm and kind. Females prefer male faces that say kindness and intelligence, while faces signifying wealth and power run a close second. Obviously, the physical attractiveness of men and women is not the only factor in face attraction.

It is sad but true that most people are extremely vain and find it difficult to live with their image "as is". As a result, faces are not only a reflection of who we are, but also who we want to be. That is why both sexes use different hairstyles to enhance and flatter their image, and men grow elaborate beards to add a distinguished and mature look to their faces, and conceal defects as well. Some psychologists contend that people have a number of facial personas for different occasions such as working, playing, and staying home.

Face reading has re-surfaced in corporate America. Human Resource Departments of some major corporations have hired face-reading experts to share their expertise with corporate managers in order to determine how well an employee fits into a particular job. Their knowledge reveals who is a hard and cold person, and who is warm and friendly. For example, a company manager is likely to associate a pleasant demeanor and frequently upturned mouth on an employee with positive qualities such as humor and kindness.

Although, faces are not reliable indicators of job intelligence, it is just as important to know who means well and who does not. Even if face reading is not one hundred per cent valid, it is a minor point. People subconsciously do it, and it will be around for a long time to come. It is an old friend that continues to survive by constantly reinventing and renewing itself.

Face Furniture

Facial features, plus their biological functions, are more than mere "face furniture". The evolution of our facial features in connection with environmental influences and the multiple genes we inherit from our parents make them particularly important. Since the expressions, features, and configurations of our faces are non-elective for the most part, they have a real genetic significance as the most visible representations of our heritage and the title page of the book on us.

Faces have a larger purpose than mere aesthetics. In fact, the face is so important that people worldwide put a face on practically everything. It is a proven fact that facial symmetry alone is so highly regarded that when newborn children are shown symmetrical faces and asymmetrical ones they instinctively respond to the symmetrical ones. Faces are important images that people care about, and thus are said to be "careworn".

Symbolic Eyes

Luckily, we are born with incredible eyes. In a sense, they are non-elective body features; however, people also use them in an elective manner. This is because eyes speak with a truthfulness that exceed verbal gestures and overcomes our fear of being misunderstood.

Common eye movements and positions such as looking left or right, up or down, and sideways or straight are special clues to what people are thinking. Additionally, the length of eye contact is indicative of people's mood. In particular, sparse eye contact indicates apathy, moderate contact indicates interest and affection, and excessive contact indicates hostility.

Eye Positions

Eye positions during the activation of the cognitive processes are the subject of a specialized field of study on the meaning of eye movements. Although falling short of universal scientific approval, eye positioning is worth mentioning. According to people trained in this field, people's eyes move in consistent patterns that indicate a search for specific kinds of information in response to questioning.

Generally, these patterns involve looking right, left, or straight ahead when visualizing certain things. For example, when we responding to a question and we look to the upper right we are visualizing something not been seen before. We are in a "thinking" mode. When we look to the upper left, we are recalling a visual memory of something we have seen before. If we look down, we are in a "feeling" mode. For example, former President Clinton is a "feeling" person who frequently looks down and to the right when speaking. If we look down and to the left, we are emotionally talking to ourselves about how we feel.

When we position our eyes on a horizontal plane, we are in an "auditory" mode that means we think more in terms of sounds than feelings. Experts say a reversal of these processes means a devious person has ulterior motives, and is trying to manipulate the signals. In actuality, brain functions are much more complicated than these helpful but oversimplified ideas.

The sideways eye glance is a widespread expression combining a lowered head and the eyes looking sideways, thus taking advantage of boldness and shyness at the same time. Too often, however, this indirect means of communication is overdone.

Blinking the eyes in spontaneous patterns often indicates untruthfulness, while a measured blinking rate indicates reflective thought. Some females use a rapid blinking pattern to say, "I'm innocent", whereas a combination of slowly closing the eyes and lowering the head says, "I'm blanking out what I'm hearing".

Eye movement is such a highly regarded indicator of behavior that veteran people watchers often ignore other body language clues in favor of this one activity as a reliable warning of what to expect.

Eye Power

Since the eye is the universal symbol of knowing, eye contact is one of the most powerful of all body language signals. For example, eye contact can be the start of a romantic relationship, or the start of a fight if held a fraction too long.

A direct stare combined with a stony expression, which is held for any period of time causes discomfort in the recipient, because eye contact has evolved from the animal kingdom as an aggressive sign of impending attack and as a warning.

Although closely related to eye movement and eye position, eye contact provides an extremely dependable indication of interest, attraction, attitudes, and internal moods that give life to ambiguous movements. Moreover, eye contact establishes a heightened visual awareness that is an important aspect of our consciousness.

The famous postmodernist artist Marcel Duchamps erred when he referred to the human eye as a "dumb organ". As a matter of record, there is no known scientific instrument as sensitive to light as the normal human eye. In short, eye contact is lightning-quick, while verbal exchanges are slow and ponderous. Frequently conversations in public, especially in the political domain, are deliberately scripted and syncopated activities, while eye contact and body language are spontaneous.

Why is eye contact so powerful? The answer lies in its long history of use. Eye contact began in the first days of visual awareness in a dangerous and competitive primordial world. It continued throughout history because it was evolutionarily adaptive, allowing animals to stare each other down and establish dominance without the dangers of physical contact.

In addition, eye contact is necessary to instinctual survival patterns since newborn babies who establish quick eye contacts have the best chance of obtaining food and attention. By the same token, humans and animals alike have a compelling need to see and be seen since certain kinds of visual contact tell us if other people care for us or not. Consequently, the body language of eye contact is here to stay as a powerful communicator in a variety of situations.

Deliberately avoiding eye contact raises many issues such as shame, sorrow, embarrassment, or the simple desire to be let alone. Furthermore, any break in eye contact during a conversation or in a meeting that is untimely and not a part of the person's norm indicates stress or lost interest, which is why many people will try to disguise such breaks by looking off and pretending to be interested in something else.

People who do not want to be sociable will avoid eye contact. For instance, joggers who take the time to jog usually are only interested in the workout and not socializing. Most of them will check others out at a distance, but when they pass someone on the same path, they invariably look off to the side so as not to make eye contact.

Prolonged gaze aversion that is obvious with no attempt to disguise it signals either complete submission such as seen in hostages, or deep discomfort, phobias, and shyness. For example, some people cannot bear to look at blood because it makes them extremely uncomfortable; other people cannot look down from great heights without getting vertigo; and small children are too shy to look strange adults in the eye.

Another rule is that eye contact has a greater significance to listening than to speaking. Eye contact is an important feedback to let speakers know you are being attentive. Normally, unless a person is looking sharply upwards, you will see white on two sides of the eye to the right and left with the pupil and iris making up the rest of the coloration, but if you are attentive and you like what you hear during eye contact your pupils will noticeably expand. Under stress the eyelids involuntarily contract, which exposes the white on the bottom side of the eye.

Sales people and marketing people know that most buyers will tend to look at objects longer if they are interested. The longer people look at an object, the easier it is to buy; hence, "eye-time" is a valuable marketing technique. Eye contact also expresses feelings such as the frozen open look that indicates fear and rapid scanning movements that reveal excitement.

Narrowing the eyes into tiny slits are signs of anger, while sadness is the eyes looking downwards. Do not pay any attention to the conventional wisdom that an honest person will always look you straight in the eye, since just the opposite is sometimes true. Professionally dishonest people are more motivated to maintain eye contact than honest people are. Many believe that men with so-called quick eyes have cold natures.

Not making eye contact in close confines with strangers helps reduce our anxiety and apprehensiveness by according those around us a nonhuman status so we do not have to be personally involved with them. People who deal with the public on a regular basis must constantly sharpen their interpersonal skills in areas such as eye contact, or at the decisive moment, they hesitate and give the wrong impression.

Eyes not only function as the recipients of external light, but also as the front porch to the house within. We are able to tell more about a person by looking into their eyes than looking at a swirl of garish, comic book quality tattoos. Moreover, the eyes guide us through life. What they see is real and forms our reality.

Other emotions such as love, fear, and recognition clearly show in the eyes, as well as reflective thought, thus making eye management a valuable personal power tool that transcends slow, uncertain, and decidedly non-reflective verbal speech.

The Stare

One of the most important techniques of eye management is the "look" or the stare. Staring plays a special role in the animal kingdom as a prelude to an attack. This survival supportive phenomenon has carried over into civilized society causing us to feel uneasy the minute we become aware of someone's stare even though we are in no danger whatsoever.

The unnerving feeling that results from someone staring at us is a visceral one and raises our heart rate, especially if we do not have a ready avenue of escape. It is natural for people to stare at nonhuman things such as art, animals, and nature, but people staring at each other forces a counter reaction such as dealing with it, stopping it, or escaping from it.

Biologically, sustained eye contact raises the respiration rate and blood pressure of the recipient causing some physical discomfort. Watch for changes in the eye-blinking rate. Most adults average approximately eight to ten blinks per minute. Spontaneous increases in the blinking rate are closely associated with untruthfulness and emotional arousal. Contrarily, maintaining a measured blinking rate makes recipients feel relaxed and trusting.

Sometimes people who stare holes through us are flirting, because they are infatuated with us, and are eagerly searching for a hint of approval in our face. We also stare at objects of great interest such as celebrities and objects of great abnormality such as the deformed or disabled, probably to help remind us how glad we are that we are not in their position.

The utility of eye contact as a nonverbal communicator and essential relationship skill is what some people call a "no brainer". Eye contact confers a dominating status, while no eye contact confers "nonhuman" status. For example, at the Performing Arts Center along with thousands of others, I had a palpable "feeling" that the people around me were silently checking each other out even though no one spoke and no one made eye contact. In close confines, everyone was treating each other as nonhumans.

Lovely Lips

The outstanding thing about lips is that they are extremely sensitive because blood is nearer to the surface due to thinner skin. Their functional purpose is to guard against unwanted objects entering the mouth and acting as speech cues whose movements enable us to recognize certain spoken words and phrases. The positioning of the lips displays attitudes, and at the same time operates as indispensable enhancements to facial expressions such as the smile and the frown.

Lips are one of the most seductive features of the body and most females place a high degree of importance on their appearance. Uncertain about their attractiveness, many women seek to recreate themselves to meet idealized goals. Thus, they spend a great deal of money on achieving certain color shades and looks they deem sexy for their lips. For example, some females like the bee-sting look they get from collagen injections, while others want the so-called "pouty" look created by extending the lower lip outward and applying a light color lipstick in the center of the lip.

Lips are important to us because we use them to kiss each other. The kiss is the first and foremost expression humans make use of in greetings and farewells, in love and passion, in sorrow and joy, and in other situations too numerous to list, which makes them unsurpassed in terms of usage. For example, people use their lips to kiss inanimate objects such as dice or a rabbit's foot, the blarney stone, or terra firma when your airplane lands safely, as well as a myriad of idols, images, and religious symbols.

The good news is that a simple kiss is able to seal an agreement, or solidify an alliance, or promise. The bad news is that a kiss also has ominous undertones as in the infamous "Kiss of death". People that bite their lips are uncertain or worried about something they are pondering.

Follow Your Nose

"The nose knows" is a childhood saying that reflects our belief in the nose's powers to detect things. The nose is an important nonelective feature that has the biological role of smelling, inhaling, and filtering the air we breathe. It is so essential to us that its predominant location on the front of our face is no accident. The nose is perfectly situated to test the air before we proceed. Studies have recently discovered evidence that each side of the nose is able to smell the environment, and that humans have a greater ability to smell than previously thought.

The nose's shape is partly due to environmental factors, since its biological job is to warm and moisten air to body temperature before it enters the body. Noses are flat and wide, or long and thin. Physiological studies have linked nose sizes to particular climates. For instance, the nose tends to be longer in colder regions than in hotter climates. In addition, nasal inflation helps breathing in a stress situation such as the fight or flight response, undue excitement, and over stimulation.

Micro expressions like a twitching nose means a person thinks something is wrong, either literally or figuratively, and needs further inspection. To register disgust, we tend to wrinkle our noses automatically by tightening the muscles on either side of the nose creating wrinkles between the eyes. Squeezing the nostrils with our thumb and forefinger symbolically means something stinks. Contortion of the nose to one side means disapproval. All of these moves, sometimes symbolic, are subtle clues to signal if something is offensive to us or not.

In addition to its functional purpose, the nose is also famous for its form and shape. For example, the "wicked witch of the west" caricature has made hooked noses famous. In fact, the third most noticeable non-elective feature of the face is the nose, which is blatant and unmistakable.

Noses have a mythological significance for many cultures. A nose can be a slightly upturned "pug" nose made famous by the Irish and English, or straight and prominent like the aquiline Roman nose. The shape of your nose does not necessarily mean you are of a certain ancestry though. The most famous of the Cheyenne war chiefs was a man named "Roman Nose".

People take pride in their noses and use them to display self-respect, pugnacity, and self-confidence. Vanity is like chasing the wind, but pride means personal integrity and dignity that places us above unworthy thoughts and actions. Raising the nose by tilting the head back is a sign of snobbery. It signals conceit, dominance, or defiance because something is beneath us and "we are looking down our nose at it". Stroking the nose means that we think someone is guilty of "brown nosing".

Aristocrats and elitists always have their "nose in the air", and sometimes they "thumb" their nose" at lower economic social classes. An overly curious person is "nosey" and sometimes their nose is sticking in your business, whereas a talented person has "a nose for it".

Prominent men have prominent noses. Think Charles De Gaulle, for instance. For some people; however, their nose is not a source of pride or vanity. For one thing, a large, bulbous, cherry red nose with spidery broken blood vessels often points to alcohol abuse, because alcohol flushes the nose area and exacerbates any physical ailments that are affecting the nose such as Rosaceae.

Excessive nose hairs indicate that personal appearance and grooming are not high on the owner's list of priorities. This aspect of appearance has become a matter of indifference to some people, especially as they age, because they have ceased being around other people as often as they used to be, and personal grooming has become less important. As social cognition becomes more and more of a potent force in everyday life, however, the ins and outs of social interdependence increase in complexity, but personal grooming will still play a big role in how people are viewed by others.

A Pair of Ears

If we do not hear something we are supposed to hear, it is not the fault of our ears, since they are natural sound wave collectors designed to capture and process diverse sounds. Of cursory note, the ear on the right side is better at processing speech than the left-sided ear. At any rate, not hearing something probably means we did not want to hear it.

Our ears are inconspicuous and humble when buried under hair, but when examined closely they are as unique as fingerprints and eyes, nobody's ears are exactly the same. Many physiological experts assert that people's ears identify them with great accuracy.

Van Gogh's ear is arguably the most famous ear in history, not only because of the back story of what happened to it, but also because Van Gogh's works are some of the most admired paintings of all time and fetch record-breaking prices. Van Gogh sliced part of his ear off after an intense argument and Absinthe drinking bout with his roommate artist Paul Gauguin. After chasing Gauguin down the street, Van Gogh wrapped it, and gave it to a female employee of a nearby brothel. This dramatic expression of nonverbal communication makes little sense, and failed to change Gauguin in any way, but it graphically indicatives Van Gogh's deteriorating state of mind, and the powerful effects of liquors aged in wormwood.

Certain common ear shapes traditionally suggested various physical traits. Large ears sticking out are unattractive, funny, and symbols of unintelligent and uninspired personalities. Clark Gable often had his ears physically pinned back for many of his movie roles in order to look more intelligent. On the other hand, small ears are a clue that the owner is distant and hard to get to know. Cauliflower ears have long been associated with athletes, especially boxers, since they are often the result of a physical pounding. A common expression of defeat is "getting your ears pinned back".

Medium-size, well-shaped ears in folklore are the marks of a con-servative, practical nature, whereas close-set ears hugging the head suggest a logical, likeable, and down-to-earth person. Folklorists also suggest that high placed ears such as those of President Bill Clinton are common on leaders and independent thinkers, while low-set ears indicate driven and career-oriented people. Before going any further with these observations, I must add a caveat. As interesting and fun as they are, the evidence to support them is arcane, anecdotal, and unscientific at best.

It is wise to take note of a stranger's ears before starting an argument. Some researchers believe that people with asymmetrical extremities such as feet, fingers, and ears of different shapes, sizes, and types are more likely to become aggravated when provoked. The rationale is that the biological causes of physical imperfections also are the cause of poor impulse control. Never mind that American women think their feet are their most unattractive body part.

The most noticeable parts of the ear, our earflaps, are not just for adornment and folklore. They help us to locate the direction of sounds. Most of us cannot move our ears, so we "angle our heads" to aid our hearing. Placing our hand behind the ear in a cup clearly means, "Speak up, I can't hear you." This gesture is more than just symbolic, because it actually assists in capturing hard-to-hear sounds.

The ear rub is an unconscious way of saying, "I want to close my ears to what I am hearing," The more obvious gesture of placing the hands tightly over each ear is often used by children as a blocking device, whereas sticking a finger in each ear means "that's too loud."

The ear scratch is a conspicuous sign of confusion that signifies we do not know what to believe about what we are hearing. We switch from confusion to insults by putting our thumbs in both ears, spreading our fingers out to simulate a donkey's ears, and waggling our fingers, which means, "Someone is a big Jackass fool."

I need to mention the ear's role in romance. The ear nibble is a worldwide gesture of love. The heavy-duty version consists of licking, biting, and tonguing. The rationale in support of this popular erotic action is simple and straightforward. Ear lobes are highly sensitive and thin skinned, which alone puts them in the erogenous zone as sexual accessories. but they also are very visual and well placed for kissing thus providing a vehicle for what people are trying to convey in a direct way without speaking.

Chin Ups

The chin begins to quiver when we are on the verge of tears, and it has long been associated with dominance and self-confidence. For example, self-assurance and defiance are clearly shown by thrusting the head and chin out and tightening the jaw muscles coupled with tight forward leaning muscular body language.

Flicking the thumb under the chin is an unmistakable insult in many cultures. A chin set firmly forward is the symbolic spearhead, advance guard, and bowsprit that lead the way for the rest of the body to follow. It signals to others our resolve and bravery, which on occasion comes off as a hostile and challenging attitude to those who oppose us.

"Keep your chin up" is an admonition to be courageous. Over the centuries, our ancestors viewed a prominent chin as a sign of a strong will and athleticism, while a receding chin was a sign of weakness. Thus, keeping the chin up is a positive signal that we are confident, self-reliant, and bold.

> A strong chin indicates a strong person.

Is the chin necessary? Does it do anything? Yes, for one thing it sets the face off from the neck, which gives people a more attractive and angular face. Think about it. Alleged aliens from outer space do not have chins in the media renderings I have seen. Supposedly drawn from descriptions of people who claim to have been abducted, chinless aliens are both spooky and unattractive.

Chins comes in many shapes and sizes, such as square and rounded, long and short, cleft and dimpled. A dimpled chin is strong, handsome, and masculine, but no chin or a receding chin, is unattractive and laden with negative connotations for men. The same is true of a female chin that juts out further than normal.

Besides being a prominent feature of the face, the chin is involved in many gestures. For example, pulling our chin down usually signals a defensive closing off and dejection, so gently lifting a person's chin up is a subtle way of saying, "keep your chin up", and "be happy".

The chin rub or stroke is usually an involuntary act indicating disbelief in what we are hearing, or it means a person is simply engaged in thought. The chin is a pointer if intentionally turned a certain direction, but if withdrawn and tucked inward, it is pointing to an internal suspicion of something.

Does the chin play a role in sexual selection? Yes, the chin does play a role in mating according to many experts. In men, the chin is a prominent, highly visible feature with links to the male hormone testosterone. A strong chin on a man is a robust body language cue proclaiming higher testosterone levels, which generally means good health and virility-two "blue chips" in reproduction.

Some people go as far as contending that a man's chin amounts to reproductive advertising analogous to the antlers on a buck. If this is true, it explains why male chins have been growing in size over the last few hundred years. They are evolutionarily determined as a species-specific survival strategy.

Eyebrows Say It First

Eyebrows call attention to the eyes, so naturally they have been the objects of considerable interest throughout history. People in some cultures do not place any importance on eyebrows and pull them completely out, and other people go to great extremes in coloring and shaping eyebrows as a means of face enhancement. In addition to adornment, and a small role in keeping forehead perspiration out of the eyes, eyebrows are powerful body language communicators. The eyebrows are the first to announce doubt and the eyebrow flash is a delightful nonpareil.

Eyebrows typically play a supporting role in nonverbal communications by helping to convey emotions. For example, eyebrows display confusion and surprise on a routine basis. Without eyebrows, we are not able to express shock, surprise, and doubt. In particular, persistently wrinkled eyebrows signal serious worry, dread, and neurotic feelings of generalized anxiety.

An eyebrow lift in conjunction with a shoulder shrug imparts a sense of helplessness, which is a common gesture worldwide. Lifting one eyebrow up while the other is down signals skepticism. Lowering of both eyebrows and pulling them together tightens and darkens the face into one of uneasy concentration, secretiveness, and suspicion.

Arched eyebrows mean a person knows the answer to a question, but if down turned, the answer is elusive. Lifting one eyebrow is a classic sign of doubt such as the famous John Belushi quizzical one eyebrow lift. Quickly raising and lowering the eyebrows, like Groucho Marx, is a universal flirting expression. Raising the eyebrows and smiling helps us to express admiration. The secret to using our eyebrows lies in combining them with other signals to form intricate expressions.

As long as they do not grow together, eyebrows are important contributors to our image and almost single-handedly have the ability to change a person's image. In the 1930s, sexy eyebrows on women were long and thin, but today sexy eyebrows are bigger. Bushy eyebrows are not everyone's cup of tea, but for some they have become icons. Think Andy Griffin or Andy Rooney for wild, bushy eyebrows.

Mouthing Off

The famous architect, Frank Lloyd Wright said that form and function are a spiritual union. The statement applies somewhat to the human mouth in that they are non-elective body features that have a dual purpose. Not only does it have the highly functional role of helping us to eat, speak, and breathe, but also it has a formal, stylistic role as an object of attraction, adornment, and expression.

> When you get into deep water, keep your mouth shut.

Mouths are very important to body language because they set the tone of the face, and after the eyes, the diverse shapes of the mouth are one of the most noticed features of the face. Therefore, it is more accurate to say that the mouth is in more of a working union of form and function than a spiritual one.

A working mouth is essential to survival. Not only is it the point of entry to the digestive tract, but throughout our waking hours, it is hard at work biting, sucking, chewing, and holding things. Our mouth works to prepare incoming food for digestion and acts as a fail-safe mechanism by testing the digestibility, texture, shape, and temperature of suitable food before we swallow it. Due to its elasticity, it is able to stretch out wide, drop down, and move sideways to accommodate us as needed.

The mouth constantly works at communicating by expressing

emotions and conveying a person's state of mind through natural devices such as a sigh, yawn, or smile, and when necessary, it amplifies emotional behavior by puckering, tightening, or quivering. For example, "gritting the teeth" has become synonymous with determination and fortitude while a pleasant smile is synonymous with happiness.

In addition, the mouth is the permanent residence of our teeth and tongue, which are two of our most important workhorses. The teeth are constantly biting, chewing, and grinding. The incisors cut food into pieces and the canines grip and rip tough food while the premolars and molars crush food. Teeth chatter when we are cold, and work overtime for people who grit and grind them during sleep. At the same time, our teeth carry the added burden of making us attractive or not. Picture a mouth with no teeth.

Teeth make a smile attractive with their dazzle and signal cleanliness, youth, and health. However, if a person's teeth are stained, missing, or uneven they become repulsive. A gap between the two front teeth allegedly gives the owner a heightened sexuality in folklore, but most of the time gaps or missing teeth are a visible sign of a person's low self-esteem or lack of finances, since this kind of person either does not care about dental care or cannot afford it.

The mouth's other permanent resident, the tongue, is not particularly attractive, but it is a significant bundle of muscles and nerves that tastes, swallows, and forms many of the configurations needed for language. According to circumstances, people use their tongues to express feelings. For example, directly sticking the tongue out at someone is an insult.

Running the tongue over the lips in a suggestive manner has sexual connotations unless it involves looking at food, which changes the meaning to, "Hmm, this looks tasty even though it's fusion cuisine!" In addition, a partially protruding tongue means a person is concentrating on the task. Since the tongue enables us to speak effectively, a person speaking unintelligible gibberish is "tongue tied" while "tongue-in-cheek" comments are not serious.

Making Faces

People worldwide are able to recognize intention from facial expressions such as "a look that could kill," a "surprised look", or an "I'm available look". Such wide varieties of expressions are possible because the human face has layered muscles it uses to form hundreds of elective expressions. For instance, antagonism results in tightened jaw muscles and lips.

Other muscles can form a frowning face, which means displeasure or possibly a state of confusion, and raising the eyebrows chiefly indicates disbelief. Anger contracts the face muscles and fear opens them as one possible rampart of the body's defense against further harm. On the other hand, a non-aggressive facial expression is a relaxed, peaceful one similar to the choirboy on a Christmas card with half-closed eyelids, a veiled smile, arched eyebrows, and no brow furrows.

> Defendants who blush and look embarrassed after the verdict is read, receive shorter sentences.

Attitudes often show up first in facial expressions. For example, jutting the chin out shows defiance, a downcast face conveys a turned-off expression, and an engaged look intentionally maintains level eye contact with another person. Hatred distorts the face, while a blank face means a person is clueless.

Complexions

Face colors reveal much about how people feel. A change in skin color signals underlying changes in psychological states and biological responses to events that challenge us. A reddish face indicates a low-level stress response revealing sensitivity. A purple or brownish face is a high-level stress response caused by a drastic increase in blood pressure and blood volume. In other words, the heart is beating so fast and hard the blood in the head has a difficult time returning to the body's trunk. A whitish face is a mid-level stress response involving anxiety or fear. If the face becomes bluish, it means there is poor circulation in that area, while green in the face usually means nausea. A yellow pallor may be jaundice.

Besides stress responses, a red, blushing face combined with averted eyes, awkward behavior, stammering, and a warm tingling feeling in the face frequently indicates a guilty conscience, shame, or embarrassment. Some observers have suggested that we probably do not blush at the thought of guilt, but at the thought that someone else knows about our guilt. Whatever the reason, we show embarrassment in about five seconds by averting our gaze, moving our eyes downwards, smiling briefly, and placing our hands on our blushing cheeks, which speaks a lot louder than mere words.

Intense shame almost instinctively causes a person to hang the head, hide the face, and blush profusely. Ethical spokespersons believe human biology and evolution have hardwired us to experience shame as a way to bring us to our senses from awkward and confused states and to compel us to set higher standards for ourselves. In this context, blushing is an unofficial standard-bearer for honesty.

Embarrassment is a likely culprit behind blushing because the exposure of certain things in our self-contained lives is highly embarrassing such as the publication of our social gaffes, exposure of sensitive parts of our body, and our innermost thoughts. Yet, embarrassment is not one hundred per cent of the reason we blush. People also blush at events that are not embarrassing such as accepting a well-deserved award.

Blemishes and Wrinkles

Facial blemishes are inferential body language clues. For example, the presence of a blemish such as a mole infers that the owner is comfortable with his image, since moles are easier to get rid of than a summer cold. Blemishes attract attention, so their location becomes a huge factor. A well-placed cheek mole is sexy in some people, as exemplified by the daft sexiness of Marilyn Monroe, but a mole on the end of the nose is a very different story.

Acne is an unwanted facial blemish. Nothing is as naturally immature looking as a pimply face. The precise cause of acne is widely debated, but inheritance is a big factor. The bad news is that cleanliness and hygiene play a role in acne, so there is some personal culpability, but the good news is that acne is highly treatable.

Too much sun causes wrinkles, leather-like skin, and possible melanomas. Due to such concerns, sun tanning is not as popular as it used to be. Nevertheless, many people still spend time in the sun since it connotes a healthy outdoors person who is able to afford spending time at the beach. If a person has a tanned face, along with other clues such as a robust physique, he either works outdoors, or has an outdoors hobby such as jogging, tennis, or swimming.

A good tan, however, without any other contextual clues indicates self-consciousness and vanity more than health. Pale skin means the owner is conscious of his health and does not spend much time at the beach or at the tanning parlor.

The longer we live the more we will have ills and troubles that cause wrinkles and lines to develop in conjunction with our biology and the natural pull of gravity. Old age forms bags under the eyes and a puffy, droopy, tired looking face that signals old age. Likewise, facial changes are a result of a variety of retrogressive activities such as drugs, smoking, and alcoholism.

Everyday problems such as allergies, lack of sleep, high-fat diets, and gravity's perpetual pull tend to lengthen our jowls, deepen, and darken the bags under our eyes and cause the upper eyelids to sag, which causes "crow's feet". However, people, can mitigate some of the effects of aging with extreme makeovers such as a facelift.

A person who is hard, cold, cruel, and vicious, and has led a tough life, is likely to have a rough and gnarly face to match, because scars, deep lines, knots, blemishes, and wrinkles etched on our faces over the years become a living record of a lifetime of good and bad experiences. For example, habitual expressions create permanent facial lines built up over time. Anger causes vertical lines between the eyebrows, and "strain hard" wrinkles also show up in the same area. Persistent worry and deep thought causes horizontal lines to run across the forehead.

Creasing around the eyes in conjunction with a smile is reliable proof of a happy person whose countenance is real and not manufactured. Lines at the corner of the mouth often mean that person is familiar with grief or loss and has become tight lipped, while small inward mouth lines indicate an inhibited personality.

Deep lines on the cheeks of the face often mean a person has known hard times, whereas fleeting expressions such as a frown hint at how a person thinks and feels minute-to-minute. Although these examples have a sound basis in reality, they are not literally true in every case, because there are so many different situations during a lifetime that it is impossible to count them all, and people's behavior is not always consistent. Nevertheless we often see others in light of our own experiences, and we know well know what causes us to have wrinkles.

Practical Pointers

Facial dynamics help people to identify with each other and center their lives accordingly. Good-looking faces are very important to us, and there is no reason why people should not look as good as possible. Besides, the power of facial features and expressions exceed oral communications and play a significant role in life's daily pleasures and problems.

Aging is the face's natural enemy. The face loses color, wrinkles-up, and gets old age spots. The skin sags and gets drier. The chin doubles, the earlobes get bigger, and the nose broadens and lengthens. For these reasons, among others, remedial cosmetics have turned into an incredible lucrative industry; however, altering our appearance too much is threatening to people.

Face reading is beneficial when combined with other body language clues, but it is not a short cut, a parlor game, or a parodistic toy to play with irresponsibly.

Chapter 9

Universal Expressions

"One size fits all."

Anger, sadness, fear, surprise, happiness, contempt, and disgust are universal expressions displayed by all humans according to researchers. They are species specific and not culture specific as many experts thought.

Universal emotions are not easy to wrap our minds around, so it is helpful to look at some expressions that are common, but are not considered universal by everyone. For example expressions such as frustration, shyness, nervousness, tension, boredom, and confidence are pervasive emotions in most all people, but manifest themselves differently from culture to culture.

Different emotions such as fear and surprise share many of the same expressions, thus making it difficult to tell which one is which. Sadness and depression also share commonalities such as the lack of any expression, turned down mouth corners, downward gazes, crying and sagging facial features. Consequently, it is difficult to tell if a person is temporarily sad or clinically depressed by stand-alone expressions that are common to both emotions.

Several other popular expressions come close to qualifying as universal expressions. For example, pain uniformly shows in a contorted facial expression with some or all of the following features: gritted teeth, eye blocking, head tilted back, wrinkled nose, wrinkled eye corners, and a cracked or moaning voice. Nevertheless, pain is shown in slightly different ways in dissimilar cultures mostly because of its symbolic nature.

For the same reason, a neutral expression does not qualify because it is more suitable for masking different emotions than acting as a complete absence of feelings. Moreover, it is not as momentary as acute affective states like pity or disgust, which are easier to read. Just because it is not universally applied, however, does not mean it is less valuable.

A neutral expression is helpful in that it signals others that we do not want to get involved, or that we want to keep our involvement minimal, which makes it ideal for activities such as judging, refereeing, and auction bidding. The lesson is that body language is complicated.

Even though some emotional expressions are universal enough to be easily recognized, most expressions are unique from person to person and situation to situation. We must go beyond shared expressions and consider all the contextual clues that signal a person's internal state of mind. Let us take a look at those expressions that researchers say all humans share.

Anger

Anger is a destructive emotion that hurts us more than the person or object that angers us. The fire we build for others burns us more than it burns them and causes us undue stress.

Statistics from a recent anger survey conducted by a management-consulting firm showed that nearly twenty-five per cent of the respondents said they had some anger while on the job. This alarming number has significant consequences to public health, since chronically angry men are seven times more likely to die of health related complications by age fifty than their easygoing counter parts.

Another study done on the workplace suggested that the most dangerous place in American society is on the job due to aggressive and disrespectful behavior. In terms of body language, angry men and women are more likely to overeat, smoke, drink, and act out their hostility, which exacerbates everything from the common cold to heart disease. When anger becomes a frequent occurrence, then common sense dictates that people learn to manage their tempers for their own sake.

Is anger more than simple biological hyper arousal? Yes, the melancholy truth is that anger is more than just a physical reaction to unpleasantness; it often involves a process of intense, consuming, and agonizing introspection that takes the slack out of one's chain. For example, domestic violence is typically about power and control that begins with various forms of verbal abuse, often disguised, but has an insidious effect because it steadily chips away at a victim's self-esteem.

Even though our strongest initial impulse is to deny anger, displace it by claiming, "I'm not angry", or project onto others our own anger in order to deny that its roots are coming from inside of us instead of others, the signs of anger are unmistakable. In this regard, keep in mind that genuine anger builds up gradually. Instant anger is scripted, and that is why body language knowledge is beneficial.

A common cognitive distortion is "personal labeling", which is a trick of the chronically anger person to refer to others with negative labels such as "jerk" or "loser". This enables chronically angry people to:

1. *Dehumanize* the victim.
2. *Oversimplify* a victim's personality, and
3. *Rationalize* personal stupidity.

There are a whole range of negative body language signals associated with anger. Surliness, hostility, defiance, aggression, frustration, defensiveness, evasiveness, and withdrawal are just a few closely associated with anger. When we bottle up anger, imagination prevails and hardens the heart. When we open up anger, it subsides, better judgment prevails, and it quickly dissipates. Delay is anger's greatest nemesis, because it allows time to think of the consequences. Until then, avoid genuinely angry people.

Anger Precursors

Precursors of manifest anger that are highly threatening are drunkenness, the loud and excessive use of profanities, contorted facial grimaces, finger pointing, rapid arm movements below the hips, tenseness, contracting eye pupils, prolonged eye contact, tightly drawn lips, mad dogging, chest expansion, and intentional invasions of another person's space.

Genuine anger that manifests itself in stages is generally self-evident because it is loud, hostile, and aggressive. The targets of anger cannot help but be aware of it, and usually react automatically to loudness by shouting back. For instance, the loud use of profanity signals possible aggression and causes most people to think the best defense is a good offense, so they tend to respond in kind.

In adults, expletive usage is more prolific among people with less education and lower socioeconomic backgrounds, which leads to the widespread use of expletives by certain peer groups that are highly susceptible to using profanity. Nonetheless, excessive profanity never makes for a good argument, and its only purpose is to intimidate and control the actions and beliefs of others.

Invasions of people's space are an invitation to trouble. During heightened emotions, many people have zero tolerance for intrusions into their personal space zone, and become rigid as a bag full of hammers. At the subconscious level, people tend to think of intruders in terms of "Who do they think they are" and "They shouldn't have done that" even though on the conscious level many territorial invasions are actually unintentional. Life is like that.

Any manifest anger situation has the potential for serious personal danger; therefore, the best practice is to avoid or defuse anger instead of confronting it. Anger is mitigated by a softer tone of voice with a strong sense of intimacy or humanness coupled with non-threatening body movements. A conversational style controls the tone better, enhances synchronicity, is more relaxing, and goes further toward defusing incipient anger.

In addition, seeking unobtrusive but hurried ways to negotiate alternatives to hostile action such as changing the subject, avoiding threatening expressions, and forgoing the use of profanity go a long way. In addition, it helps to avoid eye contact that lasts ten seconds or more, as well as putting some distance between you and the angry person's personal safety zone.

Degrees of Anger

Anger is self-induced and has an inexorable momentum that comes in degrees, which has given rise to phrases such as "a slow burn" and "reaching the boiling point". The more frustrated we become, the madder we get, and the madder we get the more likely it becomes that any club in the house will do. Internal anger is several degrees more intense than external anger, because it consists of long-standing attitudes and bad feelings waiting for release.

Much latent resentment is unrecognizable, because people who bottle up their rage seem to be mad at everybody and everything. They live in a world of perpetual resentment and borderline mania with little or no reason to back it up. The Hatfields and McCoys forgot the precise reasons for their feud long before the killing stopped. Real problems between people are subject to mediation and settlement, but if the cause of their anger is an imaginary injustice, indignation, or exasperation, then some people will stay angry for life.

Chronic anger is usually excessive and irrational. Worrisome outward signs of chronic internal anger are impatience, a cynical disposition, free-ranging hostility, the inability to enjoy anything, and self-centered behavior. Chronically angry people have bellicose body language punctuated by cursing, insults, and even yelling. They usually have a permanent scowl on their face, a chip on their shoulder, and a sense of urgency such as a readiness to let others know about their problems. They get noticeably upset and fidgety at the mere mention of anyone they do not like, and they do not like just about everyone.

> Wars start with words.

At times, external anger involves steadfastly gazing at the source of the anger as if to see the problem better because unbridled anger tends to cloud the visual center of the brain. Obvious visible signs of external anger are frowning, glowering, and scowling. Some people turn pale when angry and others "see red" when consumed by uncontrollable rage due to increased heart rate and blood flow. Although anger hardens a person's face, the worst-case scenario is when an angry person's entire body becomes noticeably tense, pumped up, and ready for action.

When we are displeased, and do not want to express it directly, we scratch our heads or furiously rub the back of our necks in a classic frustration gesture. Some of us clinch our fists at the thought of something disturbing, kick our dog, hit something, or bang on the dinner table. Other people are able to control their strongest emotions by gripping something, holding their arms behind their back, or adapting in some other personal way because they realize that most anger is self-induced.

On the other hand, external anger is easy to spot since it is manifest and usually short-term. In general, take note of any tears, face flushing, voice changes, and object slamming. A variable and reactive tableau of physiological arousal clues are a quickening pulse, escalating blood pressure, pulsing neck veins, and an increased respiratory rate. Complimentary clues are a bulging red face, flaring nostrils, fierce eyes, yelling, and stumbling for words.

Dealing with anger involves not only adopting compensating body language, but also looking for its causes, its objective, and its intensity. Bear in mind that the more angry people become, the less able they are to think clearly.

Fear

Although fear is a negative state, it is an emotion that generally promotes survival and well-being, which is a good thing, unless it turns into a phobia such as the fear of flying. When threatened by a danger we know, fear is a normal life regulating reaction with highly recognizable body language. For example, self-hugging, using the hands to clasp the top of the head, the forehead, the mouth, or the cheek are typical gestures reflecting the need for self-comfort at times of distress.

> Fear rides on ignorance

Typically, fear begins with simple feelings of unease or apprehension and progresses through various stages of foreboding as the danger increases. In the final stage, complete fright overtakes the entire body in the form of increased motor tension. When this happens, people experience, trembling, tightness, stiff necks and backs, rigid posture, and they become too scared to scream. Strained and disconnected speech patterns are also another sign.

Sometimes fear is an immediate reaction to startling external events and we lose our concentration, our mind goes blank, we are unable to move, and there is a sudden paralysis of our entire physical and mental condition.

At other times, fear is subjective such as the fear of attack, losing control, and going crazy. The mind gets easily confused, indecisive, and preoccupied with becoming overwhelmed. Fear causes a high internal state of stress, pressure, and low self-confidence accompanied by panic, physical agitation, and nervousness.

Wide-open unglazed eyes, palpitations, trembling, gulping, flushing, shortness of breath, nervous ticks, moving perilously slow, jumpiness, goose bumps, shivers, heightened awareness, and a sinking stomach manifest initial fear. The smell of fear usually provokes an attack. Full-fledged fright paralyzes the body to such an extent that it becomes frozen and unable to move, or in some instances, people assume protective body positions that turn away from perceived dangers. A classic example is the fetal position.

Quite a few people use their hands to clutch at objects such as the dentist's chair during drilling and other people turn their knuckles white while grasping the armrests on a bumpy airline flight. At the worst of such times, people get a bad case of the jitters and lose control of their body functions.

Ordinary fear is short-lived; therefore, the best defense is to confront it head on instead of hitting the panic button. Resolutely facing the music only once instead of a thousand times, reduces the lingering agony of ordinary harmless fears that are easily explainable. Thus when something bad happens, it is better to deal with it quickly instead of putting it off, with the possible exception of some inexplicable phobias.

Irrational Fear

Unbelievably, imagination and fear share the same neural networks in the brain, which causes many of our fears to be imaginary, irrational, and completely unreasonable. Customarily known as phobias, irrational fears are types of anxiety that can result from both multiple or single causes and become fixation neuroses. There are over five hundred different phobias. A person who suffers from multiple phobias has a set of related fears such as "panophobia", which is the fear of everything.

Simple phobias are those where one underlying fear is the cause of every anxious moment. Typical examples of common specific fears are "claustrophobia", the fear of being trapped in close confinement such as a closet, and "acrophobia", the fear of heights. Phobias are common in children and adults of both sexes. Many sufferers will attempt to hide their phobias, but the feeble attempt of severely phobic persons to cover up their phobias inevitably produces great panic and disruption in their lives.

Originally survival supportive, phobias continue to stay with us somehow. For example, many phobias come from our parents and peer group. We naturally identify with overly fearful parents, which cause us to imitate and copy them.

Although some phobias such as the fear of public speaking are widespread, people who are reserved, introverted, and imaginative are more susceptible to phobias. When some people become so severely introverted that they are virtual recluses, there is a danger that they will become pathological and obsessed with sociopathic activities such as being a stalker or peeping tom.

On the other hand, observation and evaluation apprehension are common social phobias. Sufferers think, "I'm making a fool out of myself" when interviewing for a job or meeting important people. However, the plain truth is that most of our peers are no different from us. The trouble is that irrational fears have debilitating effects on daily life because people try to manage them by "avoidant" strategies instead of finding a cure.

Anxiety

Almost everything we do involves a certain degree of anxiety. Consequently, anxiety ranges from low-grade feelings of "that's the way it goes" to acute pathological dread and unwarranted fear. Exactly what causes anxiety is the subject of many theories. For example, Sigmund Freud, the father of psychoanalysis, believed that most anxiety is rooted in the unconscious mind, so the trick is to bring it out by psychoanalysis in order for the conscious mind to be able to deal with it.

Biological arousal is a common facet of anxiety body language. Some general descriptors are such things as breathing problems, sweating, unsteadiness, yawning, and many over arousal signals too numerous to mention

Behavioral psychologists believe anxiety is learned from trial and error. Common behavioral symptoms are observable signs such as body motion ranging from swaying, fidgeting, stretching, and pacing to complete immobility such as rigid posture, hands in pocket, and self-hugging.

Existential type philosophers argue that humans suffer from angst, which is a form of anxiety linked to our concern for the unknown, the inevitability of death, and our vulnerability. For instance, the most damaging anxiety for many is the fear of total nonbeing like in "I'm a loser", while "status anxiety" is the result of a feeling that we are not all we can be.

One of the most ordinary examples of anxiety is when we are not quite sure what the danger is, or when it is going to arrive. For example, the anxiety a police officer must feel when he approaches a tinted-window car on a lonely road in the dark of night. In such situations, it is not a stretch to see that anxiety goes hand-in-hand with apprehension, not knowing, and tight situations. Some people might be unaffected while others are terrified.

Americans are getting more panicked and alarmed as a people every year, because America doesn't have the same ethos as a country that has been homogenous for a long time, and has unwritten rules of "we don't do it that way". America is more about laws and lawyers to hold us together.

Anxiety is in ascension. Events like 9/11, the Iraqi war, Hurricane Katrina, and the war on terror are sufficient reasons for increased anxiety. Even the unpredictability of weather such as drought causes considerable anxiety.

Typically, fear has to do with specific objects, while anxiety is less objective and more of a state of mind. In addition, fear is immediate and anxiety more general; therefore, anxiety and fear have some commonality in body language. Being vigilant and scanning for trouble are common facets and sometimes the effect on people is similar as both show up in the face and voice.

One way to illustrate the difference between fear and anxiety is to picture yourself driving a car in an inattentive fashion while talking on your cell phone. When you start to realize your driving could cause an accident, or get you a moving violation, you become anxious, but if you have to swerve suddenly to avoid hitting another car, you experience immediate nerve-shattering fear.

Another example of how anxiety and fear are distinguishable is the saying, "Woodpeckers inside the ark (e.g. Noah's ark) are far more dangerous than the storms outside". We fear the storms outside because they represent immediate danger, whereas the woodpeckers inside make us highly anxious because we do not know the effect of their wood pecking presence.

The body language of anxiety is stiffening muscles, feeling drained, tired, and difficulty in maintaining composure. Needless to say, both anxiety and fear have innumerable symptoms, some alike and some different. The interpersonal affects of both such as insecurity, vulnerability, and social avoidance can be devastating.

Anxiety can be the result of proscribed impulses or even learned behavior. At the low-end of the anxiety spectrum, typical indicators are embarrassment and minor uncertainty. Severe worries about dying, losing control, and going broke are at the high-end of the anxiety spectrum. When acute uncontrollable fear, constant internal tension causing illness, and dreadful panic-attacks are primary components, anxiety becomes a mental health disorder.

Narrow illustrations should not belittle the seriousness of anxiety. They are only microcosms of the macrocosmic world we live in, which is chock full of small everyday angst, and huge worries such as pollution, famine, viral outbreaks, and geopolitical tensions.

Anxiety may be felt as a churning in the stomach or as a faster heart beat. Sometimes it causes tense feet. People do not think others are watching their feet, so they stretch, curl, and wind their feet to release tension. Some people have a higher tolerance for anxiety-provoking situations than others do.

Sadness

Sadness is one of the most widespread expressions in the world today with thousands of potential causes given that ours is an imperfect world. People may be sad due to the displeasure, dissatisfaction, and discomfort caused by others, or for reasons involving their circumstances, or maybe they just have not learned how to be happy.

> Of all sad words of tongue or pen, the saddest are these: "It might have been."
> Whittier

For me, the classic visage of sadness is the face of the famous clown, Emmet Kelly. Typically, a sad person is said to be "down in the mouth" because the cheek muscles tend to sag with a turned down mouth and tightened lips. In addition, the eyebrows slant downwards above drooping eye lids, and the eye gazes downward. Trembling lips, tearing up, searching eyes, and attempts to shield the face from view amplify extreme sadness. Other frequent body language signs include a bowed head, slumped shoulders, and listlessness, as well as staring into space, slower movements, and a forlorn facial expression. Make no mistake about it people with these symptoms definitely need some cheering up.

Some sad expressions may be associated with the loss of a loved one or pet, a hopeless looking situation, or with any number of conditions involving excessive sentiment. Sad feelings are often the result of setting goals too high and failing.

People set themselves up to fail and they often end up with feelings of despair, misery, and helplessness, and a kind of lost-looking facial expression. A small benefit, perhaps, but when people do not know what to do next in their vapid lives; their gloominess often evokes compassion and empathy from others. Thus, the body language of feeling sorry for ourselves also makes others feel sorry for us.

> **For some, not remembering yesterday brings happiness.**

The normal distress that causes sadness also resembles chronic depression, but it is not the same thing. For starters, the body language of dysphoria is much less intense and long lasting; moreover, it is but one symptom of chronic depression.

Unfortunately, depression afflicts over nineteen million Americans, which in itself is depressing; however, sadness often is a result of life altering events such as the death of a loved one. Other causes of sadness can be daily life events such as stress, business setbacks, and extreme anger and frustration turned inwards, which in the latter case results in too much of the chemical "cortisol" being released in the body for too long which causes serious adverse effects.

While, persistent depression dogs our ability to remember and concentrate, sadness only needs to last long enough for faithful friends and allies to take notice and begin to sympathize. Once we have their full attention, friends are able to begin an investigation into the source of the sadness, and deal with its underlying causes without overly dramatizing its effects.

Crying

An adjunct to sadness is crying. While other animals howl in distressing situations, only humans cry tears of emotion. Other animals have tear ducts, but only humans seem to have the neural connections to deep emotions that cause them to cry. There are many reasons people cry such as crying for joy and crying out of sorrow, which are both positive acts.

On the other hand, excessive crying or laughter coupled with exaggerated emotions, over-activity, and hyperventilation are forms of body language behavior formerly known as hysteria in the old days.

Early on, young infants begin to cry without tears when in distress or to let us know they are present. Later this simple act evolves into a highly sophisticated form of interpersonal communication that bonds people together.

As we enter adulthood, obviously we have more reasons to cry. Our emotions become deeper than those connected only to discomfort do. We need a way to impress others that our feelings and attitudes are strong and sincere. Emotionally based tears are not always distinguishable from two other kinds, to wit: basal tears that bathe the eye and reflex tears that occur from blows to eye. Still, they are very different from the other two kinds in that they are full of proteins and hormones that manifest when we experience powerful moods and emotions linked to crying.

Crying is a way to manipulate people, like many other actions. Since crying is an effective way of getting attention, some people will continue to use this mechanism as a way of getting what they want even when they do not need it. We need to learn how to identify real crying for cause as opposed to the so-called "alligator tears" of manipulation.

In sum, crying is a powerful communication tool. Tears are a highly visible message that transcends speech. They express raw emotions, and help us to express the overwhelming feelings that we are unable to put into words such as real sadness, pain, and frustration.

Happiness

Happiness is such a fundamental good that people constantly seek out its rewards although. People differ in what causes happiness. The leading idea in Fyodor Dostoyevsky's novel *Crime and Punishment* is that happiness comes only through suffering, and not reasoning. Other people believe that happiness results from losing interest in worldly cares, while some believe that transcending external problems leads to happy valley. In the context of body language, however, happiness looks like an attitude. It is an attitude that we rarely have all the time, but when we do, it registers as a wide, distinct smile, glowing face, and twinkle in the eyes.

The body language of happy people will be excited, open, and animated. Happy people have a radiant positive energy and high self-esteem that clearly shows in their appearance and expressions. Happy people have a zest for life in their body language, whereas unhappy people seem to be chronically down, even in good times

Since happiness is an internal and subjective state, it is difficult to define. What makes me happy is not the same thing that makes you happy. For example, a review of Aristotle persuades me that virtue makes one happy, but you may disagree. Therefore, the verdict is still out on precisely what constitutes happiness.

Happiness is ambiguous for a reason. Different things please different people. Our genetic makeup also keeps us from being happy for too long. The excitement of a great time is relatively short, but so are the painful vicissitudes in life. We get giddy about bits of luck and good fortune, making progress, and salutary changes in life, but it is never enough to last long.

The latest study on happiness points toward a "set point" for being happy. Although our mood level goes up and down with life's events, it is only for a little while, and eventually we return to a set point. Experts estimate that as much as fifty per cent of our set point is due to genetics with the balance coming from recent life events.

Even though most of us rapidly adjust to good fortune, after awhile what seemed like a blessing tends to make people restless and unhappy no matter how much they achieve, because consistency and stability are what people really seek, not just the momentary highs. Would an event such as winning the lottery make a person happy for the rest of his life? No, studies show lottery winners are no happier a year later than they were before they won it big.

Circumstances such as abundant money, unlimited educational opportunities, family togetherness, high status, and happy times make some people a little happier, but they have a relatively minor and transient effect on their overall sense of well-being. In fact, some researchers contend that persons who are not focused on possessions, fame, and fortune are generally more content.

Consequently, such things as trying too hard to secure a promotion, constantly rewarding ourselves, or winning over a lover will not make life any happier over the long-term, because people eventually return to their set point. Startling as it sounds, millionaires who appear happier than people earning a minimum wage ought to thank their embedded biology more than their income. One does not have to be "the material girl" to be happy. It does not take much to bring on a good mood. Even a sunny day is enough to put people in a good enough mood to make them happy, but good moods do not last long.

Surprise, Surprise

Surprises never seem to cease. Perhaps this is one reason that surprises are the briefest of all expressions. Even though we grow older and learn more, we are still surprised all the time. The underlying causes of surprise can be almost anything such as an unexpected fourth ace, the pleasure of a great gift, or something unforeseen that results in panic or fear. Thus, surprise can be either a positive or a negative emotional state, but either way, it ordinarily does not last in most circumstances.

Although there are many causes of surprise, responses are usually automatic reactions that fall typically into the "self-protecting" category. In this category, look for wide-open eyes for better vision, a quicker pulse, hurried body movements, and a wide open mouth that enables the lungs to take in large gulps of air.

Even when news of an important event is good news to some and bad news to others, the signs of surprise can be the same. For instance, micro expressions such as a wrinkled forehead, arching eyebrows, and a startled look together with the hands either brought up quickly to cover the face or emphatically flung into the air are body language signs of surprise.

A frequent way of verbalizing surprise is the expression of a phrase such as, "Oh, my God," or by loud monosyllabic words like "Whoa," "Ouch," and "Wow," or a string of loud expletives such as "Damn," or words invoking higher authority such as "Oh, Lord" and "Jesus Christ". Mild surprise is expressed by "oh" or "gosh".

For good reason, people do not enjoy being surprised. Sudden surprises leave people speechless; they elevate the blood pressure, cause stress, and even lead to heart attacks in some cases. If a person holds his hand to his chest, gasps for breath, and suddenly jerks backwards in disbelief, he may be having an ischemic reaction due to the sudden shock of surprise.

On the other hand, some experts contend that surprise is the single most pleasant emotion in the human repertoire because of the brain's release of endorphin-the "feel good" chemical.

As people gain confidence in their ability to detect the inferential patterns of surprise, and lose their fear of being surprised, then their ability to deal with just about anything that comes their way is strengthened, and they need not have any trouble dealing with unforeseen circumstances.

Contempt

Contempt is one of the highest possible insults we can express towards someone or something. Typically, it is displayed by facial and vocal expressions such as an unctuous utterance and a sneering contorted face, but may include body gestures as well. Disdain falls into a class of speech full of derision, scorn, and sarcasm, yet it is also shown by saying nothing, looking down one's nose, turning a shoulder, and walking away.

Ridicule and contempt go hand-in-hand. Frequently, we direct our opprobrium toward other persons or groups that are so clearly different from us that we think they somehow contaminate our values even if we have few facts to support out views. For example, rebellious teenagers hold adults in contempt for not being "with it", while many adults scorn the music, dress, and social activities of teenagers.

Often, contempt is a kind of sneering with curled or tightened lips that turn up on one side, but it also can be very subtle. For example, we reject persons or things by defiantly turning our backs, keeping our distance, and moving away, or by a simple shoulder shrug and scornful eye, which are all soft, but effective ways of conveying contempt.

The body language of contempt includes such things as pinching our nose, or inflating our nose and turning our head and staring elsewhere. We "turn our nose up" at certain things that displease us, and show it by elevating our chins and looking down our noses with squinting eyes. At other times, we show contempt by narrowing our eyes and grimacing, which becomes more obvious as the strength of the emotion increases.

We show attitudinal contempt by refusing to act when ordered to do so, or by approaching a task with great insensitivity. Some people show contempt of strangers by avoiding them altogether, and a group shows disdain for an idea by collectively refusing to consider it. Thus, simply ignoring others is one of the highest forms of attitudinal contempt.

Disgust

Disgust is a subjective state of aversion or repugnance toward someone or something. Closely resembling contempt, it is deeply rooted in our biological makeup. When disgusted, we tend to use our nose as a visual analogue by wrinkling or turning it so as not to symbolically "smell" the object of disgust. The body language of disgust employs the other senses as well. Disgusted people close or narrow their eyes to block unpleasantries from sight, stick their tongues out to show distaste, and make "ugh" and "ew" sounds.

A disgusted person will physically back away to avoid disgusting objects or place his hands over his ears to block out unpleasant sounds. Consequently, if we find something internally repulsive to us, we have ways and means to signal disgust before subjecting ourselves to unwanted intrusions.

When a foul or sickening stimulant causes disgust, escape or avoidance is the order of the day. Remarkably, disgust is conditional and the actual stimulus does not have to be present, since the mere thought of it will suffice. Avoidant reactions arising out of strong, imaginary associations have developed because we know that an unseen bacterium can be harmful to us.

A predominant disgust signal that is hard to misinterpret is physically turning away in an effort to place as much distance as possible between us and a disgusting object, and at times, the "dry heaves" are an extreme sign of disgust. Not coincidentally, both are a visible warning to others of the presence of noxious stimulants.

Frustration

Frustration is brief most of the time, but sometimes it lasts a long time. The famous line from Shakespeare's play Richard III, "This is the winter of our discontent", is a piquant metaphor for long-term frustration. Usually people are able to overcome their frustrations, but at times, it seems like a bottomless pit.

People are frustrated as an indirect result of goal denial and impossible standards to meet, and directly by emotions that are a by-product of persistent anger. Aggression often results from the fear of frustration, because people are wary of becoming frustrated with its debilitating effects.

Frustration is evident in sounds such as "sheez", "tsk", and long drawn out breaths with sorrowful sighs. It is displayed by rolling the eyeballs in a symbolic "looking for divine help" expression, or pulling at the hair as if symbolically "pulling out hair", or by rubbing the back of the neck with the fingers, which says, "Get off my back".

Clinched fingers, clinched hands, and hand wringing signify a small degree of discomfiture while pointing the index finger, or using eyeglasses to point, signify frustration. Finger pointing creates antagonism and rarely has any redeeming social value. The best practice is to avoid it.

Everyone agrees that kicking at the ground is a way to alleviate built up frustration. Frustrating situations that we cannot control make us hot under the collar, which cause us to stick our fingers in our collar to symbolically let in more air. A sense of failure or disappointment causes us to turn up our nose. The potential danger in uncontrolled frustration is that it easily leads to anger, hostility, aggression, and violence if left unchecked. On the other hand, getting organized, forming plans, undertaking personal reflections, and taking pride in accomplishments ameliorate frustration.

Some events that can cause frustration are the cost of living, competition, bureaucratic gridlock, and change. One of the most frustrating things of all is not feeling connected to the universe. People who cannot give themselves the time to try to connect will never know freedom from endless searching for something, wrongheaded jobs, unrewarding relationships, and debilitating frustration.

Nervousness

Nervousness is an affective state that has been around a long time. It assures its victims much discomfort and little benefit in life. The more nervous people become the more success eludes them and the less they accomplish, which leads to bad habits that stay with them. Many people develop nervous habits that sometimes last a lifetime, thus the expressions of nervous actions such as nail biting, hair twirling, self-grooming, and wringing hands.

Medical professionals think of nervousness as symptomatic of something else, but ordinary people continue to think of it as a condition. People say, "It's a case of nerves" or "she has a nervous condition". Undeniably, however, nervousness is general in nature, and has many descriptors; therefore, the term is gradually becoming archaic and seldom in use. For this book, however, nervousness is a body language indication of anxiety and fear. Typical components are hyperactivity, over arousal, excessive worry, instability, hyper-excitability, and heightened tension.

Characteristic causes of nervousness are anxiety, stress, insecurity, and dread. Nervous energy that builds up needs releasing; therefore, repeated body movements such as toe tapping or fingernail biting are typical reactions. Related physical signs are a worried look, facial expressions of dread, and flashing smiles. Under some circumstances, perspiration and continuously blinking eyes are noticeable.

Currently, most body language experts realize that action sounds such as nervous laughing, stuttering, coughing, and throat clearing are clear signs of irritability, apprehension, and uncertainty in anxious and highly stressed people. If these commonly heard sounds converge with shaking and fidgeting while seated, turning, or pointing the body toward the doors, it indicates a more serious case of fright and desire to escape.

People who fidget in their chairs are metaphorically "on the hot seat". Also, a "pants-puller" or a person who repeatedly adjusts upper clothing is nervous and under mild stress. Lastly, a classic nervous "interrupt" gesture is tugging at the ear, and tightly locking the hands or feet behind the back is a covert attempt to get a grip upon oneself.

Tension

Many of us wonder what actually causes tension, since it is difficult to quantify and experts disagree. Sigmund Freud's mostly biological viewpoint postulates that core tension is caused by the conflict between the Id and the Superego, two things that are hard to put your finger on. Carl Jung, Freud's protégé thought much the same thing in that tension occurs when two opposites converge. Personally, math makes me tense, because I know I am not good at it. In the scientific world, tension is a completely different concept. In the world of body language, however, a tense condition is usually the result of stress.

Indecision causes tension.

As stress levels increase or decrease, tension manifests itself through body language. We do not have to wait until people say, "I'm really stressed out", to recognize that they are "tensed up." Obvious physical signs of tension are changes in skin appearance, body chemistry changes, muscle tone, ability to focus, and speech patterns. These signs are difficult, if not impossible to contain or hide, and eventually show up.

B.F. Skinner, the well-known behaviorist who ranks right behind the eminent Sigmund Freud in public awareness, maintains that psychologists need to stick to observable behaviors, because people's personalities are just a collection of behaviors with the core tendency to reduce tension.

Men and women have different responses to tension. Women tend to cry and become more emotional in circumstances that affect well-being, or the family. In addition, they tend to fiddle with their purses, blush, and bite their fingernails. At times, women will bring one or both hands to the top of their heads in a "How dumb of me" gesture and pull strands of hair up.

Men show tension by scratching and clamping their hands on the back of their necks, by clenching their fists, gripping nearby objects until their knuckles turn white, and becoming very silent. Both sexes have trouble conveying information under tense conditions and give themselves away by a slower rate of speech, taking too much time to reply, and acting as if they are picking their way through a minefield.

Tension eats energy.

Group tension created by a lack of cooperation and internal hostility is palpable and hangs heavy in the air, even though no one is talking. Similarly, social tension easily finds its way from one person to another as it winds its way through a crowd. Thus in a collective setting, tension tends to accumulate and grow exponentially as mutual relations become more strained.

The more people bunch up the more group tension builds. Built up tension is easily reduced, however, by dispersing the group. On the individual level, unfamiliar territory, unresolved expectancies, and uncertain circumstances that necessitate greater degrees of caution exacerbate the restlessness and anxiety that cause tension.

Experts have come up with a way to reduce social tension by having one side make a unilateral but minor concession, which encourages the other side to make a reciprocal concession. Finally, keep in mind that the connection between tension and behavior is loosely applied in many different areas.

Shyness

One is the loneliest number, especially if you are shy. Shyness is a behavioral condition that affects everyone now and then from the highly intelligent and socially polished to the average and unsophisticated. If a person is shy all the time no matter what the circumstances, then he is a victim of *dispositional shyness,* which is a debilitating personal problem, whereas *situational shyness* is occasional shyness in certain situations.

The chance of meeting a pathologically shy person is minimal, because they do not go out. Slightly shy people are more common, because they are just hapless, self-effacing people with a diffident manner.

> A shut-in personality is an extremely withdrawn person.

Quite a few people are shy to one degree or another. According to a research institute in California, nearly fifty percent of American adults say they have experienced shyness to such an extent that it has presented a problem for them. Chronic shyness is hard to pin down because people are reluctant to admit their vulnerabilities. No one wants to be weak.

Typical signs of shyness are such things as people avoiding social interaction and group events, passivity, low self-esteem, canceling things at the last minute, and spending excessive amounts of time on a computer because computers are impersonal and don't require face-to-face encounters. With the passing of each day, people become more aware of their potential vulnerabilities, and their first response is to shy away from them.

Numerous things cause people to have timidity troubles, including genetics to some degree, however, in my experience, the biggest contributing factors are the negative memories that people have internalized from past emotional experiences. Past experiences affect intuitive responses to everyday situations. In fact, a sign of intelligence is not making the same mistake twice.

People can be "shy" of accomplishing something, so in this sense, shyness means falling short of a goal, but sometimes, being a little skittish is a good thing, and keeps us out of trouble as long as it does not turn into a serious social phobia. Fortunately, dedicated researchers work hard to design newer and more effective ways to protect people from the worst causes of shyness.

Boredom

What are you doing with your life? A recent survey found that the average American adult spends about one-third of his waking hours bored. The cause is an overall lack of interest and discontent with life that results in the unpleasant mental and physical state of boredom. Like many of our other emotions, boredom is either specific or chronic.

The most common type of boredom is what experts call "situational" boredom, which is due to specific, identifiable causes such as visiting uninteresting people, watching too much television, or going to a bad movie, whereas chronic boredom is general and pervasive to the point that everything seems boring.

The symptomatic body language clues of chronic boredom are such things as frequent drowsiness because sufferers try to escape reality by sleeping, self-absorption activities such as long aimless telephone conversations with friends or even strangers, and fantasizing activities such as daydreaming while avoiding reality and commitment.

Nothing excites, and sufferers try to escape the relentless source of their boredom by preoccupation with creative compensating activities and other distractions. For example, the less attentive we are in the presence of others, the more active we tend to become. However, most people

> The yawn is a clear sign of boredom.

know when they are losing a person's attention because inattentive people start using their hand to support their head, let their eyes wander, or gaze into the distance.

Boredom is difficult to conceal because our body gives us away through numerous unconscious expressions such as a blank stare, a yawn, heavy sighs, and inertia, all of which have an infectious influence on the behavior of others. Other give-a-ways of boredom are a person dozing off in the middle of some activities, drooping eyes, and a classic "woe is me" groan.

People fight off boredom with self-manipulation activities such as diverse head, arm, and hand movements, scratching, hair twisting, drumming their fingers, weight shifting, and clock watching. Therefore, a valuable relationship skill is recognizing the point at which we drift into a "same old thing" attitude about daily occurrences.

At the point of boredom, resist the temptation of self-manipulating activities by positive action designed to communicate to others that they have our undivided attention. Activities such as doodling or daydreaming hinder interaction between people and interfere with open communication, which is a signal of people's waning interest in what is going on around them.

Boredom has a connection to our attitude. For example, people who disagree with us are boring. Boredom is a result of such things as a lack of variety in life, too much time on our hands, and an overbalance in

the contemplation department. Often, people who are bored with life
will have the body language of
an empty and entrenched existence. The tragedy is that lives

> Affluence is therapeutic boredom.

become "fixed".

To combat the "stuck in a rut" syndrome, it is best to get rid of
unrewarding habits, uncompromising jobs, and intransigent relationships that contribute to a life of dogged boorishness. Some habits are as
hard to shed as a '73 Ford Pinto; therefore, the best practice for those
people susceptible to boredom is to adopt counter measures.

Effective countermeasures are such things as active body language
behavior that resists collapsing into the old way of doing things, taking on new projects that promise personal emoluments, meeting new
friends, and changing jobs. Change is a key to success and goes a long
way towards a healthier lifestyle according to the famous American
psychologist Abraham Maslow (1908-70).

Confidence

Confidence, in the social sense, infers an attitude akin to trustworthiness and the ability to keep a secret. In
a cognitive sense, confidence means step-
ping up to the plate with self-reliance and
assuredness, which shows up as an un-

> No hill is a problem
> for a stepper.

mistakable radiance and positive body language. For example, observers
could not help but notice the absolute confidence clearly shining in
Harry Houdini's eyes as he performed seemingly impossible feats.
Extreme risk-taking and "laughing at the devil" are common attitudes
in confident people even though foolish, because confidence tends to
consume wisdom.

What are the visible signs of confidence? First, confident people
will have good posture. They will not bend, slouch or slump, which
makes them look meek and tired. Confidence is projected by standing
up straight with the best lofty authority people can manage. They will

maintain frequent eye contact at least 60 per cent of the time as comrades in fate, and will boldly use the space around them.

A confident person holds one arm with one hand behind their back, while thrusting their chin forward like royalty. When possible, people impart self-assurance by taking an open and elevated position above others that shows both physical dominance and a lofty attitude.

Confidence and stubbornness go hand in hand by steepling and a faint smile, but the most demonstrative form of confidence that is currently popular is the quick pull back of an extended and clenched fist or fists along with a loud vocal "yes". This is an unmistakable signal of triumph.

Staying confident in the face of life's many trials, enigmatic twists, burdens, and dangers often takes courage, sobriety, and determination. Keeping confident 24/7 is difficult because of life's inevitable uncertainties, ambiguities, and paradoxes. Nevertheless, people are able to sustain a perpetual air of confidence by coping skills and constantly reminding themselves of the pragmatic truth that "losing is not an option."

Practical Pointers

The best way to improve body language skills in problem areas such as boredom, shyness, and nervousness is to initiate the quick and emphatic directness necessary to confront negative traits that have social and psychological consequences. This approach not only builds confidence, but also steers us away from maintenance habits, whose only purpose is to get us from one day to the next.

Chapter 10

The Power of Laughter

"Laugh it off."

Laughter is contagious, which makes it a powerful social tool. When you feel low like a flat tire, try laughing more. People want to be funny so bad they are even willing to buy jokes. Laughing allows people to stand back from an unpleasant situation and deal with it more effectively. Since laughing makes people feel better and helps to put a spring back in their step, laughter is associated with a positive state of mind and good health. For instance, combining laughter and body movements such as bending forward or backward, or simply slapping one's knee help boost the heart rate. In some cases, it also may be an antidote to apprehension and panic.

Laughing and grunting are similar. People who grunt while lifting weights or returning a tennis volley expel air and bring more muscle fibers into play, which helps them bring maximal exertion to bear.

> People who laugh cooperate better.

Laughter acts in the same way by stretching muscles, which reduces high blood pressure and makes it easier to breath.

Laughter and physical movement are complimentary and may have co-evolved from the rowdy play of our early ancestors. Beginning as short bursts of vowel-like sounds made at regular intervals similar to panting.

Although practically anything is able to evoke uproarious laughter, researchers contend that it is impossible to force people to laugh. That is because laughter does not happen at random like a sneeze or cough. It occurs most often in jocular situations where a good sense of humor, a positive attitude, and the support of friends and family play a big role. It makes sense that certain elements such as temperament, awareness, and environment are involved in laughter even though their precise relationships are unknown.

The advent of modern day brain scans has provided more insight into the dynamics of laughter. Magnetic resonating images convincingly demonstrate that laughter is rooted in a maze of neural connections located throughout different parts of the brain. This suggests that laughter's reputation as a noisy but facile expression of pleasant feelings is actually a *tripartite* state that has physical, cognitive, and emotional components. Laughter is more species specific than culture specific because everyone laughs in the same basic way irrespective of cultural variations such as how loud or quiet one may laugh in different circumstances.

> When you get down, call a funny friend.

Despite the commonality of laughter, and the tendency for a smile or a toothy grin to accompany it, people still have an extremely difficult task in determining the underlying motivation for laughter, which seriously affects many relationships. For example, people who laugh but their stomach does not move are usually going to be stubborn. Laughing at jokes that are not funny often signals insecurity and self-indulgence. In addition, laughing while giving someone feedback is not a good thing.

Laughter is so infectious that everyone tends to laugh at the same time whether something is individually funny or not. The *herd mentality* can cause a laugh riot even if people do not know what the punch line is because someone else's laughter intensifies our own and often causes us to lose control.

Gender has a role in laughter. Humor researchers say they have solid evidence that men laugh at each other more than women laugh at each other, and surprisingly, women in groups don't laugh as much as men in groups even though women are generally more expressive.

Laughter has the ability to facilitate communication, encourage interpersonal relationships, and improve well-being. Not only does it help individuals by lowering stress and improving their immune systems, it also has the social power to affect whole groups. The potential to gain power, cooperation, and unanimity in a diverse group by the use of humor gives anyone who is able to induce laughter an enviable amount of social power, which helps to reduce social tensions, advance political agendas, and expand friendships.

Although humor researchers do not know for sure that laughing helps people feel better psychologically, historically the remarkable power of laughter to sway people emotionally is incontrovertible, which is why it has fascinated humanity since early Greek theater.

Practical Pointers

Whether laughter is happy, sincere, sardonic, or even malicious is a daunting challenge unless other clues are manifest at the same time. Obviously, people get something out of laughter, which makes it a positive personal skill, but not everybody agrees that it absolutely makes the body healthier or can prevent strokes.

Despite being traditionally associated with good physical and mental health, there is little supporting scientific proof. Nevertheless, given the reality that "power" is the fabric of all social relations, the ability to make others laugh is self-evident proof of its benefit.

Chapter 11

That Certain Smile

"Put on a happy face"

Putting on a happy face is therapeutically sound because it is an easy and effective way to mask one emotion with another one. When someone smiles spontaneously out of enjoyment it lights up the face by using unique facial muscles that are not employed in a feigned smile. A true smile is an easy expression that is highly visible and recognizable the world over as a positively beautiful expression.

Smiling plays a prominent role in both the functional and social arenas of most cultures. An example

> Smiling makes us feel better.

of a smile's functional use was illustrated in a recent national poll when it was revealed that seventy-five per cent of the adults surveyed thought a nice smile was important to landing a dream job. As for sociability, over eighty per cent of the people surveyed said an attractive smile was vital to meeting "Mr. or Ms. Right".

The simplest smile exposes the teeth in a bemused, nonspecific way. Coincidentally, teeth are the facial feature most people would change if they had the chance. Another functional use of a smile occurs when people smile to themselves as a means of not participating in an outgoing event. Other simple smiles are the "surprised smile" seen at times of great surprise or emotion when the mouth is wide open, because the jaw muscles relax and drop the chin.

The "concentration smile" is where people's mouths open unconsciously with the tongue partly out to help them concentrate, whereas the "frozen smile" is a continuous smile no matter what the circumstances. The frozen smile is a "social smile" due to its frequent and widespread use in social settings.

A perpetual smile signifies manipulation or subtle deception because people who have a permanent smile tend to be less sincere, open, and honest. At times, a constant smile is a safe guarding tendency, but usually the idea behind its use is to mask reality by "focus transference".

Numerous variations in the simple smile accommodate different circumstances. For instance, the simple smile is able to expand into a broad grin with no eye contact and exposed teeth when something is extremely funny or pleasurable. A coy smile that shows subordination is subject to change by bringing the upper lip inward, whereas pushing the lower lip, head, and chin outward forms an unmistakable pouting kind of smile.

Different Smiles

On the threshold, it is important to keep in mind that smiling is not always a body language signal for an affect-laden emotion. For example, smiling for the camera is a scripted performance instead of a spontaneous emotion. The same as using swearing as a heavy-handed way to increase tolerance levels for physical pain, people also can reduce pain by tightening and pulling their lips back in a stoic grin, which helps them deal with misfortune. At other times, people smile to beguile others. Thus, smiling has different effects on different people.

> The same smile has different effects on different people.

A smile is often enigmatic. It can act as a greeting sign or as a beckoning gesture for some people, and for others it invites hostility, mockery, and similar negative feelings. Can you always tell the difference between a hostile "I don't give a darn" smile, and a polite smile where the eye corners do not wrinkle and only one lip slightly turns up? It is not easy, but certainly not impossible.

The act of smiling is so fascinating because of its many subtle variations and special meanings that the challenge is to interpret all of its nuances. The most popular category has to be the emotion-based smile such as the flirting smile, the embarrassment smile, and the grin-and-bear-it smile to name just a few.

The flirting smile has an unmistakable "come on" aura about it, while the embarrassment smile usually occurs with a flushed face and ears. A mechanical smile is one that draws the lips away from the teeth in an oblong fashion. It is common in situations that do not call for any emotion like posing for a camera.

Smiling is able to mask strong emotions such as disappointment, anxiety, and grief. Certain smiles reassure, comfort others, and reduce nervous strain. Various smiles along with other body language clues create special blends such as combining enjoyment with contempt. Some people are able to affect a smile that shows they are both happy and contemptuous by turning up only one corner of the mouth in a semi-smile or smirk.

A smile is even able to say, "I'm miserable" when the lips press tightly together and the bottom lip pushes up, an expression often seen on ex-President Clinton's face when under pressure. The "qualifier" is a special form of smile people use to take the edge off harsh criticisms. Another form is where a person bites his lip when smiling to indicate uncertainty and internal question asking.

Can a smile turn away the anger in others? The answer is "yes". Notice how President Bush gives a quick smile before answering a difficult question. The act of smiling not only releases the "feel good" endorphin, it also has a good effect on others, which is the reason trial attorneys tell their clients to try to look at the jury whenever possible and smile.

Is it possible for a smile to hypnotize and transfix other people? Absolutely, with many people, all we need is a grin and we are in. Except in cases where a person smiles to himself for purely personal reasons, smiling is a form of social body language that is subject to the presence, thoughts, attitudes, and actions of other people. Consequently, smiling is one of the most pro social expressions in body language.

Practical Pointers

Smiling is a portentous act that not only affects people's opinion of each other, but also future harmonious interactions. On the other hand, the simple act of smiling can unduly beguile people with its disarming potential until they are aware of all the surrounding circumstances. Take some time to think before whipping up your enthusiasm without considering its causes. Ask yourself this question: Why are people smiling that way?

Chapter 12

Self-Presentation

"Look in a mirror to see who you wish to be."

Self-presentation is a core impression management skill. The ability to manage our image is primarily due to elective body language. We elect how we wish to present ourselves to meet the demands and expectations of others. With the possible exception of a few existing cultures that are "anti-modern" and highly repressive, most people are able to elect how they want to appear to others through a process of self-monitoring. Using their freedom of expression, people are able to build their "image" around a myriad of things such as clothes, accessories, hairstyle, makeup, the influences of their environment, and so on.

Vanity trumps sanity.

In fact, one might plausibly say that everything people do contributes to an image they contrive for themselves, including self-defeating behavior at times.

The good news is that often it is easier to fix the perception of a problem than the problem. Whole industries are built around this premise. Thus, the image that most people have is usually not a rigid, static, and preformed one for all occasions, but a flexible set of self-expression tools and accessories that fit different circumstances.

Realistically, behavior is too complex for one single thing to create a believable image, but when people join several things together, an overall elective image begins to take shape. The most important requirement of an overall image, is that it be logical, since everything must make sense together.

Social interaction in different situations sometimes calls for people to change something about themselves for specific effect. In such cases, people are better off relying on observational learning instead of haphazard trial and error to make beneficial changes.

People tend to imitate those persons who already have a desirable image; consequently, much of their image derives from the "remarkably pedestrian" observation of others in similar situations. In the childhood stages of development, most elective body language is actually the result of watching our parents. Later on, people imitate their peer group and others they see in the media.

The first step to the correct use of elective body language is how best to communicate our best image. Since nonverbal communications are best between "equals", we need to mirror and match each other to become "soul mates". The more we become like another, the more commodious we are, which leads to higher concentration levels and warmer relationships.

> When we become like the people we are around, we lose our identity and take on our peer group's identity.
> Social Identity Theory

A good example of what I am talking about is the regional sales clerk who hopes to impress others. In such cases, they should take into consideration where they are going to be when they pick out their wardrobe. Most men today are turning away from flashier clothing for something more conservative.

It is not a good idea to wear an art deco tie, an Italian-cut suit, and Gucci suede shoes in most parts of the country because they are too pretentious. Cut out large distracting jewelry, like the gold necklaces worn by "Mr. T" on the *A Team,* in favor of smaller, discreet, and less ostentatious jewelry.

Work-in Progress

Think of yourself as a work-in-progress, because your biggest obstacle is often your own self-perception. People convince themselves that they cannot change their appearance or performance, so why try they tell themselves. Nothing could be further from the truth. With a little effort, anyone can achieve a better image. All you need is a little confidence and a little creativity to overcome imaginary obstacles growing out of America's fast-changing technology, multicultural diversity, and growing populace. Appearance norms bind everyone together and provide an anchor in times of uncertainty. The guidelines are simple and easy to follow. Try the following techniques:

1. Put Your Best Foot Forward.

In sailboat racing, getting a good start is over fifty per cent of the race. In interpersonal relations, making a good first impression is eighty per cent of the objective. Although we know better than to make judgments from generalizations, numerous studies have shown people use general clues such as clothing, posture, and speech to make snap judgments about each other in the blink of an eye.

In dealing with the public, putting the best foot forward is essential because negative characteristics outweigh the positives in human perception and a single negative trait often overwhelms many positives.

There is no second chance to make a good first impression; consequently, you want to send off subliminal messages from the very beginning that announce that you are good at what you do and you intend to be a winner. If you are a salesperson you want to let customers know you have a winning product, so adopt a winner's posture that reflects confidence by standing with your feet apart and a forward body angle that shows interest.

> One negative trait trumps several positive ones.

When you sit, keep your hands open, and when you stand, place them on your hips like a sprinter ready to go. Smile and keep your head and eyes level with your customers, so they will not think they are being dominated. The position of the head dominates the attitude of the entire body. If you do some of these things, it will be easier to bring out a customer's true attitude and feelings about a product.

2. Be Sincere.

The best image is one of sincerity. It is acceptable to customize and tailor your image, and virtually everyone will change something at times, but never, ever fake it. For example, you cannot fake being good because people will find you out. Do not over exaggerate the seriousness of a situation by whining, begging, crying alligator tears, or appealing to someone's sympathy. Do not affect fake contrivances like wild gesturing or exaggerated theatrics. Do not try and act young when you are old.

Conform to the social norms of the situation by meeting the normative expectations of the people you are dealing with. For instance, when the mid-life crisis sets in, around the age of forty, do not try to become a "free spirit" and buy a powerful motorcycle, unless you have the strength and ability to ride one, because you are taking a chance of winding up in the hospital. Most people are forgiving enough to tolerate personal flaws and failures as long as you are sincere.

3. Establish Oral Rapport

To connect with others verbally, ask them to tell you a war story. Then, do your best to adapt to their speech patterns and idioms. For instance, if they talk fast, you talk faster. If they use visual words such as, "See what I mean", audible words such as, "I hear you", or feeling words such as, "I feel that", then use similar words in the same category as they do. I am not saying mimic everything the other person says, since that is impossible as well as impractical, but try to stay on the same categorical wavelength in order to establish good oral rapport.

4. Mirror and Match

Like a mirror, you want people to see themselves in you; therefore, a good icebreaker is establishing something in common with others such as supporting the same sports team, belonging to the same organizations, or going to the same church. Fit in to get in. Try saying such things as, "I'm a Red Sox fan, how about you?" or "I grew up in the same neighborhood you did." Point out similarities with statements such as, "I'm just like you. I have family too."

After making a connection, enhance rapport by mirroring and matching techniques. Adopt an open posture while talking to someone who has an open posture. If they tend to lean forward, then do the same. Head nods, eye contact, appropriate facial expressions, and eyebrow movements keep faltering conversations moving as well as "give me more" hand gestures and copious smiling.

Take notice of people leaning on chairs or unequally distributing their weight because that is a strong sign that they are seeking your moral support. Establish a firm posture base for yourself. Never rock back and forth, and never shift your weight when standing as that contributes to an undesirable "shifty look".

Practice areas
.Hand gestures
.Posture
.Walking
.Eye contact
.Voice pitch
.Hair styling
.Clothing styles
.Storytelling

5. Use Your Space

The way people use the space around them sends a strong message. Horizontal space usage connotes degrees of intimacy while vertical space usage connotes degrees of authority and power. Wide-open space usage reflects a dominant personality, whereas tight and closed-off space usage indicates a submissive personality. In a group setting, we are able to induce an entire group to assume a more defensive use of their space merely by closing off our own space.

Lecturers and lawyers know how to make the lecture room or courtroom their turf. The more space they occupy, the more important they look. In a debate, or an adversarial situation, professionals do not allow their opposition to walk through their personal space. Instead, they walk through the space of their adversary, if given a chance. Congressman Rick Lazio made the mistake of invading Hillary Clinton's personal space during their televised political debate, which brought him criticism and cost him votes.

6. Make Eye Contact

Eye contact invites people to interact with us. Once interaction is established, supercharged eye contact plays a prodigious role in synchronizing what takes place. People signal interest by slightly widening their eyes to show more white and expanding their eye pupils. The more people like you the more their pupils become dilated. If they do not like you or disbelieve what you are saying, their pupils tend to contract into tiny pin points.

The eyes are able to challenge, scorn, lie, dominate, trust, forgive, and mesmerize, among many other things. The minimum time needed for attention and interest is approximately four seconds or more, but people who like each other will engage in level eye contact longer.

7. Speak Up

A strong voice not only carries, but also is more impressive; therefore, insofar as possible speak up in a basal-toned, even, and steady voice that people hear easily. Use everyday words and cast sentences in positive, unambiguous terms. For example, it is more positive to say, "Yes, if…"instead of "Yes, but…" when explaining something. It is more positive and sounds better to say something thoughtful such as, "My position is…" instead of "My opinion is…" which sounds less thoughtful.

Try to practice speaking by varying the pitch, contour, and cadence of your voice. "Brevity is the soul of wit", said Polonius in Shakespeare's play *Hamlet*. Moreover, the sound bite is king in today's media. The orator's credo is be positive, be brief, be sincere, and be seated.

8. Control Your Environment

Control your environment to insure that it shows you off in the best possible manner. Control is the extent to which you are able to limit and restrict the environment that you want. The greater control that you have, the greater your confidence is. For example, a room that is too hot or too cold makes people uncomfortable. Also, remember that bad lighting tends to make people look fat or unreal; therefore, either lose it or keep it low.

Overhead lighting, for example, casts bad shadows, makes the nose look longer, and causes dark circles under the eyes, whereas good lighting is soft and diffused. Positive lighting is able to change the mood of rooms and people, and make or break business deals.

Too much or too little of anything is sub-optimal. Too much of a temperature or lighting extreme are negative signals that are generally construed as disrespectful, dominating, and self-serving. Too little of the same is judged to be inattentive, rude, and insincere. Finally, it is a good idea to minimize negative behaviors like the tendency to be overly casual in a formal setting, or putting more food on your plate than you can eat.

9. Keep an Open Attitude

Keeping an open attitude clearly benefits people. A huge factor that differentiates relationships is the level of intimacy. Intimacy results when one person opens up through appropriate self-disclosure and the recipient responds in kind. The benefits of reciprocal self-disclosure are a better understanding of each other, a mutual feeling of caring, and enhanced validation between partners in the relationship. At first, people reveal very little about themselves, but as they gradually open up more, their relationship deepens and they become more intimate and caring.

In secondary relationships, where people are not seeking deep personal relationships, such as a jury panel entering a courtroom for the first time, the attitude of most people is either friendly, hostile, or neutral. In addition, they will bring to court personal constructs such as a distrust of strangers, a low degree of ego involvement, a short attention span, and a limited acceptance of new information. In this situation, being open and friendly helps to overcome any hostile or neutral attitudes they harbor, as well as any inhibitory social constructs they have picked up.

10. *Avoid Cover-ups*

Avoid attempts to cover up your problem areas with such things as excessive make-up or clothes that are over-the-top. That will only make them more noticeable. More often than not, trying to cover up something is worse than what you are covering up. Women, when leaving home, are better off removing one accessory, so they will not look like a mobile jewelry box.

Incredibly, nearly seventy percent of Americans between the ages of thirty and fifty think they look younger than their actual age according to the results of a survey by a manufacturer of anti-aging cosmetics. The report said women are more likely to see a younger self in the mirror than men do, and they dedicate more of their time and attention to maintaining that self-identity.

The report also noted that weight gain was significantly more important than other aging factors like wrinkles, graying hair, brown spots, and hair loss in a ranking of chief concerns. My suggestion is to know yourself, be true to yourself, and it will show in a positive image. In other words, follow a humanistic general approach like Abraham Maslow, who put values into psychology and set forth a pragmatic *hierarchy of needs.* "Get in and get out" tips are expedient, but once you establish an acceptable and reasonable image be content with it. Know what is important and what isn't and like Shakespeare said, "Be true to yourself."

Practical Pointers

The ten steps for a better self-image are meant to be flexible and not an absolute model of behavior for every occasion. They are not short cuts to distinction that replace experience, integrity, and intelligence, but ways to maximize the benefits and minimize the costs of social interplay. Mainly, they are for social survival at those times when you have to make quick decisions and do not know what to do, or you find yourself in a unfamiliar situation in which status relationships are important.

Despite the benefits, stroking egos is sometimes counterproductive. Mitigation or elimination of this danger occurs when you stay with sincere practices that are acceptable on the local level, and do not engage in arbitrary flights of fancy, malignant narcissism, and unrealistic images of yourself.

People can go overboard with political correctness, still the best practice is to consider your audience and try not to offend anyone, which detracts from your presentation.

Chapter 13

Clothing Choices

"I am what I wear"

Clothing and accessories are one of the best shows of elective body language available. What we elect to wear signals our power and solidarity with our peer group. Innumerable sub-messages combine with the basic message to convey to people where we are going, who we want to be, and who we really are.

Not only do we dress for the occasion, but we also select the clothes that fit our idealized image as well. For example, picture Audrey Hepburn in her black dress, oversized sunglasses, and flats, Joan Crawford in her shoulder pads, and Britney Spears in low-cut jeans and bare midriff.

To a degree, clothes function as a protection against the elements, and sometimes we select our clothes and accessories for purely aesthetic reasons, but I believe the main motive behind our choices is the *communicative* value of clothes. Dressing "up" or "down" is visual and invariably rules

> Vanity knows no bounds and has no rules.

as an excellent way to communicate power and status nonverbally in a fashion conscious society. Clothing constraints signal the formality of an occasion and institutional membership in organizations such as the police, clergy, and military.

Clothes are an imitation of the life we want to live. More than just smart fashion choices, our image-conscious clothing selections reflect such things as who we are, where we live and work, what our worldview is, and our age. For example in most conservative workplaces such as those involving finance or law, people don't want to wear anything that draws more attention to themselves than their work. Another example is a particular outlook on life such as a perfectionist, whose house and clothing will be neat, precise, and pressed at all times. Anything less makes a perfectionist terribly unhappy. For instance, perfectionists would never dream of walking around with their shirts untucked.

Natural aging changes people's needs and priorities. Their need to impress others and maintain self-esteem decreases with age, and they tend to become more conservative. Thus, if a man is forty years old and dresses as if he is twenty years old something is amiss. A mature man wearing saggy "low rider" pants that defy gravity and a T-shirt depicting a skateboard is a walking red flag that people will shun.

Red flags for women over age forty are bare midriffs and miniskirts. Long hair on women lacks constraint as does showing a lot of the flesh of upper arms and shoulders. Short hair on a woman hints that she will be more submissive according to male mythology. Unless, you are attending the Hollywood Oscar ceremony, dresses that are cut too far down the front and too far up the side are red flags. Women have more flexibility than men do in clothing choices, but if they break the norms, they pay a higher social penalty.

> Some women are clothes horses.

Few of us want to appear weak, immature, or vulnerable, and clothes are a demonstration of our strength and maturity in life. Most men achieve social authority and status around thirty years of age and women a little later, but it shows up in how they dress. Both sexes begin to lose their authority as they approach the age of retirement, and they start dressing down instead of up.

As women age, they eschew tight fitting outfits in favor of more casual and comfortable inner and outerwear clothes. As men grow older, they turn to golf shirts, printed Hawaiian shirts, and slacks with elastic waistbands to accommodate expanding waistlines. Both men and women tend to dress down with advancing age and the declining need to impress others. The elderly are less attentive to how others expect them to behave and are less concerned about the social correctness of their behavior.

The cycle of life comes around when senior citizens understand that what they regarded as "klutzy" teenage wear in their formative years was actually a normal way of nonverbally communicating the common teenage issues of their day. The driving force behind teenage motivation is the idiosyncratic and usually baffling search for attention not fashion.

The Wave of the Future

In the new millennium, formal dress codes and policies will return for many public and private schools. Six of the nations' largest school districts already have uniform dress policies. After Columbine, security has become one of the foremost concerns of most Americans, which has led to rethinking regarding the scope of individual rights and liberties in relation to public safety and intensely populated environments.

Certain types of sinister clothing communicate the wrong values, draw attention, and foster behavior contrary to the health, safety, and welfare of the general populace. For these reasons, inherent in the proposed measures for dealing with terrorists and other criminals is the notion that certain kinds of attire such as bulky clothes, large handbags, and unsupervised backpacks cause group jeopardy.

On account of their unenviable experience with the correlation between sloppy dress and sloppy behavior, many of today's school administrators believe the wrong body language is expressed by teenage male students wearing sandals and flip-flops, sagging pants, clothing with holes, slashes or rips, bandanas, and clothing displaying gang symbols, tobacco, alcohol, death or drugs.

Many school districts will discourage females from wearing shorts and miniskirts hemmed six inches above the knees, as well as bare shoulder or strapless garments, and apparel that exposes low necklines, midriffs, and bare backs.

What is permissible high school attire? I predict that in the future most male middle and high school students will be required to wear clean pants in good order and conventional shirts without statements, pictures, or messages, and females will be required to cover up exposed skin.

Inasmuch as local school districts need to heed security issues, outerwear for students of both sexes will be less bulky making it more difficult to hide contraband or weapons. Moreover, gang symbols, gang colors, and other sinister graphics and messages will be tolerated less.

In the future, many adults will eschew the teen and street fashions promoted by the advertising media and Hollywood glitterati. Although T-shirts and distressed blue jeans are still popular with the Hollywood and fashion crowd because of the youthful image they present, such attire will lose popularity as fashions change. They will slowly disappear in the business and elite social worlds where adults will opt for higher quality, high-tech blended fabrics, and classic styles.

Unbelievably, some people think that if the price of reasonable safety and well-being is their youth, then the price is too high. Nevertheless, more and more federal and state courts around the country are handing down decisions that allow school districts and adult employers to regulate dress attire on the premises.

Today, adult employers are able to ban reasonably defined "sexy" dress attire in their businesses. Generally speaking, sexy dress attire for females is anything that it specifically revealing and of extreme fit such as spandex outfits, low-cut blouses, and too much makeup. For men, it is low-riding pants, tank tops, and muscle shirts.

The courts feel that businesses have the right to set reasonable dress and appearance codes because the appearance of company employees contributes to its image and success with the public; therefore, it is a legitimate management prerogative. It does not discriminate against women since it applies to men as well, yet it allows employers to require women to avoid so-called tight, flashy, and revealing clothes that traditional businesspersons seldom wear.

Accentuate the Positives

In the twenty-first century business world, I think the pendulum of change will swing back to business suits in the workplace. After a couple of decades of laidback nonchalance in men's clothing, dressing up is making a comeback. Already, many nation-wide businesses and Fortune 500 companies have issued memos to their employees doing away with casual attire for the office, especially those employees in "customer-facing" positions.

Except for a lot of "dot.com" companies, many smaller corporations are also realizing that to be competitive in today's marketplace employees have to look and dress the part, which means tailored, better-made coats and ties for men and appropriate attire for women. The dress policies of companies that allowed employees to dress down on certain days will continue only in those instances where there is little or no client contact.

American businesses are finding that casual work attire leads to casual status as well. A recent twenty-year study concluded that women who wear casual clothes to work are less serious about their job and earn less than women who dress formally.

Dress down days in the workplace allows people to loosen up, but is a mixed blessing the study says. Although casual dress days brought a new level of comfort, they also diminished the status, confidence, and positive attitude of the people who dressed down. For customer contact, a less ambivalent professional appearance for both men and women in the business world is returning with well cut, but conservative business attire in dark colors for men, and lighter earth tones for women, plus a dress shirt and tie for men.

> Wear light colors in the summer and dark colors in the winter.

After the dot com bust came a tighter job market. Unemployment remains unacceptably high today. This disconcerting fact is one of the reasons that management consultants advise job seekers to choose clothes with care because the color they wear influences the impression they make on others. Bright colors draw attention to you while dark colors are more serious than light colors and make you look like an authority figure.

Upper class colors such as navy blue and gray communicate dignity and power. Gray is one of the best colors in a man's wardrobe. It is not as dark as black, and is more striking than navy blue. Earth tones have less power, but wearing earth tones makes people seem more approachable, sympathetic, and down-to-earth.

Examples of colors that are incongruent or seem out of place are when a banker or attorney wears a white tie with a black shirt, which creates a negative impression thanks to Hollywood's portrayal of gangsters in movies, and when a man wear an all red or all yellow suit to a formal dinner. In the courtroom, a very bright colored piece of clothing is like a skunk at a picnic-you cannot ignore it.

Outerwear

The saying, "clothes make the man", is a cliché, but is it possible to become a better person because of the clothes we wear? Yes, to a degree we project the image we have of ourselves, which is always subject to improvement. If for example, we want to appear more businesslike, we need to wear a business suit and polished shoes.

People who want control and power are able to dress in a manner that makes the statement, "I am a decision maker". People hesitate to do business with a person who is careless, sloppy, or nonchalant about his outer attire.

Outer garments such as overcoats, jackets, pants, skirts, and shoes point out both the real and imaginary degree of power possessed by a person. For example, the highest power outer wear for men is an expensive three-piece business suit, plain collar white shirt, subdued red or maroon silk tie, and plain toe lace-up shoe.

The next highest power attire for men is the two-piece, off-the-rack suit, colored shirt, inexpensive tie, and wing tip shoe. Beneath that in power are the windowpane sport coat, inexpensive trousers, and loafers. Below that is a shirt and pants with work shoes or tennis shoes.

Men at the bottom of the power clothes spectrum buy things from the metaphorical third rail such as loud matching shirt and socks, sandals with socks, baggy, ill fitting jeans, sleeveless shirts, and overalls. Showing skin above the wrists and below the Adam's apple is a power no-no and the pocket square has lost its power.

Outer garments ranging from expensive two-piece suits, silk blouses, and shoes that increase height on down to a fashion suit with open heels and toes expresses a woman's substantial power. The next level on the power dress scale is the casual dress with flats, and the lowest level are things like message T-shirts, short shorts, and sweat pants with sandals.

Men send a wrongheaded message in a business setting if they wear pointy look-at-me shoes and shiny bright colored suits. Other mistakes are sandals, polo shirts, and Bermuda shorts. Blue jeans, earrings, and muscle shirts are not appropriate for business settings.

It has always been inappropriate for women to show up in the courtroom or business meeting in sandals, headbands, garish jewelry, "crocs", and tight fitting, revealing clothes. In addition, fancy shoes, handbags and jewelry that scream wanton consumption in a slow economy seem frivolous when Americans are experiencing a housing bubble and credit crisis.

For both sexes today, overly ornate anything conveys less status and power. This is important because a person's position in a group affects his or her susceptibility to the pressure of conformity. Low-status people conform more than high-status people and have less freedom and independence. The more behavior stands out the more notice it gets, and other more conservative group members consider it "showing off". Behavior that affects one group member affect other group members. The best practice is for dress attire to concentrate on pieces that reflect value and sustainability, and if that works, it has validity. Simplicity of style does not argue against intensity.

Innerwear

Inner wear garments are more personal and reflect our core personality more than outerwear because we are able to take more liberty with our inner garments. For instance, men are able to change their total clothing image by simply taking their business attire to another level with a red power tie instead of an earth tone or light-hearted theme tie. They are able to tone down a formal three-piece suit by wearing a more casual shirt and tie.

In American culture, shirts for men range from the "I look important" plain, white, starched shirts to the unbuttoned "I don't care" plaid flannel shirts. Plain collars with French cuffs are the most powerful for men and the least powerful is a denim or khaki shirt. For women, a small collar and plain cuff are the most powerful, because a woman's status decreases as her blouse becomes more flashy, open, and frilly, or the size of her neck scarf increases.

Neckties

A man's choice in neckties is visual and intentional, thus eye-catching ties continue to be popular. In 1950, Countess Mara aptly said, "Tell a man you like his necktie and you will see his personality unfold like a flower". Coincidentally, the same is true of a woman's hairdo.

Truly, a man's choice of tie width, length, fabric, and color communicates his outlook and level of confidence. The bolder the tie is the bolder the man; however, the real secret of necktie aesthetics is the knot. To create a crisp and confident look for the preferred four-in-hand knot, it must be tight and dovetail in the inverted "V" of the collar. Loose tie knots look sloppy and unprofessional.

Do you want to look younger or taller? To look taller wear the same colors to avoid eye-catching contrasts. Also, a vertical stripe and "below the belt" tie will make you look taller and slimmer, while the color and style of your tie hint at your age and social power. Although neckties come in four basic styles, the most powerful necktie is a red foulard with geometric patterns or very small dots, whereas surveys show that a maroon color signals trust. The next level on the power scale is a dark colored "Club" tie with a small logo print. Below that are alumni ties and English style "Repp" ties with so-called regimental colors and stripes. Beneath that is the solid or monochromatic tie, while the least powerful of all is the narrative tie that tells a story such as a man duck hunting.

Today, not many men wear bow ties. Bowties tend to make their wearers look "nerdy", or at the very least out of the mainstream. The only time bowties are fashionable are when they are worn with tuxedos at formal occasions such as a wedding. Keep in mind that even the right tie loses power and credibility if it has stains on it or twists like a corkscrew.

Practical Pointers

Clothes send a loud message about who we are and what we want to be. In fact, the wardrobe of most people is multidimensional and expresses matters of secondary importance to them such as their icons, geographical preferences, politics, and so on. Many business people are going back to the traditional business suit, and future school districts will return to dress codes that are more conservative.

It is easy to dress down, but not up after the first contact with others; therefore, common sense dictates looking our best from the very beginning.

Chapter 14

Elective Accessories

"Expressories reveal our innermost nature."

E lective accessories are what I call expressories because of their role in people's dress attire. They broadcast our intentions, attitudes, and spirit among other things. Expressories range from bedrock pragmatism to carefree whimsy depending on the preferred message. For example, women who are inclined toward today's individualism are able to be completely whimsical in choosing a handbag made from a variety of materials such as the new vinyl and sequin selections, a wide assortment of leather, or they are able to have a purse with a graphic print of their children's picture emblazoned on the sides.

Modern iconoclasts of both sexes telegraph a "techno" look with space-age expressories such as I-pods, GPS devices, palm pilots, multi-functional cell phones, wireless devices, and advanced applications.

The "Goth" crowd, on the other hand, find expression in tattoos, body piercing, and intentionally sinister attire such as black leather with shiny studs, heavy eyeliner, dark lipstick, dark fingernail polish, leather collars, and black T-shirts with messages of death and doom.

Old school adults have a tough time figuring out where "goths" are coming from with their horror and dark fantasy interdimensional worlds that are violent and grotesque, and vie for people's souls like flesh eating viruses. Obviously, this fashion is not suitable for grown-ups.

Watches

A wristwatch says a lot about its owner and has more meaning than many other expressories, so its gets special treatment. A brand new men's watch on the fashion scene today is the "Watchismo". It is black with silver knobs and is made of special carbon materials. The message it sends is pretty obvious. Whether or not it goes over remains to be seen.

Whether a watch is a good or bad timepiece says something about the owner's attitude toward time. For example, some people set their watches ahead because they are always running out time. Others turn their watches back a little bit to give themselves the illusion of having more time.

Instead of just keeping time, however, different watch styles convey messages such as, "I'm well to do"", I'm an athlete," or "I'm a scuba diver". For a little more money, watch connoisseurs can add a multitude of other exotic functions packed into the dial. For instance, modern watches are bigger and more complicated with crowded dials that feature things like heart rate monitors, compasses, multiple time zones, stopwatches, and even thermometers.

Watches used to be simple and small, but today they are more of a status symbol than a discreet timepiece. Status-minded people seeking a rich and powerful look can buy watches encased in their choice of red, white, or yellow gold framed with a diamond bezel. To compliment their watches they wear large diamond rings, diamond earrings, and diamond "headlights" (i.e. necklaces).

Keep it Simple

The quality, size, and type of expressories people choose gives them the cachet and self-authentication they are looking for today. Insofar as jewelry goes, it is my opinion that bigger is not always better, and people gain more from keeping it simple. If you want to trample all standards of good taste, choose something big calling attention to yourself.

Women who wear big, dangling earrings, large bracelets, multi-strand necklaces and ornate watches, and men who wear large gold neck chains, expensive rings, over-the-top watches, earrings, and bracelets are actually detracting from their image in mainstream American culture.

Men seeking a conservative image need to limit themselves to a simple wedding band and a nice watch. Women need to limit themselves to a diamond wedding ring and small tasteful earrings instead of oversized, colorful types, and shapes. Both men and women should eliminate large necklaces.

Jewelry choices underscore the difference between function and the purely aesthetic. To keep things real, bear in mind that large sparkling diamonds and elaborately jeweled rings, pins, necklaces, and bracelets are strictly ornamental body language pieces. Class rings, fraternal pins, flags, and birthstones are informational body language pieces, while watches are primarily functional pieces. In a few cases, some jewelry is neither functional nor aesthetic, but is strictly for attitude.

Practical Pointers

Our dress attire firmly establishes the body language role that outer and inner wear play in determining how we define ourselves, express our personalities, and present our physical selves. A certain suit or pair of earrings can change the energy and power of a whole outfit. In addition, if something is too weird or not quite right, one good thing is that expressories are visible flags that forewarn us of some people's dodgy personalities.

In the future, the untamed trend of "anything goes" for the workplace, along with the smell-the-roses attitude, will continue in some geographical areas, but will not last in areas of high unemployment or in jobs involving a lot of customer contact. There is little point in continuing casual trends that hinder the normative expectations of people who put their money and trust in institutions and professionals.

Chapter 15

Shades of Color

"Colors make things convincing"

Colors are symbolic and apply to all levels of being and knowledge. Although interpretations differ, colors are universal touchstones of symbolic thought, which results in their ability to conjure up deep-seated associations with ordinary visual experiences in the natural world, such as a sunset for example.

Colors are powerful adjuncts to body language since people everywhere choose various colors to make their messages more convincing for proprietary reasons, aesthetic purposes, and as markers of difference. Throughout time, colors gave given people a sense of oneness with the four basic,

> Never wear more than three colors at once.

eternal, and universal elements: water, fire, air, and earth. For example, red expresses hot, fiery, high energy below, and blue expresses depth, tranquility, and the vast skies above.

Colors have quasi-biological characteristics and religious connotations charged with meaning and power, as well as many complex meanings in the world of fashion. For instance, masculine colors, generally speaking, are black, white, blue, and grey. Feminine colors are pink, red, and earth tones.

Black is the color of evil and black animals are considered unlucky in some cultures, whereas white, the symbol of light, is lucky. Green, the color of nature, vegetation, and growth is also thought to be lucky and a sign of health. Yellow, the color of intuition, is magical to some people. Blue, the color of the sky, is the color of the spirit.

Besides Regis Philbin suits, few things are monochromatic. Colors have three essential components: Hue, intensity, and saturation. A color's name such as red, blue, yellow, and so forth is its "hue". Different hues are associated with different parts of the natural world such as blue and the sky. The "intensity" of a color is its degree of "brightness". The range of color intensity makes colors ideal for symbolic attachment to the degree and range of human emotions. For example, the brighter the color red becomes the stronger passion is. The third component of color is its purity or "saturation", which relates well to human diversity.

Usually, a person's choice in colors is subject to the circumstances of use. For example, in interior decor, colors convey either "warmth" or "coldness". Red, yellow and orange are warm colors and blue, green, and violet are cool, relaxing colors. Because each hue has its own symbolic temperature, we get an idea of another person's body temperature by their skin color, whereas emotional warmth comes out in the warm colors people wear.

In fashion, black, or the absence of color, is popular because it goes with anything, is suitable for anyone, and is "slimming". Traditionally, colors have been associated with natural objects and events seen in the everyday world such as associating red with the sun, dawn, and fire, blue with the sky and water, and green with the plants and trees outdoors.

Color associations are positive or negative. For instance, white is positively associated with good, purity, cleanliness, virginity, and the light or way ahead. Black opposes white and has a negative connotation, since it renounces and rejects the existing state of things such as the unknown "black hole" in space, which sucks in all matter close to it including light.

Deep Blue

Blue is the color of loyalty, which gives rise to the saying "true blue".

Wear red when you are blue.

Blue is the opposite of red, and is the favorite color of the majority of Americans. It connotes contentment and fulfillment. Blue is symbolic of the sky, tranquility, and peace; accordingly, blue is also the color of harmony. Not surprisingly, blue is the color of choice for many rooms where people go to relax, since studies have shown blue actually slows down the metabolic rate. A lot of people prefer blue when they are experiencing deep feelings.

Blue is symbolic of tradition in many cultures, lasting values, and the deep blue sea, which makes it the choice of institutions such as the police, the postal service, the Navy, and the United States Air Force. Blue is one of the colors of the American flag, and other flags too, linking it to the positive trait of patriotism.

The good news is that persons who favor blue are supportive, but the bad news is blue has also been connected with negative traits such as conformity and depression. The attitude conveyed by a serious lover of blue is non-aggressive and conservative. In many social systems, blue is the color of the worker function as in the term "blue collar labor". On the other hand, royalty, thoroughbreds, and the highborn are sometimes referred to as "blue bloods".

People who choose blue prefer to associate with an orderly environment free from upset. They prefer the status quo and tend to be passive and introverted.

Red Hot

Since the beginning of human memory, red has been associated with the fire, heat, light, and energy of the sun. In ancient times, the human race lived much closer to nature and even worshiped the sun for its life-giving properties, so logically red became a powerful color representing a major element in the natural world.

Henri Matisse, an important painter of the 20th century noted for his brilliant colors, claimed there is a sun inside people as well as one outside them; therefore, it is not surprising that red is strongly associated with emotions such as hot passion, anger, and sex, which is an image succored by the movie industry and print media.

Red hair, red lipstick, red lingerie, and red dresses are very sexy, both individually and collectively. Some fashion experts say red makes a woman feel vibrant and passionate, although red is not a typical choice for daywear, and going head-to-toe red is a little too much for average Americans.

Physically, red is symbolic of blood and to the stimulation of the nervous system causing blushing, increased respiration, increased glandular activity, and high blood pressure. When we become excited or stimulated, our blood rushes to a target area causing a red tinge and heightened sensitivity that gives rise to the saying "hot under the collar".

Red is the color of countless warning symbols such as red lights, stop signs, and warning labels. Paradoxically, red also has a festive meaning in many cultures, and is part of many rituals and other merrymaking occasions throughout the world.

The body language of red conveys aggression and the tendency to push one's ideas and interests, as well as impulse, anger, and excitability. People who admire red believe in winning and enjoy power, authority, and competition. They will work vigorously and ruthlessly toward their goals.

> Red and yellow are the colors of extroverts. Red for individuals and yellow for groups.

Red fanciers want to be the centers of attention and are extroverted, dominating, and individualistic with vocations such as athletes, doctors, firefighters, and racecar drivers. On the downside, people that esteem red tend to be impulsive, eschew details, have short attention spans, and think of nothing but the bottom line. The appeal of the color of bright red is cross-cultural because it is hot, exciting, and passionate in everybody's book.

Yellow Ribbon

Yellow is symbolic of light, the path or way, the fall season, and the hot sun. If your outlook is bright and cheerful, your disposition sunny, and your main desire is to be happy, you prefer yellow. Furthermore, if you truly enjoy investigating and searching for ways to get through the vicissitudes of daily living, then yellow is high on your Richter scale.

People who prefer yellow are happy, intellectual, logical, and socially extroverted. Moreover, people who choose yellow as their favorite color are projective, expansive, and active. They are democratic and love meeting new people.

Yellow adherents wear yellow ribbons for social causes such as freeing hostages and other challenging projects that have a high degree of expectation. On the emotional scale, people who embrace yellow are generally happy, hopeful, and flexible with a tendency to be fun loving, creative, optimistic, and extroverted. Typically, they will have open, cheerful, and friendly body language. When you want to appear friendly, all you have to do is wear a yellow blouse or necktie as the case may be.

In physiology however, yellow has a negative association with jaundice, fever, and liver ailments. Emotionally, yellow is associated with cowardice. Yellow's biggest use, however, is in warning signs and labels, such as the yellow caution light before the red one, yellow police tape, and yellow cautionary road signs.

Green Plants

> Green is the new red, white, and blue.
>
> Thomas Freidman

From apple green to Spanish green, the color green and its pigments are so popular that they have their own special connotations. Green is not a primary color, yet it represents such a large part of our symbolic thinking that it deserves its own heading. On the one hand, green has come to mean the beginning or starting point, which in terms of people means a rookie, fledgling, trainee, or "greenhorn". Therefore, for some a person who wears green has the slightly negative body language of an immature, inexperienced person who is inept and unskilled.

Psychologically, however, green is associated with a growing sense of pride and self-worth. People who wear green want to make an impression on others, and get recognition no matter how untrained they are. Thus, their tendencies are to be assertive, serious, somewhat structured, not too emotional, and stubborn.

> Green and blue are the colors of introverts.

Emotionally, green loving people are firm, proud, and persistent. They tend to prefer vocations where they are able to be reformers, lecturers, and healthcare providers who seek better conditions in life. At the same time, they enjoy the rewards and recognition of their efforts.

In the physical sense, green is normally associated with good health and growth. Thus, green is popular in hospitals and is often the color of scrubs worn by doctors and nurses, especially in operating rooms. Green is associated with physical signs of infection and nausea.

In another more philosophical sense, green is a cool, comforting, breezy, and refreshing color that evokes images of nature. It is the natural color of growing and preservation. Gardeners have a "green thumb", and a greenhouse is a glass-enclosed building that grows plants.

Symbolically green has been associated with a variety of things such as the St. Patrick's day holiday, the good luck of a four-leaf clover, and the beauty of Ireland. Green is the universal symbol for strength, immortality, and nature, and in the United States, it also symbolizes money, wealth, and high status, all of which command respect today. Wearing green is good luck for lawyers and clients in trials, but for actors working on stage, it is bad luck according to superstition.

Practical Pointers

Color is the big frog in the pond of description. It is impossible to explain objects and their value without its consideration; therefore, people endeavor to add color even where it is uncertain.

Colors reveal biological changes. A change in face color is a biological response to events that challenge people and functions as a signal underlying changes in their psychological states. For example if a person's face blushes pinkish to red, it is a low-level stress response revealing sensitivity, but if it becomes a darker red to purplish color then it is more likely a high-level stress response due to the drastic increase in blood pressure and volume. A very pale face is a mid-level stress response of fear and anxiety, but also could be the result of having just come out of a serious operation or prolonged confinement. Better practice argues against diagnosing a malady based just on color.

Chapter 16

Style and Fashion

"We elect how we want to look."

After clothes, the two most important concerns people have about their looks are their hair and eyes. Hair is an archetypical symbol of many different styles, and the eyes are the seat of our emotions, appetites, and inclinations among other things. Thus, hairstyles and eyewear styles have become important areas where people spend a lot of their time and money to send personal messages that suit for them.

The Mane Attraction

American men spend over $1 billion dollars a year on hair-replacement and unknown billions on haircuts. The reason is that hair is visual and directly reflects both image and maturity. As a result, a man's hair is his crown, which symbolizes his masculinity, his psyche, and his vanity. Hair protects the top of the head from the sun, but its importance lies in the perception that its owner is virile, and when it turns gray, or disappears in baldness, it conveys an aura of wisdom and worldly experience.

> **Gray hairs are a calling card.**

Since our remote ancestors, youth, good health, and reproductive ability have been associated with a full head of hair, whereas a naturally balding head and hairless face signifies a more passive, conservative, and intelligent man.

Hair is the body's most manipulated feature because we are able to cut, shape, style, and reshape it in a hundred different ways. A particular hairstyle becomes a man's pride and joy, and plays a big role in his "looks". Consequently, hair becomes important in the context of current fashion trends since the vast majority of men want their hairstyle and hair maintenance to be a visual signal saying they are "in style". This is true especially at peak times such as a first job interview or first date.

The style of a man's hair translates into lifestyle beliefs. Neat, well groomed, and styled hair that is shorter on the sides than the top instead of an even circular cut all the way around says, "I am no longer a kid. My lifestyle is making money and being successful." Unkempt or bushy hair makes the face look round, and says, "I am not flashy and I don't care." A layered haircut with side, top, and back styling is going to be more expensive, but its purpose is to impress; therefore, expensive clothes to complete the image of success should usually accompany it.

Short hair with a relaxed cut is indicative of a conservative attitude, a pragmatic outlook, and athletic bent, if it is very short, or an organizational man where uniformity is valued such as a police officer or military man. On the other hand, long hair on a man generally means he is a nonconformist, rock star, actor, artist, or scientist; however, hair that is too long or too wild does not send the right message on a grown man.

Men who cut their hair medium to short length with a neatly trimmed taper and side part look intelligent and trustworthy. The good news about a medium-length cut with a middle part is this person is pleasant to be around, but the bad news is this style is less sexy than a side part, and is may be an attempt to cover up a receding hairline.

Brightly dyed hair, long ponytails, Mohawks, and colored spikes on a man's head definitely mean he wants to look nonconformist, rebellious, hyper-trendy, or unconventional for personal reasons that probably involve getting attention. Some men who like the attention it brings go as far as cutting weird designs, initials, and strange messages in their hair.

A straight hair cut with relaxed hair is mature and conservative, whereas curly hair is high maintenance, but younger looking. Dark hair is more lustrous than lighter hair. Dry blown hair like ex-President Bush wears has a conservative look to match his politics.

Cheap wigs or sparse hair combed over in contrived ways connotes vanity and poor judgment. It is just chasing the wind. Of course, young hair is more lustrous than old hair. Hair that completely lacks any luster probably needs a thorough cleaning since mousse, gels, conditioners, oils, and sprays tend to build up and eventually sabotage style and luster.

Hats

Wearing a hat is low hair maintenance. On the other hand, when a man wears a hairpiece, or has had other hair replacement treatments, it usually means he is self-conscious about his hair and has a need to look more youthful. Maybe, he is balancing optimism with the perversity of fate; nevertheless, it is safe to say that a man who chooses to wear a hat indoors, when no one else does, is either self-conscious or oblivious to what others think.

In order to examine how hair and wearing a hat can become more complicated, think about Princess Diana and Prince Charles. In about half of her photos, Diana is wearing a hat. Prince Charles seems to wear a hat only for military reasons or for safety at a plant inspection. Although we are tempted to conclude from this that wearing a hat is a gender marker, many men and women in America wear the same style baseball cap.

In most parts of the country now, it is socially acceptable for men and women to wear cowboy hats or baseball caps indoors. The body language of wearing a hat, then, is not explicitly indicative of gender. In the case of Princess Diana and Prince Charles, wearing hats was more about fashion and status than absolute submission to discipline and safety, which one might encounter in royalty, the military, and public construction sites.

Covering the head with bonnets, shawls, burquas, stiff hats, and other ritual headgear may have religious underpinnings with a message of humility and submission to a higher authority. This is especially true if covering the head is a requirement of a particular faith.

Facial Hair

Facial hair has been a distinguishing feature on both famous and infamous men, heroes, kings, and rebels such as Zeus, Lincoln, Henry the VIII, Hitler, Lenin, Castro, and Osama Bin Laden, to name a few. Traditionally facial hair has been an adaptive signal of sexual maturity and the presence of testosterone, which aids men in reproductive prowess, although the extent to which females find men with facial hair attractive is debatable.

Today, the attraction power of facial hair seems to be more a matter of taste than conscious mate selection. Reproductive vetting aside, facial hair is one of the most powerful elective gestures in the male repertoire with significance in a wide range of domains such as religion, politics, and acting.

From time immemorial, facial hair has been a symbol of royalty due in part to the notion that beards had divine origins, which rulers sought for validation. Facial hair has been associated with religious groups, such as the orthodox Jews, Shiite Muslims, certain Christian groups, and other smaller sects. The rationale was that beards distance the wearer from infidels. For example, the gospel of Leviticus warns against marring the beard and Mohammed extolled beards as a part of Islamic tradition. Some Muslims swear an oath by the beard of the prophet Mohammed.

During the reign of Queen Elizabeth I, she decided to tax beards and clean-shaven faces all of a sudden became popular with Englishmen. Today, the overwhelming majority of American men shave at least once a day. Nevertheless, growing facial hair continues to be a rite of passage for young men because a moustache or beard suggests virility, a greater age, and more bearing than a typical clean-shaven face.

Facial hair suggests dominance and power. Men with facial hair have an easier task intimidating clean-shaven men and women, thus making it adaptive for this reason. In fact, some cynics believe male facial hair is a reaction to feminism since females cannot grow beards.

Male facial hair also says, "I'm not a corporate slave." For others, such as professors and scientists, facial hair is a tantalizing signpost of an independent mind resisting social conformity norms in favor of a deliberate enterprise to express individuality, freedom, and creativity.

The permanently unfriendly droop of a thin "Fu Manchu" style moustache may be an effort to mask weakness by affecting a malevolent visage, otherwise it should end about one-ninth of an inch from the end of the lips. Moustaches may be attempts to cover up psychic disfigurements. The desire to partly cover or completely hide visible disfigurements such as a hair lip, scars, blemishes, and other deformities may be the motivation behind many moustaches.

Outside of a few religious orthodoxies such as the Sikh faith that forbids men to shave their beards and other zealots, the rationale behind the size, shape, and configuration of facial hair seems to be a matter of individual choice.

Trend spotters predict the continuation of trim sideburns, goatees, and moustaches; however, extra long unkempt beards such as those seen on ZZ Top and the Taliban, as well as "walrus" moustaches, and "mutton chops" are "old timey" and "out-of-it."

The longer and bushier facial hair becomes the more negativity is conveyed, and for American men it is a path to becoming a social nonentity in mainstream America. Although lacking in facts, some overly superstitious people advise caution around any man whose hair is one color and his beard is another, which is Hollywood mythology more than scientific research.

Female Hairdos

Women, the same as men, place a great degree of importance on their hairdo, but have greater freedom with their hair than men do, thus they spend more time and fuss on personal hair styling. Since any style is acceptable today, how a woman wears her hair is an important hint about her entire self.

A few decades ago, fashion mavens decreed that women over forty should cut their hair short or at least to a medium length. They declared that long hair on a middle-aged woman sent a signal that she had low power and status, whereas a woman who piled her hair on top had strong opinions, and if she cut her hair short-to-medium length, she was more chic. The ostensible reason was that long, curly hair is high maintenance and shorter hairdos no longer than the collarbone seemed to be the magic length for most mature women. However, that was before the hair revolution beginning in the 1960s. Today, a longer, casual, and even negligent look is fashionable in the *haute monde*.

How women choose to style their hair plays a role in their feelings and attitudes. Age 40 is no longer old and people are living longer. For example, lifestyles, looks, and the overall condition of a woman's hair are more compelling than outdated fashion ideas.

On balance, if the hair looks good, then everything else looks better. Long, short, or medium length, women uniformly believe that their hairdo is one of the most important aspects of their image wherever they are. Hair care products flood the stores in an effort to keep women consumers paying more for less. Products no one needs are taken for granted as something every woman must have.

Eyewear

Eyewear changes how we look; consequently, wearing eyeglasses is a multifaceted prop for elective body language expression as well as an aid to eyesight. Eyeglasses are one of the first things we notice about a person, thus, they are an excellent clue into the personality and style of the owner.

> Make sure your eyeglasses fit. People want to see your eyes.

People want eyewear to make a statement. Does size make any difference? Yes, small eyewear is "in" today, but big is rapidly coming back-especially in sunglasses.

Since the shape and size of people's heads and faces are unique, eyewear manufacturers have created hundreds of different fashion styles to choose from such as the new trendy plastics, flat metals, light titanium, and rimless styles, plus hundreds of colors. The large variety of stylistic selections, the remarkable technical improvements in lenses, durability, and comfort have rendered the old adage, "Men won't make passes at women who wear glasses" as today's anachronism.

The most significant aspect of eyewear is the propensity of glasses to function as a clue to a person's outer directed identity. The image people want to project to the public is readily insinuated from the eyewear they pick and the manner in which they wear their eyeglasses.

Men who wish to project a macho or militaristic look often wear an aviator's style sunglasses with a green tint and gold-colored teardrop frames popularized during World War II. The police favor the same style today, but with a darker tint to conceal their eyes.

Security people such as the Secret Service still prefer a dark tint and heavy black plastic frames such as those worn during the 1950s and parodied in the "Blues Brothers" movies. Even though the wearers of the latter style are definitely trying to mask their identity, it is positively Kafkaesque, because their conspicuous eyewear and communication devices make it easy to spot them.

Men and women who want to project an "owlish" image of intelligence often choose larger and thicker plastic lenses similar to bottle bottoms with large frames, but unlike sun glasses, the main purpose of larger glasses is actually to see better. People who want to announce, "I'm here" are wearing custom shaped, rimless styles that were popular in the 1950s and '60s.

During the 1970s, eyewear reached ridiculously large sizes covering both the cheeks and eyebrows in an effort to make the proprietor look younger, because their opposite, small frames, were perceived as "granny's glasses". Today, just the opposite is chic.

Modern designer eyeglasses have a better design for comfort and fit due to lighter, smaller, metal frames and adjustable hinges to make them less conspicuous. Ideally, eyeglasses form a contrast with the shape of the face, rather than mimic it, which usually means choosing frames opposite to the face's shape. For instance, people are able to find the slightly angular, narrow frames that lengthen the full foreheads, chins and cheeks of round faces, while staying away from nineteen seventies inspired styles tending to exaggerate the fullness of the face.

Square faces appear softer with a round frame so people often choose wide, oval frames to downplay the angular face. Oval faces look slimmer with square frames. Oblong faces that are narrow with long cheeks look best in frames detailed on the outer edges. For heart-shaped faces, the best eyewear is a frame with a straight top that dips downward to balance out the triangular bone structure. The goal of these examples is to achieve the most flattering body language by using contrasts.

People who do not care how they look often ignore the rules of self-expression in eyewear. They wear the same frames they have worn for a long time in complete disregard of new fashions and technological improvements.

Eyewear Props

Eyewear is a handy psychological prop that people use for gesturing when they are talking or moving about. A common gesture is the time out gesture where a person takes off his glasses and wipes the lenses clean in a slow circular fashion.

A similar gesture to gain time is removing the eyeglasses and putting the earpiece of the frame in the mouth. This maneuver gains precious time for a person to ponder the ramifications of a conversation, formulate an answer, and seek more information. This person is symbolically searching for nourishment in the form of more credible information. In other words, this person is saying, "Give me more".

Another move in the repertoire of eyeglass gesturing is dramatically taking them off and throwing them down on the table with emphasis. This action is a stylized form of resistance and exasperation to what is going on by saying symbolically, "Now you've gone too far" or "Hold on". If you see this gesture, take quick action to reduce the ambient tension.

Eyewear projects people's changing attitudes about life and the images they hope to project. For example, a person wearing sunglasses indoors is more worried about his image than UV protection Look at the eyeglasses of the person to whom you are speaking if you wish to know his true sentiments, since he is able to change his words faster than his eyewear.

Practical Pointers

In the first part of the new millennium, elective body language will consist of matter-of-fact pragmatism that is less frivolous and more profound than the flamboyant 60s and 70s hairstyles. Fashion trends such as long hair and tight bell-bottoms are now out, whereas short hair and baggy pants are in. Eyewear sizes were big and then small, but are headed toward big again.

Elective body language is largely a matter of taste for the times, and usually does not make it into a social convention like the traditional dark business suit. However, some people like to play the "I am different" card. Some fashions will take the offbeat path, but most people will continue their preference for conventional hairstyles and eyewear that reflect mainstream values.

Chapter 17

Body Shapes

"The real contests the potential."

Body shapes are real, non-elective body characteristics that people are born with. Biological features such as size, shape, and weight can define people's physical potential to be this or that. On the other hand, no reliable scientific evidence supports the idea that body shapes directly influence personality. Nevertheless, nonelective body characteristics continue to fascinate people the world over because some aspects of behavior, such as sexual behavior, clearly are a result of the interaction of biological and social factors.

The traditional social standard, for example, of sexy female body shapes have changed over time, yet the notion of the hourglass figure being highly desirable lingers. Men's fashion has evolved from full bodies to muscular bodies as super athletes dominate the media, although only a few athletes reach superstar status. Often, fashion dictates seem to be a matter of cyclical periods.

While I share the concern of those who object to rigid and standardized ideas of body shapes as being the objectification of people in a judgmental world where self-esteem is all-important, everything is subject to change. Traditional views have value as historical perspective, but almost certainly will not be the standard in the future. Just look at a painting by 17th century artist, Reubens, and any today. Body shapes are not about simple biological categories, or convoluted social standards, but they are all about the relational identities between persons and their bodies.

Body Shape Folklore

Nonelective body shapes draw upon historical roots for authenticity, and as a result, they suffer intellectually. Modern researchers disdain the folklore correlating people's body type with behavior as baseless Nevertheless, nonelective body shapes are far from being a dead, monolithic concept. Instead, body folklore is organic and subject to a vast body of sentiment even to this day, which is self-evident from the saying, "Dynamite comes in small packages".

Beside the so-called constitutional theories of personality typing like the works of Sheldon and Galen set forth earlier in this book, lesser-known myths involving body shapes assert that certain predispositions are actually located in certain areas of the body. Some Eastern religions such as Hinduism, the major religion of India, make a very big deal out of this notion. Many others believe the human body is divisible into the left and right hemispheres with the right being the male assertive half, and the left being the feminine side.

It is also possible to metaphorically divide the human body into the front half and the back half. The front is the half we put forward for display, whereas the back half is less visible and is where we try to hide things from view such as pain, hence the saying, "Pain in the rear". Along the same line, quite a few people believe anxiety is often the cause of low back pain.

Slim Fingers and Big Hands

Incredibly, the size and shape of the human finger have played a significant role in folklore since ancient times as well as a functional role in a variety of pointing gestures. In mythology, the index finger is symbolic of good whereas the middle finger is symbolic of bad. Thus, crossing these fingers makes them superstitious accomplices when protecting against evil, telling little white lies, and hoping for good luck.

In Christian tradition, the hand is symbolic of supreme power. The touch of God's hand gives a person divine strength. The hand of God creates and protects, but also destroys. Contrarily, to be "empty-handed" is to have no power or rights, and to fall into someone's hands means you are at their mercy. The laying on of hands causes a transfer of energy or power to heal, and giving your hand in marriage implies possession.

Interestingly, some link the hand with the eye and knowledge. It sees all. The palm of the hand also supposedly tells fortunes, but that is beyond the scope of this book. A person's hands, however, are of especial use in communication. They help sounds and expressions become more memorable. The hands are the subject of another chapter, but let us look at how fingers are used in the new art of body language.

One finger held up for all to see is the symbol for self-hood or "I" in body language and sign language, and twirling it means everybody else. Rubbing two fingers together such as the thumb against the fingertips or the index finger is a common money expectancy gesture or implication that someone is taking payola, while squeezing two fingers together means two people are as close "as that" to each other. Pinching two fingers together in a circle means "A-Ok", while tapping them together means someone is talking too much. Pointing a finger at the head and rotating it means a person is crazier than a sack full of nuts.

Fingers are useful for self-congratulation by blowing on the fingertips and then polishing them on the lapels. Curling the finger with the palm up and motioning means "come here", whereas curling them downward with the palm down like a claw and making a growling noise is a mocking gesture meaning contempt.

A finger snap has different meanings in different cultures, but is most associated with getting the attention of someone such as a waiter if repeated several times. A finger that is emphatically snapped just once with lowered eyes, means, " that's it," or "o-k", whereas a quiet snap means "shut-up."

The finger steeple universally implies, "I am thinking". If the fingers are bunched at the mouth and then flattened out with a hand toss and blown kiss, it means, "Here is my praise". People will do this as appreciation for something or as an indirect way to kiss someone. A much slower female version usually means, "I love you." Another worldwide finger gesture is the finger strum on a hard surface that symbolizes running. Most finger strumming is unconscious, but even conscious strumming means the same thing, "I am getting impatient".

Hips

The size and shape of female hips have a place in mythology. According to some traditions, a woman's hips reveal something about her character. Some people believe that women who have large hips will be more stable and nurturing because their center of gravity is located closer to the ground. Folklore holds that small hips mean less grounding and nurturing ability as well as a flighty attitude.

Mythology about the human physique has insinuated itself into almost every facet of life, so don't automatically disregard body typing ideas as unscientific, because humans are extremely clever and innovative, and mythology has served us well over time.

Practical Pointers

Don't automatically dismiss anything. Humanity has been around a long time and the knowledge gained from nonelective body shapes and types has many links to the distant past with some of it working into the collective unconscious.

The positioning of hips indicates degrees of friendliness. Notice how friends keep their hips parallel to each other when they meet.

Chapter 18

Beauty Beats the Beast

"Beauty opens doors."

Beauty can open doors or start wars. Consider the ancient legend of Helen of Troy, the wife of King Menelaus of Sparta. She was reputedly the most beautiful woman of her time. After, Paris kidnapped her and took her to Troy, her face launched a thousand ships starting the Trojan War, which lasted ten years. If true, this ancient yarn illustrates that beauty has great power.

Looks can kill

Beautiful people and things that are well-shaped, pleasing, and aesthetically appealing have long charmed humankind, which says a lot about the expectations of diverse societies, but does not adequately explain why appearances are so important, if not essential. Could it be that a comely appearance is consequential because it means physical survival?

The advantage of having good features develops early in life due to the critical need for recognition and protection by the primary care givers. A parent's adoring gaze is vital to infants because it signals love and care, and it is easier to love babies that are agreeable to the eye. That is not the only reason.

Genes are not democratic.

Attractiveness is about more than adaptive biology; it is about personal taste and cultural attitudes as well, whether fair or not. For example, good-looking people have better jobs and make more money than their less attractive counterparts make. A recent pop up note under AOL's "Find A Job" section said that people deemed good-looking are paid 3 to 8% more than average while plainer people earn 5 to 10% less. That is a potential 18% swing in salary.

Like it or not, lovely people generally have a higher socio-economic status. Typically, they have better access to health care, and as a result, they try to keep more fit than others do on average. Moreover, researchers have found that people with the most becoming faces live longer than those who are less sightly.

Sexual selection theory asserts that when people have a choice, they naturally pick mates with biological signs of good genes. This is demonstrably true in the animal world. Of course, as a practical matter, humankind has been practicing sexual selection for a long time. For example, facial attractiveness in adolescence is predictive of future longevity, so people value it.

Beauty-Is-Good

The notion that beauty-is-good is a stereotype and socially constructed attitude that flourishes in American society today. Even when Americans know better, social accuracy collapses under the weight of long held beliefs that a good appearance also means the presence of other good qualities. To some extent, a problem exists because many people form a bias against unattractive people based on shop-worn ideas about beauty being good and ugliness being bad.

> Beauty is truth,
> truth is beauty.
> John Keats

Nevertheless, a majority of people spend a great deal of their time and money on their appearance. That being the case, exactly what do Americans consider pretty as a picture? Beauty unadorned is the soft facial features associated with infants. Aesthetically, the more childlike a face appears the better, but there are other captivating qualities as well.

In many older paintings and other depictions of females, the female form appears exaggerated. Today, females for the media appear to be overly thin. In many parts of the world today, medical doctors worry about the rise in obesity as the next trend. Nevertheless, different people and cultures will continue to have different tastes. Some will prefer the ample look of so-called reproductive beauties epitomized by Marilyn Monroe, and others like the asexual beauty of the "anorexic" look.

Presumably, both men and women will cultivate the body language that they believe will be attractive to the opposite sex. In the new millennium, men and women will be less dependent on beauty for their self-identity, social identity, and livelihood. Judging people solely on their looks will evaporate into a cultural anachronism. The allure of being a Cinderella or Prince Charming is still desirable, but discerning people know that beauty fades over time while jealousies and resentments increase.

Practical Pointers

The beautiful-is-good-stereotype is still with us, and to a degree, people still interact with each other based on how they look, but both of these things will disappear over time. Today, young men and women are learning that productivity in the business world is as beneficial as the superficial cultivation of a personality type based on physical appearances.

Chapter 19

Good Posture

"Good Posture signals spirit, health, and pride."

Good posture is unquestionably linked to good health. Astute business leaders, politicians, and successful professionals all work on maintaining a good posture, because it not only strengthens a dominant image, but also contributes to overall health by reducing pressure on the spine and core muscle tension.

Our physical posture is an integral part of moving, standing, sitting, and lying down. In these daily activities alone, there are hundreds of different arm and leg positions, body angles, and configurations; however, the normal stance we adopt is usually quite straightforward.

Good posture when standing equates to a firm posture base with equal weight on each hip, feet pointing forward level with the arm pits, shoulders back, and erect stance. Do not pace back and forth. Good posture when seated means sitting straight in your chair with both feet flat on the floor. Keep your elbows off the table. Place your hands on the table to keep your arms down so that people can see your good posture. Do not stretch or put your arms behind your back to crack your knuckles or close your fists.

> A firm posture base starts with the feet.

This is important because our posture at any given time offers an insight into our attitude and emotions. Posture plays a major role in amplifying or weakening the strength and intensity of emotions. For example, submissive posturing automatically appeases. Bending forward and holding one arm outstretched with the palm of the hand facing outward while lowering the head and looking away is a submissive posture that symbolizes an attempt to connect with and ask forgiveness of a higher authority. The more powerful a figure is the less we can look at it.

Correct, upright posturing contradicts negativity and automatically causes us to feel more self-assured. Negative descriptors associated with slouching, downcast eyes, and sagging body postures are such things as lethargy, indolence, unresponsiveness, unawareness, and tunnel vision. A great advantage to being able to read body language is the forewarning postural clues provide from a distance that enable us to choose the right approach to certain people beforehand.

Oft times, posture single handedly informs us of people's lack of interest in us, their level of sensitivity, and feelings of superiority toward us. At other times, we intentionally erect defensive postures of our own as a barrier to full interaction with others despite being vocally friendly.

Every now and then, our posture conflicts with our most soulful oral assurances. Like the fox's promise, we make oral promises to pay attention, but at the same time, we are trying to escape by leaning backwards or turning away. Good physical posturing is authoritative and authenticating in the business and social worlds. People have some latitude in this area, but as in all things, it is important to be consistent.

Good Posture Tips

According to recent medical studies, mom was not entirely right about sitting up straight. It turns out that sitting up straight is not as good for you as slouching in your chair, which causes less strain on the spinal column. Nevertheless, in my opinion, a solid posture base requires equal weight on each hip, both feet facing forward on an even plane with the armpits. Raise the sternum, slide the shoulders back, and keep the chin level with a steady gaze about twenty feet ahead.

Graceful standing, sitting, and walking includes a head held high, shoulders back, chin in and slightly tilted up, chest out, abdomen and stomach in, back straight, and knees relaxed. When walking, the arms need to be relaxed and swing naturally.

Ideally, good posture viewed from the side will show a slight inward curvature of the neck and lower back, which is entirely normal, but when observed from the front, the hips, knees, and shoulders are supposed to be level with no noticeable forward curvature.

People who rock backwards in a so-called "on their heels" position feel defeated, while people who stand on their heels are apt to slump. As said before, but it bears repeating here, a slouching or slumped over posture is vertically subservient. On the other hand, putting weight forward on the toes promotes upright posture, and equates with higher status and vertical domination.

POSTURAL ECHOING:
WITH YOU
.Leaning forward
.Mirroring you
.Head Nodding
.Open stance
. Moving closer
. Mimicking
NOT WITH YOU
.Arms or legs crossed
. Turned off expression
. Slouching
. Unresponsive
. Body angling away

Authoritative persons such as judges, the police, and politicians try to have a firm, vertical stance with low peripheral motion because it enhances their personal power. For example, most members of the clergy deliver their sermons from pulpits high above the congregation to get the proper effect. Speakers dominate over audiences from elevated podiums, and many athletes must have both height and weight. Nevertheless, it takes more than vertical height to gain effective status and power. Some tall people are still slouches.

In many cases, matching vertical postures facilitates status equality. Short actors such as Alan Ladd and numerous others often stood on boxes in scenes with taller leading people to not only give themselves a better camera angle, but also equal cinematic status. Horizontal posturing is largely a matter of personal choice. People who appear rested and fit after a night's sleep are doing a better job of maintaining the correct kind of horizontal posture, while a person who has poor sleeping habits, backaches, and chronic pain probably has poor horizontal posture. Other reasons for poor posture include prior injuries and physical disabilities.

Shoulder positioning is an important aspect of good posture. Our shoulders are visible and are powerful indicators of our resolve to deal with tricky problems. For example, retracted shoulders represent suppressed anger, while raised shoulders relate to fear. Square shoulders indicate responsibility and bowed shoulders represent carrying a heavy burden.

Researchers have linked posture and mutual attraction. People who are attracted to each other tend to adopt the same posture, thus in situations of high rapport all it takes for everyone to become more casual is one person assuming a casual stance. For example, if one person stands up at a concert, the rest of the audience tends to follow suit.

On the other hand, deliberately adopting a posture different from the people around you, coupled with a look of gravity, and a defiant attitude that says, "I'm not going to be like everyone else" sends a different message that you are independent, secure, and nonconformist.

A round-shouldered slouch, with head thrust forward and stomach sticking out, does little to make a person appealing. Not only is it unappealing, poor posture signals that a person suffers from some kind of disorder, since one of the first steps toward social incapacitation is the disregard of bad habits, posture, and appearance codes.

Poor posture often is no more than the result of bad habits or an anatomical abnormality such as an overly curved spine. Other things such as inebriation lead to stiff, wooden, and exaggerated postures as well as the effects of certain occupations and old age.

Sexual posturing is part of our inventory of romantic gesturing. Depending upon the circumstances, sexual overtures become a part of posture by assuming alluring and seductive poses. Men seek ways to drape themselves around women, and women often seek the sexiest possible way to walk, sit, and lie down in the presence of men.

Attitudinal posturing in the lexicon of the commercial, business, and political worlds is the reflexive or intentional position people take on important issues. This form of posturing is often a thoughtful contrivance in anticipation of forthcoming events and ranges from the friendly, flexible approach to the stern and stubborn "take no prisoners" approach.

Practical Pointers

Although posture lends itself to different perspectives, good posture is a visible inspiration to others, and evokes an air of wellness and confidence. The secret to good posture is drawing up to our full height to make ourselves stand tall. For example, placing the hands behind the back and drawing up the chest conquers careless posture.

Posture also plays an important role in demonstrating attitudes and emotions. People learn how to read each other's posture without saying a word, which avoids saying the wrong thing at the wrong time and hurting another's feelings.

Chapter 20

Walk The Line

"Walk it like you talk it"

Walking is a display of emotion as well as physical motion. We change the way we walk as our emotions change. It is an indisputable fact that most of us commonly adjust our posture, pace, and stride to our attitude, emotions, and thoughts. Ordinary examples of this correlation are being able to recognize happy people from the light footed, quick, brisk, and bouncy way they walk, and enterprising people by the way they hurry along with a fast walk and freely swinging arms. On the other hand, it is as plain as plowed ground that dejected people with uncertainty about their life will tend to walk in a slow shuffling gait with hands in the pocket, head hung down, and eyes downcast. Underachievers do not walk upright, look straight ahead, and move as briskly as achievers.

> Lawyers can strut, while sitting down.

Naturally, walking is subject to gender differences. Men will take longer strides, heavier footsteps, and extend their arms out more, thus taking up more space. Ordinarily, women walk with a stylistic gait that keeps their elbows tucked in while taking smaller, lighter, and quicker steps than men do.

Pacing

A fluid and natural movement, not too fast and not too slow, with the body leaning slightly forward and the eyes focused ahead is the most effective walking pace. Since people do not walk the same way every time, their pace is the most revealing. A measured pace means a person is confident and assertive, whereas a strutting pace indicates a person is an egotistical snob.

The strutting pace is something like the infamous "Benito Mussolini walk", which is a pompous way of walking to impress by emphasizing a goose-stepping, stiff legged strut with the chest and chin thrust out and the eyes peering down the nose in an arrogant and condescending manner. People who walk with hesitation and erratic paces are unsure of the road ahead, while people who carefully search the ground are most likely looking for something real or imaginary.

In a group setting, leaders know where they are going and will walk in front of everybody else thereby setting the pace. Followers will stay behind, but keep in step to demonstrate loyalty and support. By making this simple observation, we know whom the top person is when dealing with a group.

Hand-in-Pockets

The position of the hands is the second most significant aspect of body language signaling while walking. For example, people who place their hands behind their backs with one hand grasping the wrist of the other hand as they walk are meditative and preoccupied with thought. They concentrate better by not looking up and maintaining a slow pace as they ponder some fact or problem in their mind.

People that hide their hands in their pockets while walking combined with furtive glances and offhand remarks are probably hiding something, and if they rattle small change in their pockets, they have the nervous jitters. For the majority of people, however, the unconscious act of placing a hand in the pocket as they walk means they are approaching a serious matter in a casual way such as surveying their environment without being entirely open to it, or they want to maintain a critical edge without commitment. People are highly inventive, clever, and subtle at the same time.

People who walk with their hands on their hips and their elbows extended are probably exhausted from some strenuous activity because walking in this manner reduces fatigue by providing support and rest to the arms and legs. In this scenario, physical relief is the objective instead of getting somewhere.

The sum of the parts is that walking increases personal power and overall health. For example, studies for cognitive ability in six thousand women age sixty-five and older showed that women who walk regularly are less likely to experience memory loss and other declines in mental function that occur with aging. That is one reason why exercise walking was the top sport activity for Americans in 2002.

Practical Pointers

The most powerful way to demonstrate character, show resolve, and signal undesirable types, "Don't mess with me", is to walk in a brisk, steadfast, and purposeful way. Walking is an art that adds to our dignity as well as the power gained from motion.

Chapter 21

Be On Time

"Success depends on good timing."

Timing and rhythm are key elements in the success or failure of interpersonal relations. When we want something, it is smart to schedule our requests around morning breaks, noontime meals, afternoon recesses, and particular times of the day as part of our overall strategy. Trial attorneys have learned it is never a good idea to unload dump trucks of information on people at "off" times. The best practice is to set up a smooth and orderly flow of information, and when the timing is right release it, taking advantage of other energies that enrich the whole.

> "Synchronicity" is connecting your inner rhythm to the universe.
>
> Carl Jung

Timing body movements to pace the even flow of communications improve interpersonal rapport because people become more comfortable and have a higher concentration level. Proper timing heightens the impact of information. Obviously saying the right thing at the right time is more powerful than everyone talking simultaneously at the wrong time.

A good example of proper timing is its use in the art of negotiations. Negotiating is a common practice in everyday life, business, and the practice of law. Bad negotiators are old people and young kids. Good negotiators know to ask for what they want when the other side is as "open" as possible, and they wait until they see this. If they believe the other side is closing up, they let them talk and do not ask for anything. At this time, they become as open or "green light" as possible. In the event their adversaries become really closed up and there is little hope of agreement, they proceed to lay out three things they want, and change the subject until a better time. Extra time allows each side a chance to reflect on the issues.

Time is money

Time is money, and since they both are limited, they are valuable possessions at the center of people's busy lifestyles. Moreover, people with good timing are the most productive. How much time someone takes to make a point and how long they permit others to talk

> Time is the greatest of all innovators.
> Francis Bacon

without interruption provides us with a cognitive insight into who is an extrovert and who is an introvert. At the very minimum, people with good timing appear to get things done, which is something that other people admire. As the saying goes, everything in the world has a time and season, thus the effective implementation of timing is high on the list of desirable body language skills.

Attention Spans

Modern attention spans are shorter than ever. If people pay any attention at all, which is only about fifty per cent of the time, they lose their ability to retain and absorb new information after about twenty minutes. For this reason, the best practice is to break up long monologues into a series of rising and falling crescendos

> Attention spans are best early in the day and early in a trial.

approximately every twenty minutes to keep and maintain people's maximum attention. Active body language movements and expressions also help to maintain someone's attention, since they appeal to every-one's natural *effort justification* bias.

Consequential matters need bringing up at the right time, but for inconsequential and marginal matters, it makes little difference what the timing is. For example, if I am asking my boss for a raise, precise timing is extremely important. I know that, in general, the best time for initially contacting people is in the morning when people are more alert, are in a better mood, and have greater attention spans.

Even little things such as whether the sun is shining or not affects timing because sunshine helps put people in a good mood; and, when they are in a good mood they pay more attention and make more optimistic choices and judgments. Approaching people in a particular mood has a powerful effect on their behavior.

Rhythm

Keeping people waiting is insensitive; therefore, one technique to improve interpersonal skills is to speed up the rate of information flow. For emphasis, establish a communication rhythm that dramatizes a conversation by quickly getting to the point with less periphrasis and more economy. The key to rhythmic speech is being prepared with what you want to say, and in some cases not saying anything at all. For example, why waste time talking to your wife at romantic moments?

The best speech is like the dance of an elderly person-short and sweet. For example, speech economy is the artful use of one word such as "done" with a complimentary body expression that signals finality such as getting up to leave. However, do not talk too fast or be too abrupt, which is arrhythmic with negative connotations. Sometimes, people are better off just slowing things down. The preconceived idea that people have about the wheels of justice moving slowly is accurate, but for good reason. Passion destroys reason; ergo courts and lawyers are intentionally slow in order

> Being too fast or too slow are negatives.

to let the heat of a passion die down before acting precipitously upon a matter.

Everyone knows that delay has a communicative and rhythmic value when the time is not right to take action. At face value, hesitating and pausing are bad because they upset people's timing and rhythm, but if timed right, both are useful linguistic devices that help draw others out.

Practical Pointers

The use of timing and rhythm are advanced body language skills that are very effective in interpersonal relations. You can "dramatize" your actions through the smart use of timing and rhythm; however, use these skills with caution and intelligence so that others don't confuse such skills with laziness and mockery. Always, take into consideration the situation before applying these skills because the rhythms of country life, for instance, are slower than city life.

Chapter 22

Intuitive Behavior

"Get inside the defense"

Intuition is the inner sense, insight, or extrasensory perception that we have about people and things without the benefit of scientific analysis, or in some cases, without conscious deliberation. It is behavior that results from an inner feeling without prolonged thinking about it. We just know or understand some things without proof, which is a deep-rooted part of our cognitive processes; therefore, an intuitive understanding of human relationships is a large force in basic survival.

> "I go by my gut".
> Calvin Klein

Around 1225, Aristotelian logic that characterized the orientation and content of all western civilization in terms of the five senses and rational science dominated most of the world. At this time, the Church hit a home run when intellectual and philosopher, St. Thomas Aquinas, the patron saint of students, established a two-part epistemology that postulated that people know some things through sensory experience and reason, and other things through faith and revelation, or intuition. Interesting history, but what has that has to do with body language?

First of all, St. Aquinas was able to support Aristotle's predominate idea that humans are reasoning beings, and the mind of the infant is a blank slate with the power to extract ideas from experience. Secondly, the contribution of St. Aquinas is consequential because people do not have time to apply inductive reasoning to everything that confronts them, especially body language, and the five senses are not one hundred percent reliable. The influential work of Aquinas helped establish Christianity and gives comfort to many believers.

Often, there is no time for learning through trial and error, yet people have to make decisions and move on. Consequently, they use their intuition to evaluate and make judgments in the absence of hard evidence.

In most cases, intuition lies beneath the conscious level, and in this regard, is more like an instinct (i.e. a drive to satisfy primitive needs) than conscious reasoning. All of us make split-second assessments that happen so fast we are not even aware of the process; therefore, we need our gut responses to keep us from an endless effort to analyze everything.

Since most of us don't like to be bogged down in limitless detail, many people are placing renewed emphasis on gut checks as a legitimate tool in making sense out of the vast array of signals and signs that exist in everyday life. It is my belief that people need to develop and cultivate more right brain activity by paying more attention to their inner feelings about people and situations.

What is intuition? Is it just common sense? No, since common sense is the knowledge that most adults have about the normative expectations of

> We feel that we are more than we know.

their daily life. For instance, when we approach a blind corner, it is common sense to proceed carefully until we see if anything is coming, and if so, how fast.

Common sense tells people not to touch something red hot or to drink cloudy water while intuition, on the other hand, is more like an abstract "knowing" that comes without thinking about it. For example, foresight is the ability to sense something coming before we actually see or hear it. People need self-protecting devices to warn them of impending danger.

Some experts believe that intuition is the complex surfacing of an encoded positive or negative memory that is largely subliminal, while other researchers maintain that it is only simple instinct. The fact that intuition requires more scientific inquiry does not argue against its continued use as a handy tool in reading people's body language behavior.

Jo Ellen Demetrious, the leading jury consultant in the first O. J. Simpson criminal trial, afterwards said fifty percent of her jury consulting work was intuition. It is my view that it is foolish to look only for logic and reason in the vast recesses of the human mind. Gut feelings and emotions tend to affect people's decisions more than conscious reasoning.

"Women's intuition," was worth more than laboratories and should be taught in police schools, announced Vivian Merchant in the 1972 movie *Frenzy* directed by Alfred Hitchcock So, how do we teach ourselves to have better intuition? The answer is we must improve our database of information that is "out there".

Try to connect with everyone you meet, engage people in conversation, look for obvious and not so obvious characteristics, and note any patterns that emerge. Focus on activities that induce intuitive thoughts like running, driving, and people watching. For instance, a classic focus activity is meditation where a person is able to concentrate on specific things without interruption. If possible, create a silent and quiet, stress-free environment, then make sure everybody knows about it and leaves you alone.

Intuition is possessed by everyone, but its skill level is not the same for everybody, because it is more than a simple idiographic visualization that is inherently good or bad. Much like a value judgment, factors such as experience and background count. Also, just having a hunch about someone's body language behavior is not enough, since intuition is subject to faulty memories, incorrect data bases, and other cognitive factors. People are asking for trouble if they try to follow all of their hunches blindly without considering the underlying factual evidence that might contradict the easy, stereotypical value judgments that cognitive misers love to use to get through their day.

Suppose you have a sales call and you intuitively sense your customer is reacting negatively to you. Following your gut instinct, you look for obvious signs of negative body language knowing that business people with negative gestures are the most competitive and require the most attention. For example, does your customer lean away from you and avoid eye contact while crossing his arms in the self-love position? All of these are negative signals.

What is up with people who frown while looking sideways? Do they turn their heads to the left or right when answering tough questions? For example, I noticed that during the nomination hearing of Associate Justice Alito for the U. S. Supreme Court, he turned his head up and to the right when listening to conservative senators, and to the left when the more liberal senators talked.

I know that when tough issues come up in an argument or negotiation people will raise red flags such as one or more of the participants beginning to frown, turn away, lock their legs, or forms a partial arm barrier with one hand in front of them. When a compromise is struck, the participants start to uncross their legs and arms, move toward each other in forward body language, place both feet firmly on the floor, and smile.

Although having a hunch about people based solely on their body language behavior is occasionally all we need, we need to remember that there are "different strokes for different folks", and intuition works for them in different ways. Sometimes, we have an immediate thought about something, and we go "aha". At other times, a calmer inner voice weighs our options.

Sometimes, we get premonitions that manifest themselves as physical feelings such as goose bumps and chills or as queasy feelings of dread. Inasmuch as intuition typically speaks to us through our emotions, we all need to practice distinguishing intuitive emotions such as that "funny feeling" we get about things from non-intuitive ones by evaluating the context in which they occur and comparing first impressions against subsequent well documented consensus information.

Powerful intuition is a positive skill we all wish we had at our disposal upon demand. However, in the ordinary course of daily life, a lot of things just are not clear enough, and we have intense moments of personal uncertainty about them. Help comes in the form of two kinds of clarity. The first kind occurs instantly from deduction, while the second kind is a process of becoming clear, and although the second kind is slower to emerge, it is more durable.

Practical Pointers

What history and experience teach is this-nothing dies as hard or comes back as quick as intuition. It is a valuable interpretive resource that helps people interpret body language behavior quickly instead of having to resort to time-consuming studies of infinite possible causes.

In addition, by using their intuition, people are able to supplement the processes of clarity and thus organize decisions faster. Remember, however, that intuition is one of those skills that require practice and use or it will be lost.

Chapter 23

The Language of Legs

"Legs are an open and shut case."

Having "a leg up" is leg language for having an advantage. On the other hand, if our legs fail us our heads have to take over, which is why a majority of people consider themselves lucky if they are able to maintain a strong pair of legs throughout their lifetime. Not only are legs essential to good posture and the distinctive way we walk, run, and express ourselves in everyday living, but they are also one of our best body language tools.

Since the movement and positioning of our legs are highly visible and convenient, there role in nonverbal communicating is very broad. People's legs are not involved so much with communicating their inner-most natures, but actively display openness and defensiveness, which are two of the most fundamental human attitudes familiar to everyone.

Leg Positioning

Suppose you are trying to sell a product and the buyer props one leg over the arm of his chair. What is he signaling? It probably means he is neither open nor willing to listen to your sales pitch. The buyer is pretending to be more comfortable, but the real meaning of this maneuver is "I'm unconnected to your presentation" or "I am hostile to the idea of buying your product".

People who assume extreme positions of comfort such as placing both hands behind their head and propping their feet up are openly communicating supreme confidence and the power to do anything they want. The message is that they are in control, know everything, and are superior. If you go to your lawyer or banker's office and he crosses his legs and props his feet up on his desk, he is insensitive to your feelings and your problems.

If the way you sit or walk appears to be insensitive to another person, it is possible to approach them a different way by leaning toward them with open palms extended and saying, "Look here, I can tell you have thoughts on…, so let's get down to business"? Another tactic is to place some paperwork just out of reach, which forces the other person to change positions. Of course, mimicking the same open gesture means you both agree.

> Context is everything.

On the other hand, if someone comes to see you and over relaxes in your office, he is telling you he is superior to you, even in your territory. By symbolically trampling on your territory and feelings, the real meaning behind this open but informal and casual pretense is domination, control, and territorial aggression.

Leg crossing is a subtle way of including or excluding members of a group around you. Some people sitting at the aisle end of a long bench in church or a row of seats at the movies, or the local performing arts center will cross their legs and slump down a little bit to make it difficult for anyone to get by, thus deterring newcomers from sitting next to them.

If you want somebody to sit on your bench, signal your openness by getting up and letting them enter without having to crawl over you. Crossing the legs is so common that even one person in a room crossing their legs triggers others in the room to follow suit in a "postural echo".

The special way people cross and uncross their legs is significant. In America, men learn that the macho way to cross their legs is the "figure four" position where one leg rests horizontally on the opposite knee. This signals that a man is guileless, unafraid, and poised for a challenge.

A man who uncrosses his legs and extends them forward while leaning backwards has probably lost interest in the social interaction around him, and is symbolically relaxing in an imaginary lounge chair. A person shifting weight from one leg to another is nervously anticipating something, or suffering from a medical condition such as static ataxia. Additionally, people who shift their weight from side to side are most likely bored with the conversation and activities around them.

Bare legs are a display of female sexuality in some cultures. For example, Betty Grable was a highly regarded pinup girl during WWII because of her shapely legs. People we find attractive have a *referent power* based on their ability to be a model for others.

Practical Pointers

"Instant conclusions like gunpowder are easy to explode", goes the ancient proverb. Leg positioning is also very subtle, and we need to be careful before forming any instant conclusions. For example, some people cross their legs simply because they are tired, or uncomfortable.

At times, crossed legs mean nothing at all at a particular moment. A woman wearing a short skirt typically sits with her legs slanted and crossed merely as a graceful way to be comfortable. The bottom line is allow time for other probative clues to develop before jumping to any conclusions.

Chapter 24

Hands Down

"Let your hands do the talking."

Our hands are kept busy with touching, grasping and holding objects. However, we also experience the sensation of temperature through touching, and we experience texture, weight, and inertial strength through grasping and holding an object. The degree of dexterity we have often determines our choice of vocations.

Since hands are symbolically associated with work, they often reveal the nature of a person's work. For instance, we might have the delicate hands of a piano player, or surgeon, or we might have the less delicate hands of a lumberjack, farmer, or construction worker. Hands are also symbolism for the idea that if you cannot put your hands on something- it really is not yours.

Hands in conjunction with the arms are very visible and as such are the second most expressive part of the body after the face, which gives them a high position in the hierarchy of body language. With a flick of the wrist, we summon a person, wave them off, or deeply offend them. Hands are particularly helpful in addressing a large audience from a distance where some words are inaudible.

Talking Hands

Skilled conversationalists use their hands to reinforce what they are saying. Placing their hands in an outstretched position to each side with palms up means let us be reasonable, or what more can I do. Putting your hands palm out in front of you, means wait a minute, stop, or hold on. Placing the hands palms down and pushing them up and down means slow down or calm down, whereas pushing them upwards above the head indicates praise in some sub-cultures. Therefore, a skilled person is able to use his hands to appear reasonable, deflect criticism, or indicate praise.

The hands help emphasize that you are getting your point across. An extended finger on each hand in an identical position lets the speaker compare points, whereas forming a kind of spade or hoe acts as an exclamation mark to what he is saying. In general, always point single digits with care, so as not to appear threatening; however when done properly, extending a single finger is like an exclamation mark.

Professional speakers like ex-President Clinton know they are able to get their point across better by breaking down complicated issues. They use their hands to cut the air into slices or boxes. These hand-bracketing measures make hard issues easier to understand.

Positive hand language consists of such things as waving the hands in greeting, giving the thumbs up gesture, pinching the fingers in the "A-okay" sign conveying that everything is all right, and by clapping at a public function to show approval. Similarly, we express sympathy and affection by gentle touching with our hands and loyalty by saluting. Two thumbs up mean positive approval and says, "Way to go".

> We must kiss the hand that we cannot bite.

Negative hand gesturing connotes underlying psychological concerns. For example, hand wringing, clenched fists, nail biting, and perspiring hands are signs of nervousness and anxiety. Pointing two thumbs down means disapproval, and pointing with the thumb is a sign of thinly veiled ridicule, which is not good unless you are hitchhiking.

By being on the lookout for unconscious hand movements such as face and neck scratching, ear tugging, and mouth covering, we are able to tell if people are anxious about the words they are speaking. . Putting a hand with the fingers bunched to the mouth means, "Oh, no, I've made a mistake" or "Have I done wrong?"

Some hand gestures have serious ramifications. For example, giving someone the bird is highly offensive and is bound to provoke trouble. Placing fingers in the mouth is a sign of being under pressure with roots to thumb sucking as a child.

In the middle of the road category, some elaborate hand gestures are intentionally ambiguous and incomprehensible to outsiders because they are only for members of a certain gang, group, or social organization.

One of the most common hand movements worldwide is opening the hands and spreading them outward, which means let us begin, yes, and I am open to suggestions, so give me more. The further apart we spread the hands, the more open we are. Closing the hands means something is finished, or it is a subtle way of saying "no", or signaling the end of something.

Another common gesture is the unmistakable shoulder shrug with raised eyebrows and flat palms up hands, which means that we do not know or understand what someone else is saying to us. It says, "What do you want from me", which is not intended to be subtle, and is found practically everywhere people get together. In effect, this gesture shifts the burden of explanation from the person making the gesture to others in a self-serving attempt to put everybody else on the defensive. A less exaggerated shrug that lasts only a few seconds with hands pulled in means, "Leave me alone".

> Other parts of the body may assist, but the hands speak for themselves.
>
> Quintilian

The speed and direction of hand gestures increase the emphasis of the message. For instance, fast-paced gestures in the upper plane are aggressive while open, slow-paced gestures in the lower plane are friendlier. Vertical hand gesturing above the ribs creates a sense of dominance and is more forceful than lower plane gesturing, which is less aggressive.

Directing a hand gesture to the side of a person is friendlier than one directed straight toward them like finger pointing. Happy hands are moving hands. Nothing helps to facilitate communications and build rapport more than the liberal use of the hands in all forms of gesturing because this action conveys the feelings associated with oral messages and the relationship of the body to the soul.

Some movements, although valuable, simply do not have the wide range of eloquence and possible nuances of hand gesturing. For instance, we raise our fist to exhibit anger, clap our hands to show approval, and rub our stomachs to suggest hunger.

Hand usage involves three basic positions: palms up, palm down, and palms sideways. On the vertical plane, we try to get people's attention by waving with open palms forward as high as possible. People use the "Tomahawk Chop" in an up and down fashion with the side of one hand to prompt others to finish what they are doing. People tuck their hands under their armpits to signal frustration from waiting on something and behind their head to show confidence.

At a distance, hand placement such as finger pointing, waving, and throwing the hands in the air to surrender is easy to understand. Placing our hands in a vertical "T" means

> Gesticulation-it is half the language.
> Marianne Moore

time out, and the vertical hand fan means, "I'm too hot. Fingers bunched together and then opened and closed rapidly means "yak"", yak", or someone is talking too much, and if placed in front of the mouth it means, "I'm hungry."

A clenched fist with the arm raised and palm forward is a form of salute and symbol of unity. One or both hands outstretched above the head mean, "I worship you, Lord, "or "I accept you, Lord." Open palms symbolize openness and outstretched hands symbolize acceptance.

Raising the hands to touch the chest with palms in is a male gesture of honesty, devotion, and loyalty like in the pledge of allegiance, but with females, it means shock or surprise, whereas closing the hands on the neck, mouth, or chest is a covering up gesture. Covering up gestures are negative body language signals that both sexes use in much the same way.

Moving the hands in a circular motion by the ear means there is a telephone call for you, and a hand flap with the back of the hand means leave. If we put our hands in our pockets, we are being secretive, and placing them behind us means we are thinking, we are meditating, listening intently, or have become preoccupied elsewhere. It is a way to express less than full cooperation and commitment

Showing the back of our hand is an unfriendly and menacing gesture, especially when the hand is in a clenched fist, which strongly denotes hostility, tension, and anger. Because obscene gesturing uses the back of the hand when we do not care for someone, we will use the back of our hands with more frequency. A man placing the back of his hand over his crotch area is a common masculine gesture of superiority, reassurance, sexuality, and at times nervousness.

A side of the hand gesture is for emphasis and drama. A person trying to dominate us will use the side of his hands more frequently. Placing a hand in a pocket with the thumb out is a sign of superiority. The hands signal a myriad of other gestures as well. We tuck our hands under our armpits to show frustration.

We scratch our heads to show confusion and slowly rub our hands together in simulated satisfaction when considering something devious or manipulative. The palm in palm gesture is a display of authority, whereas clenched hands signal a negative attitude.

Rubbing the palms together right before using them is an indication of internal tension, or at other times, it means, "Oh good". Consider the overall context to determine the right meaning. For example, rubbing the palms together is a positive expectation gesture, but how fast the palms are rubbed together changes the meaning by degrees.

Handshakes

The handshake plays a significant role in the social matrix. In American culture, we shake hands to greet each other, congratulate each other, say goodbye, seal an agreement, and to make peace. Handshaking began as a good faith way to show others that you did not have a weapon in your hand, and over time it evolved into a powerful nonverbal communication tool.

Handshakes are important because they make or break the first impression people form of each other. A firm handshake expresses trust and commitment, whereas a flaccid handshake is wimpy and lacks character and reassurance. Additionally, the loss of perceived sincerity and competence by a weak handshake the first time around is hard to recapture later.

What are today's rules of handshaking and do they apply equally to men and women? The same rules apply to both men and women equally, but women do not have the same background in handshaking as men do, and do not see their weaker and softer handshake as wimpy-just feminine.

> Handshaking basics:
> 1. Stand up.
> 2. Look at them.
> 3. One big shake.

Traditionally, women extended their hand with the palm down so that men were able to kiss the back. If they shook hands at all, it was a limp or partial finger handshake with their arms straight out to protect their personal space by keeping a little distance. Today, discerning women will close the gap a little yet continue to maintain distance by bending their elbows slightly.

Knuckle touching is currently in vogue with certain groups, and has its benefits, such as not spreading germs for one thing. The normal standard for a good handshake, however, is being the first to stick a hand straight out; keeping the arms down, and firmly grab the webbing of the other person's hand. Make sure all your fingers are around the palm of the other person's hand, especially the little finger; shake one-time with a good squeeze; smile and make eye contact as long as the handshake continues.

> Handshaking Don'ts
> 1. Pastor pat.
> 2. Hand over.
> 3. Limp wrist.

People will return a smile if greeted with a smile, so if you smile and they do not, it may signal that something is wrong.

Avoid the two-handed handshake at the first meeting, and save it for close personal relationships. Grasping someone's hand with both of your hands is ultra friendly and is much too familiar for the average business setting. The same goes for grasping the other person's arm as many politicians do, because it is too intimate for ordinary business settings where that degree of closeness still requires earning.

The firm, sincere handshake is the best way to solidify a personal or business relationship. Most of the time touching someone else quickens and increases the chances of agreement. A good grasp causes some sensation and says, "Here, I am for you, and my handshake proves it". In times past, a person's handshake was as good as his word. It was his bond. Nothing else was necessary to seal an agreement. In the new millennium, however, the best practice is to get agreements and confirmations in writing. As social cognition increases, interdependence become more complex, but the time-tested handshake is still a quick and effective way to begin a relationship. It is a simple act that everyone understands.

Practical Pointers

Hand gesturing expresses the degree of psychological involvement we have with what we are saying. For example, the impression of eagerness and effervescence accompanies the different ways to shake hands. We use our hands to get others involved and persuaded to our position.

Chapter 25

Talking Heads

"Hold your head up when you are down"

Head talking is an important aspect of effective body language. By constantly moving our head this way and that, we attract attention in both talking and listening. Without head moves, consultations and agreements are boring, and of course, robust disagreements are not the same without head butts.

Appropriate head moves help get our point across, whereas the wrong head moves have an adverse effect. For example, lifting the head when we need to be bowing it, shaking the head sideways to signal "no" when we really mean, "yes", and head beckoning to people in an arrogant and disrespectful way are costly social gaffes.

The head's position reveals attitudes, acts as a substitute for speech, and bolsters oral speech. An arrogant snob will hold his head up with a slight tilt backwards, curl or push his lower lip upwards, and thrust his chin out thereby tightening his facial muscles.

A head pointed down signals a negative and judgmental attitude. Additionally, submissive people also lower their head to show humility. The bottom line is this: unless you get a person's head up, you will have difficulty communicating with him.

Head moves are good speech markers in oral communication. For example, people who want to add emphasis to what they just said can add a quick head nod that says, "So there". A rapid, slight sweep of the head to one side and a whistle means "zoom", something went by fast, or the same move with one hand over the head means an idea went right over the head without stopping.

We give directions by using our head. For example, we point out the direction we want someone to move in, look at, or consider by motioning with our head. If someone gets right in our face, we are able to use our head to defuse the tension by tilting it to one side, which means that what we are saying is not very serious, and functions as a softer way of talking to someone in lieu of a head on confrontation. Similarly, using the head as a means of recognizing someone else's presence or turn to speak is friendlier and more appropriate than pointing our finger.

The head is an important asset in listening as well as talking. For example, a worldwide species-specific gesture is using the head nod to signal our agreement, consent, or affirmation in a conversation. Research has shown this form of miniature bowing shows up more in listening than talking because frequent nodding encourages others to speak longer and say more.

Several head movements are important to listening as well. The slight "head tilt" shows interest, and measurable head tilting is flirtatious. Likewise, the orientation of our head when gazing at people makes a difference in how they will perceive our behavior. If we turn our head to look somewhere else instead looking at the speaker when they talk, speakers will most likely conclude we are not "with them" even though we hear them.

Swaying movements of the head from side to side often express reluctance and doubt while we are mentally weighing the merits of a proposal or request. It says, "I don't know about that," or "I'm not sure", especially if we roll our eyes at the same time, whereas a firm headshake means, emphatically "no". A head scratch means, "I'm puzzled", and is clearly different from a head tap, which means, "I'm fed up." Slapping the back of your head means, "How stupid of me", or when done to another, it means "dumb move."

At times, we move our heads diagonally to summon others along with a shout or a wave. The more we move our head, the more urgent the request. At times, a head beckon is permissible as a surreptitious motioning to a confederate or person we want to meet discreetly. Less subtle head moves signal consent, but we do not want anyone else to know.

The popularity of hats ascended and then dwindled dramatically in the last century for both fashion and comfort. Today, men and women wear baseball style caps with logos that announce a diversity of things such as what company they work for, what sports team they support, and places they have been. In a small way, many people believe that changing caps on their heads also changes who they are and how they want to appear in the world.

Practical Pointers

Head moves evoke a sense of shared understanding. Instead of being an immobile "talking head", use your head to convey your degree of involvement, and add a few head moves to your conversational arsenal for deeper subtlety and versatility of expression.

To nod or not to nod involves different issues. Nods at appropriate intervals keep conversations moving because it says, "Give me more, I want to continue this conversation". On the other side of the coin, refusing to nod or make head movements usually cause speakers to dry up.

Chapter 26

The Right Angle

"Angle out of tight spots."

At first glance body angles seem to be insignificant, but body angels are important signs of our disposition to respond favorably or unfavorably to other people. Additionally, when two people openly face each other, the way they angle their body is a telling clue to what they are feeling. For example, if people lean toward us they like us, but if they lean away, they do not care for us. If people lean sideways, they want attention, but if they back up, they are unsure of us.

In social interplay, we use our bodies as blocking devices by turning at a 45-degree angle to partly close someone else off and decrease any sense of friendliness. If we turn our body at a 90-degree angle perpendicular to others, it translates into an unfriendly, closed off stance.

Maximum rapport always requires full frontal exposure, so using body angles as blocking devices protects us from unwanted communications or physical contact. Sometimes we find ourselves in situations where we have a waning interest in what is going on around us, but do not wish to be impolite. In this situation, we just turn our head when speaking instead of our whole body.

The positioning adjustments we make to specific situations are solid clues to our physical and mental feelings; however, we get in trouble when we make body angle assessments based on a single move without considering the overall picture. Always look for other body language signals that converge with body angles.

Edna O'Brien, the Irish writer, said in a 1984 interview that women are not chattels and have expressed their right not to be the *Second Sex*, especially in the area of earnings; however, mating, physical attraction, and sexual love are spurred on by instinct and passion, not social consciousness. It is biological she says, and men have the greater autonomy and authority.

When it comes to sex appeal, however, women have the upper hand in my opinion. For example, women are much better at using body positioning to attract others. Female models do more advertising than men do because they have more body angles, and their body language says much more than men's does.

Practical Pointers

The angle of people's approach shows the degree of their apprehension. Interpreting other body angles, however, is not a cakewalk, since diverse body angles are heavily context dependent. Consequently, the secret to success in reading body angles is to learn the nuances of body angles in different situations. Once we learn the meaning behind different body angles, we are smarter, more patient, and socially interwoven with others.

Chapter 27

Give Me Space

"We live in a shared world."

We live in a shared world, and since many of us live in tight confines, we must use the space we occupy wisely. In body language, space usage falls into either the vertical or the horizontal category. On the vertical plane, body movements fall into the upper and the lower body with the waist being roughly the middle. On the horizontal plane, there are four invisible social zones of space surrounding our body called the intimate, personal, social, and public zones. Smaller zones are the distances between two noses.

The nose is a key variable in social interaction,
Size Matters and plays a role in how comfortable or uncomfortable we are in the presence of others. For instance, not enough nose distance and we are uncomfortable.

Maintaining defensible space against unwanted intrusion is the main motivation underlying social spacing rules because violating someone's space has serious repercussions. For example, people who lean against other people or who place a hand or a foot on objects are showing a territorial claim to that person or object and aren't likely to give up their claim without an argument even though this is very intimidating to the person who is being intruded upon.

People who get in someone's face without an invitation run the risk of a hostile or aggressive response from that person. When riding in an elevator, it is not a good idea to touch or stare at others present for the reason that territorial defenses are weak in tightly confined spaces and people's self-assurance and security declines. It is best to treat each other as nonpersons.

Different activities such as going to school, working, and socializing all require special kinds of normative space usage that we pick up mostly from the observation of others. Space usage is not a static system of behavior, however, and is constantly changing.

Vertical Space

In most cultures, height is dominating, superior, and authoritative. For instance, people build huge towers, tall buildings, and large vertical monuments to express their greatness and strength. Vertical height even gives humans a sense of heightened will power and triumph. Since height implies authority and power, veteran public speakers know it is best to be elevated above their audience, which is why many teachers prefer standing in front of their students.

Taller people have a physical advantage in large groups such as the movies, in waiting lines, and in sports. Sometimes, however, the unrestricted use of a height advantage causes tension because towering over a person is psychologically intimidating and physically aggressive. The best approach to smaller people is to move slowly closer and tone down any height advantage by using soft language with no threatening gestures.

The particularized way we use vertical space sends a strong message. Hand gesturing is more threatening on the lower body plane than on the upper body plane because hand movements above the waist are easier to see and follow. For example, a person with a knife (or any other object) in his hand is much more threatening if the knife is held below the waist.

Trial evidence is a different matter. A rule of thumb is to deal with favorable evidence higher up on the vertical plane making it more visible, while keeping unfavorable evidence lower down where it can't be seen by the jury. Evidence that is higher up is sharper and more dramatic, while putting something lower down softens it effect.

The power in height ranges on a scale from very little to extreme. A short person is able to ask a taller person to sit down to negate the height advantage, and temporarily at least, taller people are able to bend down or kneel on one knee to the same eye levels as others when conversing.

Horizontal Space

On the horizontal plane, size is dominating and even frightening. The rapid expansion of horizontal space is threatening to strangers because the more space we occupy on the horizontal plane the more power and authority we express. As in the animal world, the ability to spread ourselves out and present a larger image gives us more superiority. For example, public speakers project authority, confidence, and dominance by placing their hands on their hips with elbows out and feet apart. On the other side, shrinking the horizontal size advantage promotes intimacy and rapport between two people.

Horizontal space consists of four social zones:

1. The *intimate zone*, is about one foot or closer to the body, and is reserved for the most intimate friends, family, and lovers.

2. The *personal zone* is one to three feet out from the body, which is close enough to allow people to touch each other, but not hug or kiss. The personal zone is for faithful friends and people we trust.

3. The *social zone* is three to four feet away from the body and is reserved for acquaintances such as co-workers or casual friends sitting at a lunch table.

4. The *public zone* is anything more than four feet out from the body, and is generally reserved for strangers.

Examples of zone usage are people sitting at a large dining room table. The "head of the table" is the person with the highest status, which is usually the master of the house. The zones radiate outward from his position. For example, the closest seat on the right of the master is a few inches away in the intimate zone. The person sitting there has the status of being the important "right arm" of the master. People sitting a few seats away from the head position are his in personal zone, while lower status people sit the farthest away in the social zone.

Sex and gender are factors in managing personal space. Generally, females take up less horizontal space than males. Thus, women are able to approach both males and females more closely without being threatening. As a result, women find it easier to gain rapport on the horizontal level than men do. For instance in a public gathering place, if a woman strikes up a conversation with a man or woman two or three bar stools away, she will invariably move closer, but two men who begin talking will usually keep an empty bar stool between them. Since females take up less space than men occupy, they will stand closer and face each other more directly than men do when talking to each other.

Law enforcement personnel know a loose crowd is much easier to handle than a tightly packed one. As a crowd gets larger, tighter, and more compact, it also becomes more difficult to deal with. Similarly, no one likes cars on their bumper while driving because tailgating is invasive. Our zone of privacy extends to our automobiles; consequently, our reaction to intrusion in this zone is ugly and can potentially erupt into road rage.

The way diverse people try to share the irreducibly messy nature of a fast changing, crowded world will be a continuing problem until the population understands that the egocentric, old school rules of space usage may be inadequate for say, sharing a modern super highway. Sharing the versatile and context dependent multi-space in which we live today may require updating the rules.

The egocentric perspective that the world is the problem, and not the people in it, is no longer viable. The strong presumption that the space around us gives us a real visible and tactile reality of the public world just as it is, or always was, now seems to be naïve realism that ignores the very contextual individual nature of space. For instance, our homes have a very familiar feel for us, but not for people who do not live there.

Space in a social sense is the environmental space in which people live and work. The concept of space, however, is used in many different contexts such as the spatial zones surrounding personal space, the distance between two objects in mathematics, outer space, and so on. How we use space in the future and what conceptual framework we use for the study of the human factors in a hostile world that is too crowded and complicated for individuals, when all they have is their own personalized space around them, will be the challenge.

At present, maintaining awareness of acceptable spatial zones is a key relationship skill. Depending on how we use space, we make things easy or hard for ourselves. One way to use spatial zones more effectively in the future is becoming less egocentric in order to move in people's social or personal zone without alarming them.

The individual context and our mental representation of space improves as we become more familiar with people through the knowledge of body language behavior. The closer we approach people without increasing their stress levels, the better contextual rapport is established. People who are close have higher concentration levels and warmer relationships.

Practical Pointers

Most of people are largely unaware of the unwritten rules of space usage even though violating the rules is consequential. Proper spacing is most important at key first encounters since allowing someone in your space is a form of acceptance, and the closer people allow you to enter their space the more they accept you.

Although increasing technology and changing demographics in the richly layered spaces of American society requires many relative nonperson positions like entry-level clerks and other functionaries to keep low-level things running smoothly, people will still try to maintain some distance from each other and avoid eye contact until some of their psychologically vital shelves can empty.

Avoiding any emotional bonding by contact, people can give each other the status of nonpersons. Normally, it is our call. We can invite interaction by direct but gradual space usage, or we can back off intimacy by not making eye contact, turning our backs, and walking away.

Chapter 28

Power Seating

"One can be in the right church but the wrong pew."

U pon entering a meeting or room full of seated people, is it not true that the first thing we do is try to decide where to sit? Invariably, new arrivals do not know where to sit because it involves the ceremony of being recognized more than it does physical comfort. No matter if we have an

> People do not like to be on either end, but in the middle where they have the most in common.

invitation to take a seat, or we enter a room with assigned seating, we instinctively do not want to invade anyone's territory, so we send out submissive body language signals such as lowering our gaze and moving quietly and slowly through the seats attracting as little attention as possible.

Late arrivals seldom go to the front row. Even when seats are clearly empty, some people will ask if they are taken just for recognition. Finding a good place to sit becomes more difficult when people who are already there build subtle barriers around themselves to anyone from joining them. I have stood while some people keep entire tables to themselves in busy restaurants. Others seat themselves in corners or on the aisles of a long row of seats to send the message, "Sit here if you must, but leave me alone". People maintain their privacy by setting up territory that excludes others.

People avoiding others will sit at the smallest tables facing away from the door in the back of the room, or against a wall, and bury their face in a newspaper, whereas people who are open and less interested in defending their space will choose to sit at roomier tables facing the door. In terms of social power, the most dominating position in a business meeting, or at the dinner table, is at the head of the table. Likewise, the nearest seat facing the door is a choice power seat because it monitors everyone that comes in or out, and it is the quickest exit route.

In a public facility such as the park, the most dominating position is sitting in the middle of the park bench because it controls the entire bench. For instance, if I sit on the far end of a park bench, I am saying, "Others may sit, but not next to me." If I sit in the middle, I am saying, "I want this bench all to myself." If I want to share, I will sit at one end, but not at the very end, and maintain an open posture. At times, I will beckon to others by giving the bench seat next to me a gentle hand pat that means, "You are welcome to sit here."

By slyly arranging their seats in relation to the environment, people say, "stay away", if they sit behind a curtain in back, or "I'm better than you" by sitting higher up than others. Sitting on the back row in church, or in a classroom allows anonymity, whereas sitting on the front row confers the best exposure. In the unique situation of a sporting event, play, or concert, seats nearest the players and actors are the most powerful and privileged because people are able to see and hear better. Most people prefer sitting in the same spot every time, since it's a habitual response based on their self-identity.

> Don't give trouble a seat in your life.

A person who blithely swoops in and sits down next to someone without any hesitation is violating that person's social zone, saying in effect, "I can move in on you." While seated, if a person spreads his arms out and grips the edge of the table he is nonverbally saying, "listen to me". Eighty seven percent of right-handed people will move their hands first before they want to interrupt or start talking.

The person that moves closer to your seat with a lowered voice, secretive look, and gives the impression you are going to be told something in confidence has a couple of motives. The first possibility is that a narrowing of the distance between two people implies an endorsement of each other, and the second possibility, is that it is an attempt by one person to dominate the other. In either case, be wary of a scheming person who affects friendship as a tool to move in on you before you respond to transparent "narrowing the gap" activities.

Chair choices matter, because swivel chairs have more status and power than fixed chairs; and, the higher the back of the chair the greater the power and stature of the person sitting in it. The chair is a universal symbol of authority and to raise it higher shows superiority. Chairs with armrests are better than chairs without armrests since the best chairs embrace people. It never hurts to ask your host which chair to sit in, because sitting in someone else's chair risks their resentment. The bottom line is that powerful people do not fumble around with great hesitation in seating themselves.

Seating location in a room full of people is important. For example, the more confident people are, the closer they will sit to the front in a large room. Along the same lines, if people are in a business meeting, or negotiation with others, and choose their location at an average table, the persons seated beside them are usually the most cooperative with the person on their right being more cooperative than the person on their left is. Usually, the most resistance to ideas comes from the people seated directly opposite of each other.

Practical Pointers

In navigating the social seas, seating is more significant than we think. Amazingly, people are so sensitive to where they sit that a "pecking order" often emerges. All-important relationships hinge on seating arrangements; consequently, it is important to follow the local rules of power seating.

No matter where you sit, always take note of the available exits and the ease or difficulty in getting out if necessary. You never know when negotiations will break down, or when you will have to leave suddenly with little or no warning. Also, be creative and leave a different way than you came in.

Chapter 29

Crowd Survival

"Go along to get along"

Do you feel lost when you enter a crowded room full of people you do not know? What do you do when people seem to be avoiding you, or worse, they just stand there saying nothing when you enter? What if there is no host to greet or acknowledge new arrivals? How do you overcome this type of social dilemma?

One option is not going, but this option is nihilistic and wastes a good networking opportunity. The other option is to go with the hope of finding someone that is approachable. Fortunately, proven techniques exist to help in such situations.

The first step is to know a little about who else is going to be present, and what they do in life. Do they make things, educate, sell, or do something else. Next, you need to know in advance what the dress code will be so you wear what everybody else is wearing. Mirroring the people

> A good icebreaker is to ask someone for advice.

in a crowded room is a relationship skill that allows you to approach those people with similar attire first, or short of that, those people who at least look like they have something in common with you.

We begin telegraphing our attitude the minute we move onto center stage. Do we stroll, swagger, shuffle, slink, limp, waddle, tiptoe, or strut? Ideally, we need to keep our heads up and shoulders back while looking straight ahead and take surefooted steps with arms down swinging freely.

It is not necessary to rush into a conversation with the first person we see upon arrival. Instead, take time to size up the crowd. Single out the loudest person in the room and note how they move around using space. If they tend to go to one side and attach themselves to one person, or a particular group, they are uncomfortable. Who seems friendly and open, and who is sitting alone? Notice who is walking upright with enthusiasm, a smile and friendly demeanor, and who seems to circulate around with little or no enthusiasm.

Avoid people who look like they have nothing in common with you, and seem unenthusiastic about being there. Don't bother approaching them since they probably have a silo mentality that is defensive and closed off to any conversation with newcomers.

Likewise, mock fiddlers who are busily tapping or drumming fingers or feet are too bored to be engaged in conversation. People who move closer together when approached are signaling that their conversation is not open to third persons.

When using a lectern or podium for the first time, do not constantly grab it and lean over it, but stand back so you are able to see the audience above the lectern. Ideally, a lectern is no higher than four or five inches above your navel. Lecterns are too high if they tend to make you look small.

Make face contact by looking slightly over the heads of the audience. Look at notes, but look up when you have a change in voice inflection, and go down in pitch for points you wish to emphasize, but stick with your notes instead of trying to wing it.

Stay away from people who are nervous, finicky, and constantly on the move because they prefer to move about instead of conversing. Do not interrupt people who obviously will not like it. For instance, who is using a cell phone? If it is a person

> Crowds are not company.

standing at attention with coat unbuttoned and a serious look, he is probably calling his office or boss and does not want to be disturbed.

If a cell phone user starts doing something else while talking, rests the phone on his shoulder to free his hands, or looks around most of the time he is most likely talking to a friend or spouse and could be interrupted for something very important. However, if the caller shields his face, tilts his head, hunches his shoulders up, turns his body away, and cups the phone delicately, he does not want anyone to hear his conversation, and it is better not to interrupt him.

Crowd Survival techniques are quick and easy by design in order to meet situational demands and the expectations of others. It is counterintuitive, but one way to reduce your anxiety at a social gathering is to set your sights a little lower and select individuals or small groups to approach that are not movers and shakers, but seem a little lost. They will not be the loudest, most animated, or best dressed, and they may be located in the back of a room instead of the front, yet they probably appreciate company more than some others do.

In making your entrance, use some imagination and pretend the person you are going to talk with is your best friend. Naturally, the larger the group of people you engage, the larger your options, since higher numbers make it more likely someone will be responsive. At first, not saying anything is the best course to chart. Walk in briskly, merely say hello, unbutton your coat, and find a chair while keeping a cheerful, lively, and curious look. You want to communicate you are at ease, happy, confident, and secure as you scan the room. Try to be relaxed and unhurried.

Do not automatically extend your hand for a handshake until someone else indicates a readiness to shake hands, and maintain a pleasant smile. Instead of trying to promote yourself, be honest and openly admit you do not know anyone there. Try using flattery on others such as, "I like your haircut", or "Nice dress, you have on." If you do not overdo it, try acting helpless, and ask about the food. Usually, someone will offer to help.

Always strive to keep the conversation going by maintaining good eye contact and nodding your head. While nodding, you are able to turn your eyes anywhere else in the room and still appear involved in the present conversation. A great opening line for an instant conversation is asking people their name because people like to hear their name.

One notable caveat is that the more ego involvement a person has the narrower their latitude of acceptance, so do not talk about emotional issues that arouse instinctive feelings about such things as religion, politics, and sickness. Furthermore, in my opinion, it is rude to talk about business at a social event.

Humor sometimes backfires if you do not follow special guidelines for being funny in a crowd. Do not try too hard to be funny and do not risk a bomb by telling a stupid or obscene joke. Do not make your funny story too long or laugh too much yourself. In general, do not make fun of other people or try to be a perpetual punster.

Do not touch others unless it is to interrupt, calm someone down, or show them affection. Excluding athletes and contestants on the *Price is Right* television show where people high-five, chest-bump, and use touching as a gesture of assurance or reassurance, people usually do not need to touch another person. Many people resent being touched, and at the very least will recoil from it, because touching implies rights of possession and spreads germs in high flu seasons.

Escape Strategies

Suppose it just is not your night and everything you try is a failure, or you feel miserable because you cannot escape a drunk, a bore, an egomaniac, a wolf, or someone who wants to borrow money. Do not be heroic, simply disengage, and quickly move on.

Another way to escape is to just fade away and say you need to get some food before it is all gone. At lulls, you are able to change the subject or introduce someone else into the group and fade out. If someone else enters your group, you can move away at this time.

Practical Pointers

Crowd survival puts pressure on ordinary people to find their spot. Instead of "winging it", the best practice is to know a few survival techniques for unforeseen events. Body language movement in a crowd indicates change, and changes present opportunities.

Chapter 30

Intimate Relationships

"Love is a quest for an end and the end of a quest."

That love thang makes people happy and it feels good. It seeks mountain tops, blue skies, and a togetherness forever that transcends life's daily realities. Yet love has many paradoxes, many tragedies, losses, and vulnerabilities. The good news is that a simple "I love you" may be able to turn even the most harrowing separateness into a romantic bonding between two people. The bad news is that it may not last. There is an urgency factor is sexual longing, but *le petit mort* follows. Now, experts are conducting research that shows the brain chemicals that initiate romance are different from the ones that sustain long-term relationships.

> Love is like line work. Either you go forward or backward. You cannot stand still.

Some experts say love is a Darwinian adaptation of natural selection to insure the procreation and protection of children, while a creationist believes it is spiritual. But what is the "love thing" in terms of body language behavior.

On the threshold, logic and rationality take a back seat on the love train. The seminal conundrum for people is that they are rational beings in a mental state of irrationality. First, love is different for all people. What behavior is love and what is just lust are not the same for everyone.

Therefore, it follows that love must be self-determining. If someone thinks and behaves like they are in love then they are in love. If love is different for each lover, then what uniform signals and clues can we look for in the body language of love?

One thing that is certain and has been around since biblical times is the *Golden Rule*: Do unto others as they expect you to do unto them. Flower givers want flowers. People want to see themselves reflected in those around them for validation. If the object of your affection says, "I love you," she or he wants to hear back the words "I love you". In case you have not heard those words lately, do not despair, because people in the thrall of romance are very good at expressing affection nonverbally.

Romantic signals are as simple and reliable as a big smile, or the animated gesturing of two people conversing with each other, or the way couples freely move in each other's intimate space zones. What is important is that couples emphasize loving feelings rather than logic and reason.

> Nothing ventured, nothing gained.

The objective of romance is deepening love, which never seems to be satisfied, and is full of self-sustaining tricks. A precursor to the transmission of life, romantic behavior between men and women comes in stages to help insure they get it right.

The Courtship Sequence

A consistent template of the courtship sequence is elusive because it changes with the era in which it occurs. Most of the time, romantic attachments evolve in a sequence, so can people fall in love at first sight? The answer is yes. If people can fall in love with themselves the first time they see their image in a mirror, why not someone else? Self-love, however, is a limited example of idealized be-

> Love is like lightening. You never know where it is going to strike.

havior, and probably is more survival adaptive than romantic, therefore

I will not dwell on the body language of self-love, or why people stare at themselves in a mirror.

Anecdotal evidence of love at first is abundant. For example, the great Italian poet Dante was inspired in later years to write two of his best poems after meeting Beatrice Portinori at her parent's home in1274 when he was only nine years old, and she was eight. He only saw her one other time nine years later, but she appears in *The Divine Comedy* as the symbol of faith who guides Dante through the final section, *Paradise.*

Another example, is the enduring romance of Queen Elizabeth II and Prince Phillip Mountbatten, Duke of Edinburgh. Elizabeth was only thirteen the first time she saw the tall and handsome young Prince, but reputedly never even looked at another man. They married in 1947 and had four children. Other examples are too numerous to mention.

Even hard-core cynics admit that love at first sight is not only real, but often leads to deeper relationships. In the animal world, instant attraction is commonplace. Perhaps, as some experts believe, humans also

> Love at first sight is often cured by a second look.

may have an inherited ability for instant attraction. It is more probable; however, that novelty is more stimulating than commonness at first sight, because new, exotic things cause the release of dopamine in the brain, which stimulates attraction. The same is true of activities such as flirting, risk-taking, and even physical exercise.

Polls of Americans show that love at first sight is often the underpinning of many long-lasting and surprisingly strong marriages. More than half of the survey members experiencing love at first sight eventually got married, and two-thirds of those stayed married. This is strong evidence for love at first sight and the power of body language with little or no verbal communication.

After passionate feelings begin to fade; couples learn from experience that it is

> Love trumps sanity.

sustained friendship that lasts and not just lust. True love has a higher spiritual existence than either socially organized rituals of approval or physical cravings. It is the bonding glue between people in an intimate relationship.

A simplistic explanation for love is that it is something people need to keep from feeling insecure in our vast universe. However, true love is seldom simple. The reality of both courtship and love is that it is a sequence of events from an initial meeting to full intimacy. It is too important to leave to chance. First of all people must meet each other, and this takes place during everyday social life, or at prearranged display grounds where men and women are able to strut their stuff in front of each other.

Possibly, the display arena is something like a straightforward computerized dating service, or a place where people meet under the pretense of doing some other activity such as eating, drinking, worshipping, and so on. This helps overcome initial fears and acts as a safety valve in case nothing happens At this time, an understanding of body language is important since there is a great deal of preliminary body language taking place that is primarily visual.

As people check each other out, they note the physical characteristics, clothing, and movements of each other. Frequently, nothing happens because many people are constrained by inexperience and low self-confidence. To make matters worse, people tend to go to social gatherings in self-supporting cliques that inhibit the courtship sequence. For example, many women will go out in small groups of two or three, and one is always designated as the "We gotta leave girl." Once there is contact, however, most people move on to the next sequence to see if things are going to work out.

After people get past the initial problems associated with meeting each other for the first time, they anticipate their future according to their personal constructs, which is the meaning they place on events from their own experiences. Even though everyone construes events differently, they quickly make vocal contact, begin to exchange information designed to uncover mutual like, and dislikes.

As people spend more time with each other, they engage in small talk about mundane and trivial topics. By repeatedly saying the name

of the other person, they signal their interest. At the same time, they are
mentally comparing each other with
their preformed ideals of a mate. At
this point, it is easy to find fault and
break off from each other without
super consequence.

> Men usually start a relationship and women end it.

The next major exciting step is making physical contact. Since everything big starts off little, the first contact is usually incidental to
something insignificant like making a helpful adjustment to clothing or
holding hands. The next classic maneuver
is putting one's arm around another,
which is a prelude to a full body hug and
kiss.

> Romantic love brings people together and companionate love keeps them together.

Serious sexual interest begins when
couples begin to explore each other with
their hands. This kind of contact is hard to disguise and all pretense
disappears. At this point, either party is able to drop out and only be
slightly embarrassed, but if no one drops out, full sexual intimacy soon
follows. In fact, the main advantage to romantic sequencing is that either
party is free to quit before going too far.

What happens after the full intimacy stage? Does love become
a "second hand emotion" as a popular pop song suggests, or does it
become a relationship between two people with normal interdependent
needs? Passion does subside, but both of these choices fail to factor in
the huge affective state that romantic chemistry has on people.

Couples move from affect-laden states of romantic love to more
sedate and longer lasting states of companionate love. The chemistry
of these states involve more than mere co-dependency and exaggerated
concern, so how do people get there?

The traditions of courtship are exquisite and courtly, essentially
human, and at the beginning, somewhat impersonal until the expression of divine union encompasses the whole. At the risk of redundancy,
but for simplicity's sake, I will breakdown the body language of loving

into three fundamental categories: infatuation, passionate love, and companionate love.

Infatuation

Infatuation is a wonderful but mild form of interpersonal attraction that draws one person to another such

> Infatuation is another word for love at first sight.

as the fascination of Sir Lancelot for Guinevere, who was already married to King Arthur. As a categorical concept, infatuation is the subject of countless books even though it is difficult to quantify or define. Going back to its roots, the word itself seems to derive from the Latin term "to make foolish".

Logically, I believe infatuation is associated with youth and "puppy love", because for one thing, its endurance record can be poor. Young people want their infatuation to be transcendent like a "story book", but novices often expect way too much of each other and overlook the harsh realities of daily getting along together.

The body language of infatuated people is carefree and uninhibited, but infatuation is not the eternal flame, and does not involve an intense relationship like the one between Lord Byron and Lady Caroline Lamb, one of his mistresses, who said he was "mad, bad, and dangerous to know".

So-called puppy love, however, does give young people a new sense of individualism. For the first time, they love someone outside of their family. A little bit of emotional suffering and a great deal of flirting body language that eventually fizzles out are the hallmarks of infatuation.

Passionate Love

Passionate love is turbulent and indescribable. It is that intense "love thing" between two people that encompasses much more than mere infatuation. It is a bonding that insures the procreation of the human race. It is the stuff of dreams, Hollywood movies, and millions of books.

Hot, passionate love consists of powerful biological arousal, a consuming physical interest in another, a sincere caring for another's needs, a possessive jealousy, and in my opinion, game playing. Playing the game involves anxiety, insecurity, reciprocity, promise, readiness, mystery, and deep feelings for another. As the King of Siam said, it is a "puzzlement".

Passionate love is best when it is an adventure and sweetest when it is taboo. It engages people in bodily intimacies, explorations, and revelations. For the average female, true love is about emotional closeness, the chase, and marriage. For the average man, it is about the chase and catching the girl of his dreams. Aside from locker room boasting, most men enjoy the chase and do not appreciate easy love because of the "paradox of value", which holds that anything easily obtained has less value.

> Love means not ever having to say you are sorry.
> Erich Segal

Lots of eye contact, body contact, intense interest, making excuses for being close, and overlooking the flaws in each other are the benchmarks of passionate love. Both sexes expect the other to know their likes and dislikes. Repeating the name of your lover many times is a sign of passionate interest. Another sign is endearing little names for each other like, "Pumpkin" and "Sweetie".

Hot passionate erotic love, however, comes at a high cost. The search for a blissful union leads to a vulnerability with each other. The unforeseen price people often pay for their passion is intense jealousy over each other and a world of hurt if things do not work out. For example, the Russian poet Alexander Pushkin paid with his life. In 1831, he married a "wild thing" in a seventeen year old girl named Natalie, who made his heart sing. However, she became romantically involved with a guards officer, Baron Georges d' Anthes. Beside himself with jealousy and self-pity, Pushkin insulted the Baron and his family, which led to a pistol duel in 1837 that mortally wounded Pushkin.

As we age, however, passions, sexual urges, and reproductive desires wane in favor of responsibility and long-term commitment to companionship as opposed to short-term fantasy, excitement, and physical arousal.

Companionate Love

Most people believe that companionate love is the best of all. It involves loving each other in a different way. Love between companions is more permanent without the momentary ups and dreadful downs of passionate love. The characteristics of companionate love are strong bonds between family, siblings, friends, and even quasi-friends like teammates, and it is more stable and rewarding by many accounts.

Love between companions is more about a long-term commitment, responsibility, and interdependence than hot, intense, consuming passion. The body language of long-time companions will naturally echo each other. They will be in accord with little reason to be jealous and insecure. A long-term marriage often encompasses a companionate love based more on spiritual identity than a consuming passion. The history of humankind's evolution from small primitive groups to complex societies is the history of love between men and women. Humanity is obsessed with love and that is good thing.

The Game of Love

Experts believe that humans have unique brain circuitry for loving that allows them to send a variety of romantic signals through posturing, gesturing, smiling, gazing, and so on that allows men and women to make a game out of loving. In 1920, the English writer John Galsworthy wrote a classic book about love called *Skin Games*.

> Some things do not have to be true before you can believe in them.

If you want to be a player, stay alert and keep the lines of communication open. Both sexes have such a high degree of visual awareness that it does not take much to trigger a romantic spark to the brain that sets certain chemical changes in motion, which is one explanation for the archaic term "sparking". After the spark, couples bring the body language of novelty and appreciation to the table.

Courtship specialists say that most romantic relationships begin with a good opening line. "Haven't we met before", "What's your sign," and "I like your perfume" all fall in the male overused pick up lines category, whereas female clichés are some variant on, "I like your tie," or "I like your haircut".

Instead of antiquated clichés, the optimal opening line is one that establishes something in common between two people. It is counterintuitive, but after commonality, the next best opener is the playful insult. Unbelievably, lightly insulting the opposite sex in a funny, harmless way is a proven attention getter and icebreaker. Other useful ways to bring down barriers are touching each other in a light way such as a lingering handshake, or a helpful adjustment to a man's tie, which establish that all-important first contact.

Preening Gestures

The provocative way some people tilt their head to one side in the direction of the object of their interest, open up their eyes, smile, and give short, clipped answers show sexual interest. When seated, people signal interest by propping their chin up with their fingers as they listen to another person.

> Love is something most people don't see coming.

Male preening involves tie-straightening, cuff link adjusting, unbuttoning of coats, breath spraying, and conducting subtle personal inspections. Insouciant sexual interest turns serious when a male places his thumbs in his belt or pockets or if he unconsciously grabs his crotch.

A heightened intensity is expressed by moves that are intended to maximize fertility clues such as pulling in the stomach muscles to tighten the "Abs," standing straighter for better posture, pushing the shoulders back, expanding the chest to look bigger, and putting on a sexy outfit.

Women express interest by a variety of preening gestures such as the "air kiss", smoothing their hair, arranging their clothes, glancing sideways, looking in a mirror, leaning forward, making eye contact, gradually exposing the smooth soft skin of their wrists and touching. Women that are more forward will sit with legs a little more open than need be, fondle a cigarette, beer bottle, or man's necktie, and even fiddle with their shoes.

Correct nonverbal behavior is especially significant in romance because of the need to protect the high degree of ego involvement yet still get feelings across such as marking their territory. Another correct female expression is the romantic eyebrow flash, which is direct and delightful. Incorrect behaviors are such things as using vulgarities, loudness, over-assertiveness, and talking incessantly.

Opposites attract, so women looking for romance need to put a little sway in their hips, take off their jacket to expose bare shoulders, touch their lips seductively, and pretend to be somewhat helpless, which encourages men's desire to protect and help them.

The use of appropriate gender gestures during the courtship ritual serves both the man's image of being a strong, but silent provider, and the female's image of being the total woman. For both men and women, the trick is to know precisely which body language movements send the right message at the right time.

Overdoing body language during courtship is counterproductive, since it invariably comes off as an obvious contrivance or as "having an attitude". The best reality therapy, however, is not to put too much emphasis on single aspects of romantic body language.

Romance has a high maintenance requirement. Lasting romances are the ones that two people have devoted much of their time and energy to preserving as they move from a state of idealizing love, which re-creates loved ones anew and suppresses the negatives of what they are actually like to a stable relationship based on durability.

Stability-based relationships occur most often when romantic behavior changes from infatuation and passionate love to long-lasting companionship. The good news is that companionate love is the end-result of a natural evolution of people growing old together, becoming more mature, changing their priorities, and making choices based on a rational calculation of what serves them best over the long term.

Family Love

The primacy of family love is self-evident. We are all the product of our formative years in the family constellation, and the intricate development of interdependent family relationships through ordered but overlapping stages is a major wellhead for acquiring body language.

The importance of the parent-child relationship actually begins during pregnancy. In extreme cases, for example, infants with depressed mothers are significantly more likely to make a sad face with angry expressions.

From the moment of birth, nonverbal communications play a decisive role in the functional interactions between parents and children. Infancy is the critical time for learning which behavior brings rewards. Infants must learn how to communicate their need for affection and sustenance nonverbally until they are able to communicate verbally.

Babies signal their parents about their needs and physical comfort through a variety of clues like mimicry, and mothers, in particular, know how to interpret the signals and respond in "motherese", although fathers also play a significant role.

Infants quickly learn the facial expressions and sounds that get attention such as when to smile endearingly and when to cry to evoke sympathy. Children often become insecure in later life if left alone in early childhood without the chance to form strong affective relationships through mutual body language

Children are dependent on the family unit and a small number of friends, but as they mature, their dependence transfers to a larger number of close people. Being less dependent upon the family translates into growing individualism as a child's options increase. A wider concept of self emerges from the broader interaction with others along with an expanded utilization of body language.

People love their selves as much as they love others. That is their natural nature. People think they are genuine and deserving even if others do not. They would liquidate their not-so-genuine behavior if they could. Therefore, self-love is not all bad. It is a necessary ingredient in positive individualism, expanded awareness, and raising the level of our consciousness if it is not overdone.

Practical Pointers

The state of love is something average Americans do not know much about. Of course, so-called experts do not know much either. However, the irreducible nature of love seems to be a design for keeping future mothers and fathers together.

A large part of what constitutes the right romantic relationship depends upon what happens during the all-important sequencing of courtship into lasting love. When lovers stop gazing at each other and gaze into the future together, their love is on the right track. At the end of the day, love is very insistent, blindingly persistent, and resistant to all planning. When it comes to passion, however, it is a tiger.

Chapter 31

Prosocial Body Language

"Openness and trust go hand-in-hand"

Openness is a positive state, and is an essential element in maintaining trust, which is the basis of our social capital. Declining trust is sub-optimal, whereas openness is a positive trait and a highly desirable frame of mind. It allows new and possibly better things to come into our lives. It also forces us to re-examine ourselves on current affairs and important issues such as living and working together. Furthermore, openness is an indispensable body language tool in maintaining both primary and secondary relationships.

Open hand gestures, the universal signals of openness from time immemorial, are readily associated with sincerity, warmth, trust, and friendliness. A signal of openness not only gives us a warm feeling, but also invites reciprocity. When trying to convince others to change their minds, or to pursue new and diverse ways of doing things, projecting openness is best.

People with a high degree of openness shun dogmatism and are more extroverted, ecumenical, and tolerant. Their downfall, if any, is the propensity to become uninterested in routine activities, an inability to remain attentive, and a tendency to forget how important other people are in their lives. On the other hand, people who are not open naturally tend to be introverted and conservative, and often become completely closed-off, dogmatic, biased, and intolerant.

Anecdotal evidence of openness is abundant since it is such a productive trait. A good example is the modern day criminal trial. In my experience, people called to jury duty in a criminal trial tend to be defensive upon entering the courtroom. It is a new and unfamiliar experience for most of them and they do not know the people around them. To compliment matters, they rarely admit they cannot be open-minded, because society views that as a negative character flaw. Can they truly fulfill the open-mindedness requirement?

Ideally, most jurors feel they have a duty to listen to the evidence no matter how boring or complicated, to uphold law and order, to keep their neighborhood and families safe, to do justice to both sides, and be completely open-minded.

Prospective jurors have vital social functions to perform and individual imperatives, but at the same time, they must be completely open-minded about something that has never happened to them, by people they do not know and have never met, and could care less about. Trial attorneys know that jurors who are taking notes are still on the fence. When they put their notes down and lean back, they have made up their minds.

Openness Gestures

Openness gestures are unfolded arms, uncrossed legs, and hands between the waist and shoulders with palms up, a big smile with facial cheeks up, and good eye contact. Related shows of openness are steepling the fingers at either the waist or the chin, and unbuttoning or removing a coat in a business meeting, which communicates that some agreement is possible.

Forward body language is the key. If you are sitting, uncross your arms and legs, move closer to the edge of your chair, and lean forward. If anyone approaches, stand and welcome them warmly to show openness and potential cooperation.

Other signs of openness are fully facing the person you are talking to, positioning yourself in the social zone of spacing, maintaining appropriate eye contact at least sixty per cent of the time, and keeping a pleasant countenance. In addition, good signs are people lightly pacing the floor and waiting quietly for recognition in your presence.

When is someone not open? Behavioral opposites of openness are intimidating actions such as raising the shoulders, crossing either the chest or hips with the arms, and sticking out a finger and either shaking or wiggling it, which cuts off questions. Therefore, a person may intend to be open, but negative information is typically weighted more heavily than positive information.

Acceptance

The highest form of acceptance known to the human species is a mother's love for her children. The psychologist, Carl Rogers, called it *unconditional positive regard*. In other words, anything a child does is all right with mom. Acceptance such as this has a beneficial social purpose. As a baby or young child growing up, it inoculates us against the problems of the world and gives us the strength, courage, and fortitude to go on. When we do wrong, and mom still accepts us with open arms and loving body language, she is giving us her unconditional positive regard.

Unconditional positive regard is something people get without earning it, but if we crave acceptance from a particular person or group, the best approach is to emulate them as much as possible without being obvious about it. Why, because there is no getting around the fact that people prefer similar people.

Matching and mirroring another person's behavior are effective tools for communicating openness and acceptance, since this technique conveys the notion that you regard others as equal in status and worth. For starters, try using the same jargon they do. For example, attorneys, physicians, bureaucrats, and others purposely use devised

> Take the tone of the company you are in.
> Lord Chesterfield

"industry speak" to dialogue with others in their field, and befuddle the public at the same time.

Attorneys, for example, employ words such as misfeasors and miscreants for wrongdoers and villains in addition to Latin phrases such as "mea culpa" for my fault or simply, "I'm guilty". There is a story about a man who lost his wallet one night, but only searched for it under a street light. When asked why, he said, "That is where the light is". Lawyers also use language to spin their phrases to fit desired conclusions that tend to mirror and match their clients with innocence and reasonableness.

Since many institutional workers such as law enforcement, the military, and federal employees have their own industry parlance, the best approach is to secure a mentor who is able to teach us the "linguistic ropes" if we don't know the "group speak" and common body language of a highly structured group.

Touching, or lack of it, shows how close people are. It has long been a sign of acceptance and affection between two people. Exactly which kind of acceptance touching implies depends on diverse factors such as who, what, where, and when it occurs, as well as how long, the amount of pressure involved, the presence of others, and the context of the touching. Therefore, contextual details determine the significance of touching.

Touching suggests a bond or close acceptance, or at the very least, touching indicates a person feels comfortable around another even though the purpose behind touching simply may be to calm another person down. Leaning toward or physically moving closer

> Touching is a power gesture.

to another person shows trust and acceptance by closing the gap without touching, as well as providing the collateral benefit of keeping intruders away.

Sustained eye contact and the thumbs up gesture signal acceptance. In another popular gesture today, men will tap a clenched fist on their chests to show acceptance, loyalty, and devotion. It says to others, "My heart goes out to you". If you point at someone, it is specific to that person. This gesture is much like the ancient salute of a Roman Centurion.

On the other hand, women usually limit touching their chests to protective gestures or expressions of shock and surprise such as when they want to say, "Me, you're talking about me," and they will splay their fingers instead of making a fist.

Once again, imagine how President Lincoln is sitting in the Lincoln Memorial. His pose is highly representational of the principle of postural acceptance.

Cooperation

Cooperation is pro-social behavior closely related to openness and acceptance, and is usually measured in degrees. Its importance cannot be underestimated however. If you do not believe in cooperation, watch a wagon when one of the wheels comes off. In a relationship, our cooperation is trivial or substantial, premeditated or impulsive, and so on, depending upon the degree of empathy we have for the person or persons who need our cooperation.

Along the same lines, our willingness to cooperate depends upon our mood and the emotions we are feeling at the time we assess the causes underlying another person's need for our cooperation. Being in a good mood helps a great deal, but good moods are ephemeral. In egotistical logic, even bad moods help or hinder the spirit of cooperation depending on whether people think cooperating with another will do anything for them.

Since egotistical behavior is motivated by self-benefit, some cynics believe that the main motivation for some people to help others is no more than the desire to reduce personal unpleasant emotions associated with observing others in need.

Another important attitude in cooperation is the phenomena known as *pluralistic ignorance* that occurs when numerous bystanders at a sudden emergency use the body language of others to determine whether their cooperation is actually required. They tell themselves, "No one else is doing anything".

A real confusion of responsibility occurs if observers believe a person who is actually cooperating has the body language of someone responsible for the problem. Whose side do they take? In ambiguous situations such as these, a proper understanding of body language gives people an advantage in deciding whether to cooperate or not since some people do not want our cooperation.

Garden-variety body language gestures that signal cooperation involve ways to move closer to people such as scooting up to the edge of the chair and leaning forward in a round table meeting. Show acceptance of what another is saying by frequently nodding your head in agreement and cooperation by offering to help pass important papers around. In addition, tilting the head communicates to people that we are listening. We signal that we are ready to get down to work by unbuttoning our coat and rolling up our shirtsleeves.

Secretiveness

Secretiveness is the opposite of openness, acceptance, and cooperation, and is unsocial, although necessary at times. In an open society, people do not trust secretive people, and a hidden agenda is a negative trait. Of course, at some levels of government keeping secrets and hidden agendas are essential; however, secretiveness is rarely advantageous to interpersonal relations since it has a sharp edge that sometimes jabs the keeper. Besides, in the social context, secrets are difficult to keep, and a simple observation of people in a variety of social situations informs us about what to look for despite efforts to keep things secret.

Secretive people are not secretive all the time, but because secret knowledge to them is like buried treasure, they will attempt to reveal as little as possible by covering or hiding personal items, keeping their distance, staying aloof, avoiding eye contact, and showing no emotion.

> We don't seek advice so much as we want an accomplice.

A telltale sign of secretive behavior is people whispering or partly covering their mouths with their hands. Some people will talk in hushed tones out of one side of their mouth without moving their lips in an effort to keep people from hearing or reading them. Other types of secretive behavior are changing the subject and hiding things from view.

Another well-known sign of secretiveness is the unconscious eye rub. A person who uses his forefinger to rub his eye or skin next to his eye is using this action as an excuse to temporarily look away or close his eye to a deception secretly taking place. At any rate, we cease to be a child when we realize that hiding the truth does not make it better.

Practical Pointers

In a way, people are like an umbrella: The more open they are, the better they function. Nevertheless, in some cases, it behooves us to keep some secrets for a couple of legitimate reasons: 1) Security and 2) once a fun secret gets out, it ceases to be fun. Overall, acceptance and cooperation come with increasing maturity, while secretiveness is immature and unnecessary.

Chapter 32

Tell The Truth

"Stretching the truth is lying."

Mark Twain called lies "stretchers". This mostly covert subtlety is a form of deception more akin to *duping* than overt *concealment* and outright *falsehoods,* which have no basis in truth. Stretching the truth is funny at times, and can be a positive act that does not create internal stress, which is what Mark Twain artfully sought after in his stories.

Twain's colorful and benign "stretchers" metaphor, however, fails to address the immense problem of deception today. We halfway expect lawbreakers, the advertising media, and certain salespeople to deceive us from time to time, but not jurors, Wall Street stockbrokers, elected representatives, and loved ones.

Unfortunately, deception has become one of the most serious problems in society often playing a major role in our interpersonal relationships. On the other hand, some people believe that deception serves a valid social purpose at times. For example, how would you like to know the exact truth, even if it makes you worse off, or causes you to avoid doing some good?

Since some deception is socially or morally beneficial at time, under what set of circumstance does deceit become socially harmful? Deception is clearly bad when a person intends to mislead another, in a deliberate manner, without prior notification, and without our consent.

Do you tell little white lies to keep from hurting someone's feelings? Is it okay to be a pragmatic prevaricator? Are your peers less than honest with you? Today, if for no other reason but self-defense, we need the ability to detect falsehoods whether told to us on TV, in the bedroom, or on the job.

In our age of hyper-reality and sensationalism, the unvarnished truth does not seem to be enough, and a peccadillo or two is not that bad. For example, big name media reporters routinely embellish upon ordinary events in an effort to aggrandize themselves and make their stories more interesting and spectacular.

Prominent writers embroider the truth to sell their books, and nobody thinks twice about Hollywood rewriting documented history to produce a larger than life movie, even when it does more harm than good such as Oliver Stone's movie *JFK*.

More is not always better. Short answers are probably more truthful than long answers, but professional spin-doctors specialize in long-winded explanations about government abuse and political chicanery. Of cursory importance, a recent TV documentary said that the father of spin was an advertising man named Ed Bernays.

> Liars talk too fast or too slow.

Euphemisms and word parsing help hide the truth. For example, former Secretary of State Alexander Haig called lying "terminological inexactitude", while other government officials call lying "inoperative statements". Ex-President Bill Clinton came close to impeachment after lying about his love affairs. Under questioning, he played word games saying his answers depended upon what the meaning of the word "is" is.

Occasionally, even our friends, co-workers, and neighbors exaggerate, equivocate, and parse words with us, whereas some telemarketers, salespeople, and advertisers constantly bombard us with hucksterisms and half-truths.

Why are people untruthful? Some sociologists theorize that children are taught to lie at an early age when they are instructed to say things such as, "Tell Mary you had a good time at her birthday party," even though the party was dreadful. Likewise, children begin to tell wish fulfillment lies at an early age such as "I'm going to the circus tomorrow", or teasing lies such as "My doll is a person and yours isn't", both of which seem harmless enough at the time.

The stark truth is that the genesis of deception begins early and is a major dynamic throughout our lifetime with serious consequences. For this reason, detecting deception is a major imperative. The biggest difficulty is that most of us do not have any training or experience in spotting deception, and that is where knowledge of body language can help.

Technically, spotting deception in a "close" relationship is a simple matter of looking for the right clues by keeping our eyes and ears open to behavioral indicators such as movement in the hands and feet, physical changes, arousal signs, and obvious fluctuations in anxiety levels in people we know well. For example, deception clues are something as minor as a person we know appearing controlled and unemotional when relating scripted testimony, but suddenly developing the jitters on less than honest testimony.

Many deception clues are far from being simple. For instance, a difficult clue to spot is a faint blushing around a liar's eyes, which is practically undetectable without a thermal imaging device. In addition, it is difficult to decipher half-gestures that people use by extending their arms and hands only partially as if trying not to overextend themselves. People who are unsure of themselves noticeably moderate their gesturing.

> Whoever blushes is already guilty; true innocence is ashamed of nothing.
> Rousseau

Another consideration is the fact that some people have a throbbing pulse in their neck veins when lying and others do not. Additionally, it is a proven fact that a liar's nose expands slightly, because the tissue inside the nose swells as a result of a hyped up nervous system, but that does not help much because it is barely visible. Misjudgments occur because people fail to take in account the stress of a truthful person that nobody believes. Think about it.

Basic Signs of Deception

Basic signs of deception are finger tapping, scratching, and dancing feet; however, some hand and foot movement are entirely innocent, so watch for hand and foot movements under threatening circumstances or at inappropriate times before becoming acutely suspicious.

In close relationships where we know each other extremely well, lying is much easier to spot because we know the normal, unstressed behavioral patterns of the person lying, and we are able to make telling comparisons.

If a co-worker is an hour late to an office meeting and you ask him if he got lost, but he hesitates with an answer and mumbles something about traffic, or touches his face and looks down when answering, there is a good possibility that he is being untruthful. He probably has been lost or preoccupied for the last hour or so, but does not want to admit it.

Signs of treachery are such things as unusual swallowing, noises, and changes in vocal patterns. The eyes are the best indicators of treachery and falsehood. Our eyes reflect stress, and if a person looks away or blinks when he or she answers a crucial question, it is safe to assume they are not being honest with you. The same is true if their eyelids flutter or blink constantly.

Suppose you are meeting a friendly acquaintance in your office and this person tends to frown and look down when talking, pauses before answering, and responds to simple questions with noticeable changes in

> Exaggeration is making a mountain out of a molehill.

speech patterns and elaborate answers. The frown and gazing downward are inappropriate to a friendly meeting, pausing before answering is a damning speech pattern, and long drawn out answers are out of place.

Another example of an inappropriate gesture or expression in a conversational transaction is the woman who asks her date if he ever cheats, and he waits a minute before answering then smiles and says "no". Should she be on guard? Yes, because the smile is incongruent and a smile arriving too early or too late has a hidden message, which contradicts the spoken word. In this example, the man needs a serious expression for a serious question, while saving the smile for when she says she believes him.

Changes in vocal patterns are signs of deception. To catch a liar, listen to the sounds of the voice as much as the words. Did a suspected deceiver speed up unnecessarily, hesitate, add tag words, or otherwise change speech patterns that indicate stress? Once again, it is not "what" a person says, but "how" he says it.

Lying voices will tend to climb the pitch scales. Also, using non-words such as "sheez" and "uh" are common ways to stall before giving a complete answer.

Pillow Talk

People are more open without the overlay of marriage or work. So, is your marriage an honest one? The bad news is that a recent survey revealed that many married couples were dishonest with each other during the past year.

Men, it seems, lie more often than women do. Thirty-eight per cent of those surveyed lied about how much something cost, twenty-five per cent lied when they told their marital partner they looked good, and nineteen per cent lied about their marital partner being a good cook. The good news is that marital lying diminishes with age.

Suppose hypothetically, a man and woman meet at an office soiree and are consumed with passion. After a little conversation, she asks, "Are you married?" If he says "no" and is lying, she needs to notice if he raised his glass to his lips or tries to cover his mouth with his hand, even momentarily.

Did he cough or avert eye contact? If he shifts his feet, adjusts his tie, or just fidgets, either he is shy or he is married. Our hypothetical woman still is not sure about this hypothetical man until he says jokingly, "Do I look married?" It may be a joke, but a diversion is more likely. Smart liars know how to use indignation or some other strong emotion to mask fear and guilt.

Untruthful statements are not always intentional lies. For instance, if someone is telling you about his car accident a few weeks ago, and you know what he is saying is not exactly what happened, it is not a lie, but what lawyers call a "memory slide", or how he remembers it.

The farther away from the event, the worse memory becomes, which is why spontaneous declarations close to events are more accurate than declarations farther away in time. Too far out and they become smaller, jumpier, and less critical. Nevertheless, memory flaws are so well known and understood that they remain a solid part of American jurisprudence.

Structured Lying

Lying in a structured environment such as the office of a supervisor, or higher authority, is different from conversing with people at a party, so it deserves special treatment. When someone with authority puts us on the spot, or asks questions with an accusatory tone, our response potentially has some very serious consequences.

Authoritative interrogators will have a plan of attack and a special place to conduct it. For example, a few years ago, I was friendly with a couple of detectives that I frequently saw in court, and they told me their favorite place to interrogate suspects was to drive them around the local cemetery! Some of my court appointed clients confirmed their story.

Latency spells uncertainty.

In a structured Q and A scenario, the authority asking the questions probably expects some lying and knows the answer before asking the question. They are deliberately looking for signs of deception by using the science of kinesics instead of listening to explanations, while the person on the spot is busy sizing up the questioner in an attempt to tell a plausible story and control his behavior at the same time.

During Q and A, any physical or behavioral changes need to be fairly consistent and timely. That means they need to occur often and close to the asked questions to be of significance.

Lying comes in many forms, so let me unpack them a little bit. There are little white lies to keep from hurting someone and big exaggerations to gloss over the truth. Half-truths are statements that are hard to pin down because they are partly true. Imaginary lies are fibs the teller believes are true, whereas large-scale deceptions are the "big lie" that, ironically, are the easiest to believe.

Broadly speaking, there are two kinds of lying clues: thinking clues and feeling clues. Basic feelings are hard to conceal. For example, people experiencing the fear that exposure brings, or the pleasure of putting something over on someone will try to hide their true emotions. However, a give-away will immediately show up in their body language like a slight flicker of expression in the face.

STALLING TACTICS
.Pausing and hesitating
.Use of non-words
.Repeating the question
.Rephrasing the question
.Nervous laugh

Thinking clues take place because it is harder to lie than tell the truth. Liars have to make something up, which leads to biological changes, hesitations, slip-ups, and lack of detail in what they are saying. At times, the distortion of facts is little more than an unintentional memory slide or by-pass, but unfortunately, intentional deception is more likely.

Even though falsification is highly ambiguous in ill-defined situations, it is possible to assess patterns of behavioral clues associated with deception. For example, the liberal use of flattery is an indication of deception. Keep in mind, there are some exceptions to normal rules of lie detection that are due to the presence of arousal causing agents such as mental problems, alcohol abuse, and numerous medications that distort the perception of reality.

Patterns of Deception

The speech patterns, voice qualities, and other paralinguistic devices we use to answer pre-designed diagnostic and structured questions are just as important as the selective words a questioner uses. At the point of deception, the rate of speech tends to increase or decrease with noticeable stammering and hesitation, nervous laughing, and other sounds such as "whew". For instance, answering two, three, or more questions quickly, but pausing on the fourth one is a pattern of deception.

Another indicator of prevarication is the pause or hesitation in concert with drawing a deep breath while trying to think of an answer. A person who avoids specifics and tends to use "soft" words such as "borrow" for "steal" is trying to circumvent harsh realities.

When a person invokes a higher authority, suspicion is in order. Along the same lines, statements similar to the line made famous by Flip Wilson that, "The Devil made me do it" are obvious attempts to shift the blame, and long, drawn out answers such as "noooooooooo" tend to be attempts to mislead.

Someone who has a sudden memory failure when it comes to incriminating evidence, but easily remembers facts beneficial to them is "selectively" trying to avoid giving the full truth. A *parapraxis* or minor slip of the tongue, sometimes called a "Freudian slip", indicates a person's subconscious thinking is in conflict with what he is saying. Since Dr. Freud believed people are habitually in conflict with themselves, he believed "slips of the tongue" were the royal roads to their subconscious.

Why do guilty people tend to look guilty and innocent people tend to look innocent? Liars will make fewer hand gestures, move their heads less, speak slower than normal, and sit more rigidly. However, if a guilty person thinks someone is watching closely, he will tend to relax his facial muscles and pretend to have pleasant emotions. A liar will hold a facial expression too long indicating false emotion, or show different colors in the face such as blushing red, or turning pale white.

Besides showing stress signs in the arms, legs, and hands, dishonest people will invariably touch their face when lying as if to cover up or check what they are saying. They will rub their eyes, scratch their nose, wipe their mouth, or sniff audibly. In addition, people will use half gestures so they will not look overextended and employ props such as pencils, toothpicks, and eyeglasses to bite, chew on, and fiddle with as tension masking diversions and attempts to reduce stress.

During questioning, if people twirl their thumbs or twist their hair relentlessly they are waiting to see or hear what is coming next. Placing a hand on the back of their neck signals uncertainty, and stretching signals boredom.

The truth comes out when the liar is ready, not when the interrogator is ready. People who are ready to come clean with the truth will indicate their readiness to do so by sobbing, by looking at the ceiling and blinking as if beseeching the divine, and by striking a submissive pose like rounding the shoulders and looking sheepish.

Many times, people ready to confess will rub their chin with a "Ya got me" smile, or assume a posture similar to Rodin's famous statute of "The Thinker". If any of these activities, or other pre-confession clues take place, then the time is ripe to stop asking questions and start listening. How well interrogators synchronize with others is an important aspect of interactive Q and A because synchronization fosters comfort levels that induce people to talk more openly and freely.

Valid Excuses

People do not relish questioning. It can be jarringly unpleasant, embarrassing, and degrading, especially if the tone is accusatory and their ego becomes threatened. Normally, people do not expect that they will have to account for their actions. Caught off guard, everyone is nervous and stressed under questioning about unpleasant experiences, personal motives, and forgotten memories. Distinguishing normal stress from guilt-based stress is the challenge.

> "Who cares" is the ultimate excuse.

Old school interrogation methods of constantly asking leading questions calling for simple "yes" or "no" answers are not optimal. Trick questions such as "When did you stop beating your wife", and constant interruptions by the good cop-bad cop routine like, "My partner wants to shoot you, but I want to help you" are sub-optimal interview techniques. Under these circumstances, an honest person sometimes appears to be dishonest. It is similar to that unsettling question or unforeseen insinuation from a trusted friend that just happens to catch you off guard.

A person is in a bad patch when he is exaggerating, but manages to stay calm, and his companion standing close by becomes demonstratively nervous because the companion knows veracity is lacking. In situations such as this, the bystander who knows better will become agitated, nervous, and stressed in place of the actual liar. Husbands and wives are bad about committing this indiscretion, so if you jointly plan a deception keep one or the other away, or better yet, tell the truth at all times.

Practical Pointers

Picasso once said that all he wanted to show in his paintings was the "unexpectedness of the naked truth". Do we expect people to lie? If that is the case, it is a sad commentary on modern day life. Nevertheless, deception is ubiquitous enough that the best and perhaps the only defenses are to learn how to spot the patterns of lying behavior as opposed to honest behavior.

Lie detection is a skill we need in other areas as well. For instance, Senator Tom Coburn said during the nomination hearing of Chief Justice Roberts that he was using his skills as a physician to observe the body language of Justice Roberts to discern whether the judge was being honest with his answers.

Overall, it all boils down to this: Truthful people will be calm and give simple answers that make sense, and untruthful people will give elaborate, unrealistic explanations accompanied by animated expressions that do not make sense under the circumstances.

Chapter 33

How To Sell

"Relationship building comes before tasks"

A secondary non-kinship relationship is the everyday commercial transaction between a buyer and seller. The decisive period in buyer and seller relationships is the first meeting when each party sizes up the other and decides if doing business together is a good or bad thing. At this crucial moment whether on the phone or in person, each party must be able to convey who he is, and how he is able to fulfill the other party's needs.

The seller needs to facilitate the buying decision of the buyer because buyers purchase according to their buying patterns and not that of seller's. Identifying need-based behavioral clues is half the battle, and like a city mayor knows his wards, that is where the knowledge of body language becomes irreplaceable.

Buyers and sellers ordinarily have the physical need to be comfortable, which makes the environment important to the transaction, the social need to look good in front of others, the personal need to be accepted, and the mental need to manage stress while trying to make the best possible deal. In most cases, sellers have a high degree of ego involvement with their products, whereas buyers have a preconceived mental picture of how much they are willing to pay for a product.

The best way to discover a potential buyer's needs is to begin with appropriate self-disclosure such as talking a little about the family, sports, the weather, and other generalities. Then ask the a buyer about his feelings on similar matters employing "open-ended" questions, instead of questions that call for a simple "yes" or "no". For instance, say something such as, "I bought this product for my kids. What do your kids like?" Open-ended questions increase the amount of verbal and nonverbal information you receive.

Follow self-disclosure questions with broad easy-to-answer questions before asking specifics, since this helps to set the tone and rhythm, which will increase your effectiveness and efficiency. Remember that appeals to a buyer's fears, worries, or apprehensions are not typically useful. When a buyer uses the word "I" instead of "we", it indicates his assertiveness and dominance. The expansive use of gestures tells people that person tends to control his space. First person answers are a sign of personal responsibility, while third person answers indicate a tendency to accept group decisions.

I will never forget a statement once made to me by a real estate agent Aspen, Colorado. I asked him to show me a certain condominium, and he asked me if I was going to buy it. I replied that I did not know until I saw it, and he said, "If you aren't going to buy it, I'm not going to show it to you". If you don't buy it today, tomorrow it will be gone." I said, "No thanks", left to see for myself. It was a tiny, very old, viewless, converted motel room priced at sixty thousand dollars plus outrageously high management fees.

Informational "Tells"

The new art of body language is data driven. The more information you have the better. That is why background information is helpful. In many respects, informational "tells" are the same whether it is potential trial jurors or commercial buyers and sellers. Ideally, information "tells" show up by asking the right questions along with pertinent data mining.

Before I agree to tie up my client's time and money in a trial, ideally I want to know as much as possible about potential jurors, or potential buyers and sellers in a business transaction. For example, I want to know what a person does twenty-four hours a day, so I ask questions about how his spare time is spent when not working to see if he "has something going on or not". I try to collect all possible information that will "tell" me how strangers, jurors, or parties to a business transaction are going to behave. At the bare minimum, I want base line information in four areas:

1. *Occupation:* A person's occupation and workplace tells me if he is an individual or institutional type, and if he works with people or things. Work history is important since it represents the safe thinking of the middle class that operates as a base line for all other human endeavors.

2. *Family status and age:* The family status and ages of people are clues to their responsibilities and lifestyles. The goals and responsibilities of married people are different from the goals of single people, and their priorities are different.

Some respected psychologists say that people have a *range of convenience,* and if they go outside of it, it causes them anxiety. For instance, it is "convenient" for pre-adolescents to reflect the primary values of their parents, although these values are highly permeable. College age people prefer "status convenience" and are the easiest to persuade, while Americans over the age of thirty-four find it convenient to stay in attitude stability.

The psychologist Erickson said everything is "age related". He believed that our ego identity develops over our lifetime in stages. He coined the term *identity crisis* for adolescents struggling with the maturation process. As people age, their behavior becomes more conservative and they understand life's frailties better.

In addition, older adults are more experienced in their assessments of problems. They are able to put things in context better than younger adults, and govern themselves accordingly. They have greater flexibility and can regulate their emotions better.

3. *Hobbies and activities:* What are a person's hobbies and activities, and how does he or she spend their spare time? Does he belong to

certain kinds of civic or political organizations? Does she hang out with social, professional, or athletic groups, and does he spend his spare time on himself instead of others?

Research has shown that people who are active in community, school, or church activities have *high social integration,* and will do things for other individuals and their community.

Officers in social and business organizations are structured people with high regard for rules, schedules, and authority. Highly structured people are more comfortable with institutional values and prefer to work for "C" corporations, banks, the school system, and the military. Their body language will be more conventional.

Unstructured people are free spirits who do not mind bending the rules, and have not fully bought into mainstream society. The unstructured person is more individualistic and works in sales, independent contracting, and self-employment occupations.

4. *Attitude:* What is a person's attitude? Attitudes are beliefs and opinions that tell how someone will be predisposed to respond to other persons, places, or things. Attitudes develop early in life and form strong "anchor-like" constructs in the personality. If a product is tough to sell, then find a buyer with a strong "can do" attitude that allows him to make tough decisions.

Clues to a "can do" attitude are such things as talkativeness, a willingness to give first person answers, and the control of nearby space, whereas buyers with a poor attitude will be passive, quiet, shy, unmoving, and apathetic.

To Buy or Not To Buy

Buying decisions are either emotional or rational. Everyone develops a preference early in life and sticks to it. The emotional buyer makes decisions based on ego involvement and subjective, internal values. Emotional buyers are subject to emotional appeals such as, "Buy this now, and half will go to the needy kid's fund". Oral clues are buyer

> Sell the sizzle not the steak.

statements such as "I love it" and visual clues are emotional expressions such as a warm, friendly look, expanding pupils, and an open posture.

The opposite of the emotional buyer is the rational buyer. Rational buyers tend to be logical, detached, analytical, and driven by objective facts. They prefer not to get involved personally with sellers. For them, reasoning is more convincing than appeals to emotions and sympathy.

Oral clues are statements using words such as, "I think not", or "Let me think about it". Highly visual clues are evaluation expressions such as chin stroking or a closed hand resting on the cheek. When the index finger points up and the thumb supports the chin, the buyer is having disinclined thoughts about the transaction.

Since people do not apply logic to buying a teddy bear and do not get emotionally involved when they buy a trash compacter, we need to get a handle on a buyer's attitude toward the sale as quickly as possible. It is advisable to take note of body language signals that answer the following questions: Is the other person's behavior spontaneous or deliberate? How fast does an attitude surface? How strong is this person's attitude associated with the object of the sales transaction? There is no such thing as coincidence.

Body language behaviors that are "turn offs" and reduce people's credibility and personal power in commercial transactions faster than a tumbleweed in a tornado are such things as wasting each other's time, contradictory actions that are at cross-purpose with each other , disorganization, repetitive actions, constant interruptions, and holding cell phone conversations.

In short, if buyers and sellers in most commercial relationships make crucial buying and selling decisions based on emotions and preformed attitudes, then knowing the right body language "tells" is essential to making a sale.

Practical pointers

Psychographics is a commercial market research tool that has been identifying and mapping consumer preferences by regions for years.

Essentially, at the culminating point, psychographics systematically divide consumers into inner and outer directed types based on variables such as regional values and lifestyles, and of course body language.

Commercial transactions require managing the same as money; therefore, we must possess the personal communication tools necessary to manage the buyer and seller interface in a way that satisfies the values and lifestyles of both parties, while building a long-term relationship at the same time.

A good salesperson should have four things going for himself: An ability to read a buyer's needs from his body language; the behavioral profiling skills to interpret potential purchasing behavior; the ability to take hard rejection without showing it; and the persuasion skills to close the deal.

Chapter 34

Group Behavior

"Go along to get along."

Do you spend time computer "networking" or nightclubbing with thesame people two or three nights a week? Perhaps you are retired and play bridge with close friends. Whatever the activity, groups, are social engines that range from small everyday groups to large institutional ones.

Whatever the size of a group, we prefer to hang out with the persons that we perceive to be most like us, except in those instances where we choose to hang out with social and financial inferiors only for the dubious reason that they make us look and feel superior.

Humans are very relationship dependent, and after making up our minds about what we are interested in, and where others with the same interests as ours hang out, we go there. We eagerly pick up the same lingo and mannerisms of our chosen group and over time we gradually become interdependent.

Go with the flow.

Those people who allow us to be ourselves are a healthy and positive influence on our lives, but occasionally we pick the wrong people whose Faustian influences bring out the worst in us. At times, we find ourselves in small groups with people we do not know, and our status then depends upon the magnitude of our contribution and degree of personal charisma.

Since few of us spend time alone, group relationships are extremely important. Why? Because belonging to a special group is often a source of pride and getting the stamp of approval from peers means the difference between having self-esteem and not having it. Participation in a group causes us to behave in ways that sometimes conflict with our individual behavior. Many psychologists say the mere presence of others arouses our emotions, which leads to evaluation apprehension that causes us to perform better on familiar tasks, but worse on unfamiliar ones.

Groups that are highly motivated to achieve a consensus often have a special kind of "group thinking" that envelopes the members and causes them to mysteriously lose their ability to think independently. Group acceptance is more important to some people than thinking logically.

Practically, all trial lawyers fear groupthink. It not only impairs independent thought, but also diffuses personal responsibility. For this reason, many trial attorneys will stress during jury selection that each juror review all of the evidence and make up his or her mind independently from the others.

Overall, general standards regarding appropriate behavior within a group develop over time and become well- established in most areas of the country. Interestingly, there was a paradigm switch in the 1990s regarding jury selection. Instead of which jurors are favorable or unfavorable to a litigant, the key today is knowing which jurors are the worst for a litigant. Nowadays, lawyers want to concentrate on getting rid of the most dangerous jurors, instead of keeping the most favorable.

Leaders and Followers

What if you are a contestant on the TV series *Survivor* and they leave you in a remote place with a small group of people. Are you a lion or a mouse? People who suddenly find themselves part of a small group tend to submerge their individuality and direction, which naturally creates a need for leaders. However, who is going to lead and who will follow? Let us look at real life.

We are constantly required to pick leaders for such things as organizing social events, picking a foreperson for jury duty, electing officers in neighborhood associations, and countless other group activities. At such times, we need to know how to evaluate small groups of people for leaders and followers.

Pursuant to the "great person" theory of leadership, certain people are born to lead others; although, most experts agree that leaders are people who are born with vision, discipline, passion, and conscience. They will come to the forefront, while people who are passive with no vision and no skills will stay in the background.

Some cultural allegories teach that great leaders will come out of the wilderness. However, realistically, it is more likely that great and small leaders will be people with special skills or knowledge in areas such as public administration, contracting, and engineering.

Leaders should be careful thinkers, with organizational abilities, good memories, and the ability to speak convincingly. They will have personal opinions, and will make fifty per cent or more of all the statements and gestures made in their group. Normally, they will adopt friendly and caring body language. They are open and warm, but confident too.

Usually, leaders are between the ages of thirty-three and fifty-five years of age. They will have higher social and economic status, more education, more skills than the average person will, and some managerial experience. They will have a sense of purpose and think in terms of goals Leaders are forceful and consistent with clarity of direction. One caveat, however, is that some people are leaders in some situations but not others.

Followers will be passive with closed off body language and little participatory movement. Under different circumstances they could be leaders themselves, but most of the time they are disinterested, bored, and apathetic with a disconcerting tendency to wander off to "la, la" land both cognitively and emotionally. They will say things like, "I could care less."

Typically, followers are under the age of twenty-five, or over sixty-five years of age, unemployed, retired, and working for somebody else.

They have poor memories, poor detail recall, and poor experiences with life. They dress casually and are unkempt, unorganized, and evasive.

Naturally, a group is better off by an early determination of who are the leaders and followers. Leaders rise to the call, but that is subject to change under different circumstances, so learn the body language of each type. One caveat regarding followers is that even the most faithful sometimes will be hard to lead. People can be unpredictable at times.

In an egalitarian society, being a part of a larger group is highly desirable. The degree to which the members of a group find the group attractive is known as group cohesiveness. Members of a group committed to each have high cohesiveness and low cohesiveness if not very committed. At times, the influence of groups brings out the best in people. But, the dynamics of small groups are more invasive and require more self-protection strategies because people often say things and behave in ways that are stupid. Because group members are affected by the pressure to conform, a false consensus occurs that reinforces the dominant view.

Practical Pointers

Leader and follower relationships usually emerge in accordance with the normative rules of small group formation, which is the subject of countless books. The body language of courtesy, smiling, openness, and etiquette help to overcome early masking barriers, and enable group members to deal with each other since these actions mimic friendships.

Chapter 35

Interview Strategies

"Have you got game."

A vital concern in our economic life is the employer and employee relationship. Employment begins with the job interview and

> Conscientiousness is highly correlated to discipline and organization in the workplace.

sometimes ends there as well. At this critical time, both parties strive to find out as much as they can about each other within the guidelines of applicable federal and state employment laws.

On the threshold, the interviewer wants to set up a relaxed atmosphere for truthful Q and A, and the interviewee seeks to be at ease and put his best foot forward. Good interviewers assure interviewees that the initial interview is simply a conversation to get to know each other better with no right or wrong answers. For example, rigidity and shyness, as well as closed off posturing, correlates with the introverted per-

> The truth is more visual than auditory.

sonality, whereas a sense of humor correlates with intelligence.

The tendency of introverts to admit common faults correlates with a high tendency to "agree". For example, research has shown that workers who demonstrate honesty on the job are also less likely to exhibit negative body language activity such as shouting matches, fights, and using drugs in the workplace.

Studies have shown that the average job applicant is not only tense, but also reluctant to talk to strangers, and will reciprocate only if there is some self-disclosure from the employment interviewer; therefore, the experienced interviewer "primes the pump" by setting up the atmosphere of the interview as a friendly and open exchange of information and not an interrogation. Ipso facto, the interviewer will establish a "turn-taking" technique where both participants in the dialogue takes turns at speaking, which is constantly encouraged by techniques such as partial lead-ins, patience, timely pauses and overall patience.

Evaluation Behavior

In addition to a person's experience and qualifications, interviewers will be judging candidate's nonverbal confidence, competence, and ability to fit in. If a candidate's nonverbal approach contradicts that of the interviewer, he has a problem. The potential employer's style differs from job-to-job. For instance, a potential boss who leans forward with head tilted and places a hand on his cheek is signaling a pensive and evaluation mode. Normally, he is trying to evaluate a candidate's capacity to develop a particular ability for a job.

Evaluation, however, makes most people uncomfortable. For example, if an interviewer is talking, lowers his eyeglasses, and starts peering over them, it produces a negative reaction in the interviewee, because it is condescending with an air of superiority, and creates an uneasy feeling of being under scrutiny.

When an interviewer takes off his eyeglasses, it is probably a gesture to gain time, but if he flings his eyeglasses down, breaks a pencil in two, or slams his telephone in its cradle, he is clearly frustrated by something.

On the other side of the desk, interviewees need to be able to handle their potential boss as well as the job in question. Right off job seekers need to identify the employer's interview style. For instance, a traditional style employer likes signs of success around such as a fancy office, nameplate, desk and awards on the wall. He will wear expensive clothes; stay seated behind his desk with erect posture, expressionless face, and squared shoulders. Also, he will erect barriers by closing the door, putting things between you and him, and controlling his movements. As for job applicants, they should treat the traditional interview with respect and formality.

The interview is not going well when interviewees start pinching the bridge of their noses, slapping their forehead, shaking their legs, rubbing the back of their neck, or closing and squinting their eyes. Such things are negative gestures that convey their concern about the direction the interview is going, or what they are about to say.

Posture is very important to interviewees. They should employ forward body language and a happy facial expression. They must present their views clearly and concisely, while refraining from asking negative questions. Interviewees should make sure they are suited for the job. For example, a person who values independence is not suited for a job in a highly structured, organized, and team oriented occupation. See Appendix "B" for occupational categories.

Interpersonal Job Skills

Career development and job search experts place communication skills as number one on the list of qualities employers are seeking in job applicants. Interpersonal skills are more important to employers than analytical, computer, or organizational skills. A recent study that interviewed CEOs who had lost their jobs revealed that the reason for their torpedoed careers was not due to a lack of technical skills or job knowledge, but a lack of people skills.

> Make 'em laugh,
> Make 'em cry.
> After 20 minutes,
> say goodbye.

Teamwork is the mother lode of business skills. Big corporations place an extraordinary emphasis on belonging. Good job interviewers listen for plural pronouns such as "us" or "we" instead of singular pronouns such as "I" in a potential employee's conversation. Companies are trying to find employees who support team issues instead of individual performance. They like to say, "We are all on the same page here" or "We are one big family".

Probable team players use hand gestures such as crossing the fingers and bringing the hands together in ways that indicate togetherness. Usually, team players have helped to build successful teams once before, so job interviewers look for applicants who have recruited or worked with other team players in the past.

Speaking style is important to employers. Many interviewers believe faster-paced and articulate speech is more credible. Other interviewers favor a homey style reminiscent of President Reagan, which alternated from a loud to soft delivery.

An "intimate voice" and natural rhythm style is ideal from a body language viewpoint, while hedging and excessive hyperbole are suboptimal linguistic tools that tend to free the speaker from full responsibility for the truth. In addition, interviewees need to avoid being too precise and refrain from using "hyper-accurate" speech patterns that the interviewer does not use.

One aspect of employment that many job applicants overlook is longevity. Being number one in the graduating class is unimportant to a typical employer if that person does not intend to stay in one spot long. Employers like law enforcement and the military place a high value on loyalty and continuity if they are going to spend time and money on training new employees. Besides good job skills, employers want employees who will stay put.

> Body language can help you get what you want.

Interviewing for a job, or a new client account, is stressful for many people, because they are not comfortable with talking about themselves, and do not feel comfortable being put on the spot. Too often, the wrong body language emerges to sabotage the relationship before it even gets started. An obvious example is failing to make good eye contact. We know that direct eye contact gives us more credibility and trustworthiness, but at times such as the first job interview, we forget.

When we are under performance pressure, we lose points by coughing, or actually paying too much attention, which breaks down our natural focus. The best practice is to have a sense of humor in case things go wrong. Positive facial expressions during an interview are essential, because interviewees who look distressed are less likely to be successful than those who smile and look happy.

Abe Lincoln said that storytelling is usually self-effacing, and this would not be an asset in an interview. It is advisable to avoid the temptation of telling personal stories. Self-disclosure should be appropriate and limited in scope. Oversharing personal information makes people uncomfortable and is counterproductive.

Practical Pointers

Business no longer takes place exclusively in formal office settings, but at the golf course, health club, and restaurants. Companies expect their employees to be able to perform in all settings with civility and the body language of poised and confident people. Interpersonal communication is a two-sided coin. Reciprocal self-disclosure should be limited and avoid undue prolixity.

Chapter 36

Listen Up

"Real friends listen to each other"

D ue to the postmodern influence of time compression, people are reluctant to spend a great deal of their time patiently listening to others. The constant crowding of our space leads to the crowding of our time, so we fight back by tuning others out, and building dismissive excuses of perpetual deferral such as, "Let's have lunch sometime". As a result, we nurture poor listening habits that inhibit success and happiness in both our social and professional lives. Yet, listening is the other half of intercommunication.

> Learning comes from listening.

The dismal fact is that we spend forty-five percent of our waking hours listening to something, yet promptly forget fifty percent of what we hear. Interaction between people depends on communication, and if we want to get the full benefit of robust dialogue, we need to take our listening skills up a notch or two.

Although average people have the physical capacity to listen to six hundred fifty to seven hundred words per minute, the typical speaker in an average conversation usually talks at the rate of one hundred fifty to one hundred sixty words per minute.

Normally, people listen at the rate of about one hundred twenty-five to two hundred fifty words per minute, despite being able to think at the rate of one thousand to three thousand words per minute. This allows time for people to evaluate, accept, reject, or contest what they hear. As a result, the temptation to interrupt is a difficult impulse to control if it affects people emotionally or morally.

People that are afraid of hearing bad news will try to find a diversion but this strategy runs the risk of creating an impression of being self-centered and impolite. In addition, having to listen intensely and carefully causes some people to experience a sudden paralyzing anxiety that manifests itself as dry mouth, closed- off body language, and mental blocks. People continuously suffering from this malady may not have a clue about how to listen, or have a learning disorder and do not want to be conspicuous.

Listening Efficiency

The first rule in listening well is sensitivity to the speaker and the topic. Many listeners only hear what they want to, and are easily distracted, forgetful, or preoccupied seventy-five percent of the time. In the movie *Cool Hand Luke,* the bad-guy overseer uttered the famous line, "What we have here is a failure to communicate" as he calmly looked down on the downtrodden maverick inmate played by Paul Newman.

Few things are past the infinite of thought, so every communication, both spoken and unspoken, has a purpose, including how and when presented, so we do not always get the full meaning of something unless we are sensitive

> We learn more using our ears than our mouths.

to the many nuances of communicating. For example if something we hear seems inane or ambiguous upon its face, treat it as a good opportunity to gain additional information by open-ended questions like the soft command, "Is that all?"

Sensitivity includes being more careful about "how" we listen. We need to be on guard for harmful listening errors such as trying to rush a conversation or getting ahead of ourselves. Trying to top a speaker's story, letting our interest wander, and frequent interrupting are not conducive to listening.

Good listeners put attitude aside in favor of a consistent listening mode that pays close attention to the needs of the speaker. For example, most speakers need emotional sympathy for what they are saying. People seldom talk just to relate the cold, hard, objective facts. People want sympathy for their position. For this reason, ignoring speakers or disagreeing with them carries a hefty price tag, unless someone is paying you to be contentious.

The second rule to good listening is to agree with people on easy issues and frame difficult issues as "meeting challenges" instead of impossibilities. For example, to keep a conversation moving lean forward slightly, nod at regular intervals, and shake the head understandingly when people relate their problems. Next, follow up with oral feedbacks when appropriate openings occur. Say, "I agree" or "I understand" often, and use the other person's name as frequently as possible. People like hearing their name.

A good listener avoids confrontation. Instead of disagreeing outright, the trick is to focus on shared opinions. Keep personality out of it and stick to the facts. Avoid describing differing views as "yours" or "mine". Be alert to where you are. A big factor is where the conversation takes place. When disagreeing with people, do it privately one-on-one so they do not lose face in public.

Restate what you hear before "venting" on something. Say what you think the other person thinks or feels and do not send off negative body language signals such as rolling the eyes, audible sighing, and speaking in patronizing tones, because people will react to those things instead of what they hear. You do not need to raise your voice to make a point.

Weak Arm Positions:
. Arms crossed.
. Hands in back.
. Hands in pockets.
. Fig leaf position.
. Hands crossing face.

If you are going to disagree, maintain a positive non-threatening voice and body language. When listening on the telephone, the best practice is to speak up and more often. Show interest by changing the contour, pitch, and inflection of your telephone voice at various times.

Good listeners avoid quick movements and nervous distractions such as jiggling coins, shuffling papers, and constantly looking at their wristwatches. Level the playing field by aligning yourself with the speaker eye-to-eye during the conversation. If there is background noise, move closer so that you are able to be easily heard. This sends a positive message that you are interested.

Avoid displacement gestures such as picking the imaginary lint off your clothes. Lint pickers do not approve of what they are hearing, but are eager to give their point of view. Raising your hand with the palm out in front of you says, "Talk to the hand, my face isn't listening".

Maintain open body language and concentrate on understanding, instead of looking for opportunities to respond to every single thing. It is a yellow light when listeners begin to fidget or put a finger to their mouths, which means "enough". In addition, it is bad to cross the arms or sway from side to side, or nod too much as if to say, "You've made your point, now shut up". That makes the speaker feel rushed to finish, skipping valuable information. A good listener's attitude is to make it clear we are listening with the intention of learning, and not just waiting for our turn to "fire back".

Most speakers know they are losing listeners when their listeners appear less riveted to the dialogue or quickly forget what is going down in the conversation. The same is true for listeners who become preoccupied with other things such as clock watching or looking for opportunities to interrupt so they can redirect the conversation. In addition, it is not a good omen when listeners use negating phrases such as "Yes, but…"and "Say that again".

Practical pointers

If you want to make enemies just talk a lot, but if you want to make friends-listen. People will not continue to speak unless they believe that listeners are taking them seriously, and that what they have to say is fairly important.

Normally, people only remember about twenty percent of what they hear over extended periods, but by practicing listening techniques, we can do better. Forget your ego and nitpicking attitude, and learn something by listening, and once you establish a listening strategy stick to it.

Chapter 37

Smoke Signals

"Smoking is a roadblock to intimacy."

Cigar, pipe, and cigarette smoking is a roadblock to intimacy. That may explain why people light up after sex. At any rate, smoking is an excellent real-life lesson in how body language and props work together. Notice how people handle their cigarettes when lighting, smoking, and extinguishing them. For example, if smokers angle their cigarettes and eyes upward, and exhale the smoke up instead of down they are confident that what they are saying will not get them in trouble.

If smokers look down, blow smoke downwards from the corner of their mouths, stare at nearby ashtrays, or take longer to extinguish their cigarettes, they are anxious about what they are saying or feeling. A smoker who lights up in an enclosed room or vehicle is insensitive to the well-being of others.

Smoking gestures are excellent clues to people's attitude because they are habitual and stylistic in ways that are easy to see and interpret. For example, the rate of exhaling smoke is a good clue to a person's attitude. The faster smoke blows upwards the more superior the smoker feels, and the faster it has exhaled downwards the more negative this person feels.

In a game of cards, maneuvers such as these are telltale signs of whether a smoker has a good hand or not. In a sales transaction, blowing smoke upwards means smokers are ready to buy, but if blown downwards, they are not ready to buy, so give them more time to consider purchasing.

A smoker who holds a cigarette between his thumb and forefinger, and barely touches his lips with it, while taking a long draw that he holds in longer than normal, is trying to get the maximum kick out of it. If someone passes what looks like a homemade cigarette to someone else, it is probably contraband. People who dangle a cigarette from their lips while doing something else are veteran smokers who go about daily life and smoke at the same time.

Sometimes people smoking extra long cigarettes are unconsciously using this activity to erect a barrier between themselves and others by symbolically saying, "Keep your distance". Most smokers will smoke their cigar or cigarette down to a certain length every time, so if a typical smoker lights up and then quickly puts it out, he has made a decision to terminate the situation and move on.

Pipe smokers have more to do than cigarette smokers because they are required to fill, tap, stoke, clean, and keep a pipe lit, thus they have more evaluation, pause, and pondering time. Since pipe smoking takes more time, it owes its biggest popularity to people who are required to think abstractly such as theoreticians.

As it happens, pipes have all but disappeared from the smoking landscape of adults, although small pockets of young smokers such as "surfers" smoke pipes just to be different. Other than these atypical groups, nobody wants to smoke a pipe because they produce a heavy, odoriferous, low hanging cloud and have a strong taste, but mainly pipes never caught on with young people, or became acceptable to women, so pipe smoking is a social failure as well as a proven health risk.

Although smoking evolved into a great body language prop, its health risks outweigh any socially redeeming merit. To this day, a few people swear that smoking helps them to concentrate and calm their nerves, while others believe smoking helps to keep their weight down. These beliefs, however cherished, put smoking into the role of providing emotional support and act as displacement activities for smokers to release the emotional and physical tension that build up from daily social and professional encounters.

Of cursory note, some observers do not buy the "tension relief" argument because they believe people are simply addicted to smoking and are unable to quit, latching onto any convenient excuse to continue smoking. Although smoking clues communicate people's attitudes and intentions, some people continue to smoke long after the original attitudes that gave rise to their behavior have completely vanished. They keep smoking because the behavior has become habitual and occurs without conscious thought.

Practical Pointers

An unanticipated psychological effect of smoking is that nonsmokers and healthcare providers are putting smokers on a serious guilt trip. Therefore, people who disappear for thirty minutes from their desk, or at a party, or who huddle with others at building entrances are smokers who have to physically and socially isolate themselves.

Chapter 38

Things We Have

"Possessions control us as much as we control them."

Everyday possessions have a body language all their own. In the context of body language, material things do not move or gesture by themselves, but they do have characteristics such as size, texture, structure, and the suggestion of movement. Therefore, inanimate objects play a huge part in everyday life, and in special ways communicate the thoughts, attitudes, and feelings of their owners.

How much of our life we show to the outside world is a creation we construct from our possessions. Often, people are measured by what they possess as much as by what they do in life. In addition, if we have to make a quick assessment of someone, we learn from the everyday objects that surround him or her.

Home Sweet Home

An eternal quest of mythological proportions is our desire to go home. Like Dorothy in the *Wizard of Oz*, we follow our own "yellow brick road" out of habit in order to get home. Home base, home plate, homecoming, no matter what we call it, home is a special place that everyone cherishes. Why is yearning for home at the heart of many good fables? Is it because being home is relaxing and makes us feel safe and secure, or do people just want a comfortable place to rest their heads?

Actually home is a lot more than a fuzzy sentiment or roof over our head. Our homes are where we feel secure and keep our most prized possessions, raise our family, and spend most of our time. Our homes give us a social identity and the location, type, and condition of our homes reflect what is going on in our life and what matters most to us. Without a doubt, our homes send some very strong messages us.

People pride themselves in where they live and work and this will continue in the future. After 9-11, Americans have a renewed sense of national pride to go along with their sense of local and individual pride. They want a home in a place where they fit in, and their expectations are higher than ever, while interest rates are lower than ever.

Many Americans will put most of their income in a home instead of expensive clothing and luxurious transportation. Most Americans will continue to take pride in where they choose to live and raise their family instead of moving every year or so. For those Americans who choose not to buy a home, mobility, expensive clothes, and lavish transportation is more important to their self-esteem than being tied down to property upkeep, house mortgages, and yard work.

Domestic "Tells"

Is a house cold, damp, gray, and shrouded in fog with a yard full of weeds like in a Dickensian landscape, or it is bright with new paint, flowers, and a manicured lawn? Americans spend as much as forty billion dollars a year on their lawns and landscaping, which is fifteen percent or more of a house's value, and indicates attention to detail and respect for authority.

On the inside, does a house need wallpaper and interior paint? What colors did the owners choose? Are the colors atrocious or appealing only to a narrow few? Interior decor can range from disaster to a tour de force; consequently, the answers to these questions say a good deal about the homeowner.

Houses that are cold, damp, and dark with few openings to the outside are probably that way for insecurity reasons such as the occupants being fearful of letting the outside in, or for economic reasons because the owner does not have enough money to fix or change property characteristics. In many homes, look for signs of priorities. Take into account the relationship of the owner and the property. For example, unfinished work often means the owner underestimated the time and money it would take to finish the job, or the owner is just a procrastinator despite the best of intentions and never seems to get anything done.

Three Unseen Roommates

The three unseen roommates in every house are sight, smell, and sound. Does everything look to be in good working order or do things leak, groan, and smell musty? For example, visible stains, mildew, roof leaks, and foundation cracks are obvious clues about how the owner maintains his property, and if his public image is important.

In many homes, bad house smells such as tobacco smoke, indoor pets, and illness are noticeable, and the homeowners either ignore them or try to mask obvious odors with room fresheners, scented candles, and open windows. The presence of bad odors in a house says a lot about the owner's socialization, cleanliness, health, and sensitivity toward others.

The third unseen roommate in every home is the sound and noise level. Is it noisy and uninhibited, or relatively serene, or quiet enough for home schooling? Is the stereo playing loud, raucous rock and roll, the TV blaring, and children cavorting noisily from room to room? Answers to each of these questions provide a sense of whether the people living there have calm and quiet lives, or lives full of constant, noisy hyperactivity that makes it almost impossible for the occupants to listen to and understand each other.

The style, design, and layout of a house are fundamental clues pointing toward the age of the structure, but also the tastes of the occupants. Young professionals are more mobile today; therefore, first time homebuyers are looking for homes with a good "flow" from room to room and an easy resell.

When "baby boomers" reach their peak earning years, they are ready to enjoy a life of convenience and comfort. Thus, the style, quality of construction, and furnishings suggest whether the owners are flamboyant, cosmopolitan, or conservative.

People cannot be abstracted from the home in which they live. Intangible feelings of harmony, rhythm, and balance resonate in homes and reflect the occupant's strengths and weaknesses. Harmonious and linear house designs telegraph positive messages about the occupants, their status, maturity and potential. Disharmonious, unbalanced, and conflicting arrangements such as ill placed out-buildings, junk scattered about the yard, and uncut grass send negative messages about the occupants and their socio-economic status.

Home Expressories

Interior design is about material relationships, but it is also about contrasts. The furniture and other accessories inside a home warrant special attention. Much the same as the inner clothes we wear, a home's expressories bring the various rooms together and are essential to achieving the overall desired effect. Household furnishings should avoid conflicts with other pieces, and should create the right balance in color, form, and comfort, while taking maximum advantage of the space available.

A sofa and table crowded in a small room seems larger in a less confining space. While symmetrical balance is formal and static, asymmetrical balance is informal and suggests movement.

> "Things are in the saddle and ride mankind."
> Ralph Waldo Emerson

Even small things displayed inside someone's home have a story to tell no matter how seemingly insignificant. For example, weird, offbeat nostalgia items straight out of Kafka are indicative of unusual personal idiosyncrasies. Photographs, degrees, certificates, and trophies reveal interests in life and levels of achievements, while curios and tourist souvenirs disclose trips taken and places visited.

The things we collect are a wealth of information about our hobbies, secret interests, and investments. For instance, does someone's home have a particular style of artwork on display such as modernistic, romantic, or impressionistic paintings, or none at all? Decorative artwork and personal items are clues to emotions and values.

Furniture ranges from the practical, conservative, and inexpensive such as Early American furniture to expensive imported continental antiques. The former indicates a rural background or frugality because the owner does not need to show off, or cannot afford to, whereas ornate, imported, and original antiques mean the owners do not mind spending money on home decor.

For the most part, expressories are either functional or decorative. Some decorative items such as pillows also might serve the functional purpose of providing a protective barrier when laid across the stomach or something to hold onto when lonely.

Items that look good, but have no true taxonomy, and are tied to discretionary income are primarily decorative and reflect taste, whereas dedicated functional possessions such as phone lines, entertainment consoles, computers, sports equipment, hunting, and fishing gear reflect what the owners do in their leisure time.

Clutter Bugs

People who keep everything are obvious clutter bugs. For example, America's beloved poet, Walt Whitman, reputedly never threw anything away, but as far as I am concerned, clutter sucks up our energy the same as disorder sucks up our time.

Clutter bugs are simply unable to let go of things, which gives them an excuse not to get on with life and to let things drag on forever. They are irrepressible xenophobia's, that is, they fear empty spaces. Furthermore, they must surround themselves with possessions to feel secure and reduce anxiety.

Some say the packrat's compulsion to keep everything is the result of a lack of childhood attention and love. Packrats gather things around them to love, but the downside is that material things end up controlling them instead of them controlling the things they so love to stack and pack.

Memorabilia are more decorative than functional, but reflect people's inner identities and aspirations. Psychologists say that obsessive-compulsive people tend to group objects into piles or clusters, which they subjectively believe belong together, but others fail to understand. Piles of newspapers, books, personal papers, magazines, and other things reveal attitudes about health, politics, commerce, and science.

The Neighborhood

"Location, location, location", is the real estate agent's mantra, because they know location sells real property. Putting location aside for a moment, however, the neighborhood is where people sleep, worship, and shop. It is where their biggest asset is located. Moreover, it is where people raise their kids and spend most of their time.

The neighborhood for a vast majority of Americans today is in a fast growing suburb of a major city on either the east or west coasts. Some families will choose where they live because of a desirable school district, while others want a cohesive neighborhood, or close access to a golf course. Whatever the reason, common interests, friends, hobbies, and preferred lifestyles are revealed by the neighborhood where a person lives, whether close in or far removed from a city's center.

In the past, neighborhoods often arose out of a sense of area history and local sentiment, whereas modern neighborhoods are organic communities organized out of a sense of material unity that sends a clear message about the wealth, status, power, and attitudes of its residents, both real and imagined. Some well known neighborhoods have become power points in the body of American society.

Real estate agents are keenly aware that most potential buyers will not even get out of the car if a neighborhood lacks "curb appeal". Gentrified neighborhoods are safer investments and make reselling homes easier; consequently, real estate agents correctly figure they are halfway to making a sale if potential buyers like the looks of the neighborhood where a house is located and aren't afraid to get out of their car.

The Workplace

The workplace and furnishings of most people is no accident. They reflect who the occupiers are and what is important to them. Realizing this, the prominent CEO of a highly successful computer company recently stated to the news media that he knows within five minutes whether the company he is thinking of buying is the right fit or not.

This CEO was able to tell whether an acquisition was a good match or not by observing how the other company's CEO set up his office. Telling clues are the size of an office and its configuration. There should be no barriers to interaction. He said that office furnishings invariably signal clues about the ego of the occupant, the office's comfort level hints at the occupant's sensitivity, while its location is a statement about the occupant's power in the company.

People do not display things with which they have no ego involvement. For instance, hanging calendars indicate the importance of time and its impact on daily life, while artwork gives a sense of the tastes and humor of the owner. Does a person's office have any family pictures on the walls or something else? Things like coffee cups and clocks are "mood" and "time" regulators.

What other props are present? Some things like certain books are "thought" regulators. The number of books in a person's office indicates how much attention he pays to a particular subject, whereas different types of books indicate different attitudes. A neat and ordered office shows fastidiousness and organization, but if stacks of unreturned phone calls lie about on a person's desk, that person is not making sure the customer always comes first.

Automotive Body Language

Ever since the invention of the automobile, Americans have fallen in love with their cars. We think so much of our automobiles that we make cars an extension of our world. In other words, some say we are what we drive! For example, practical people buy an economical car that is small and compact, or a sedan that is dependable and conservative. Materialistic people encapsulate themselves inside expensive and luxurious vehicles with amenities such as tinted windows, temperature controls, adjustable seats, and entertainment packages to meet all their comfort needs. Such cars also let them be anonymous without having to deal with outsiders.

Cars signal the big three ego trips: Money, power, and success. As a rule of thumb, the bigger the vehicle the bigger the pocket book of the drivers. At the other end of the scale are the older, junky cars known as "ghetto sleds". Big vehicles for females indicate big families and big houses in middle-class suburbia.

There are a few fundamental ground rules in automobile acquisition. While large car owners want comfort, safety and luxury, small to mid-size car buyers want reliability and mileage. Most convertibles show up in areas where there is good, warm weather, thus a person who buys a convertible sports car is probably single, young, upwardly mobile, and likes the top down in warm weather.

Minivans are for people with pets, kids, and extra-curricular activities, and are most popular in regions like Chicago, whereas Suburbans are King in Texas. A person who buys a SUV physically elevates himself above other automobiles, controls more space, and is able to afford the cost of driving one.

Pickup drivers are mostly males, and if they add after market equipment such as brush guards and fog lights, they are a bit more independent than the rest. Sedans are popular with families that want safety, more head and foot room, and large trunks. Light trucks and SUVs meet the needs of folks who need to haul things. New compact car owners need to save money because they are on a frugal budget and are often just getting out on their own.

Many car purchases reflect buyer emotions instead of intellectual reasoning, and this is why a choice in car colors also sends a message.

For example, white is the all-around most popular color and the choice of drivers who like to blend in and not get traffic tickets. Red draws the most attention including the most traffic citations, which is the cost of being hot and sporty.

Black is a favorite choice of young males because it is aggressive and macho. Blue is rich looking and is the choice of conservative middle-aged folks. Silver is very popular and represents success, speed, and class. Yellow is in your face and screams expensive, which is why it is never on sedans, but is the color of a lot of Corvettes and Hummers. People make color choices based on a very subjective calculation of what will serve them best, and not what other people will like.

Practical Pointers

Material possessions, and where we display them, are clues to who we are. The home place, the neighborhood, and workplace are a pastiche of power and solidarity indicators. Most homes are full of illuminating clues to who we are and aspire to be, and such clues are less likely to be a contrivance due to a home's intimacy and its "anchor-like" attributes.

Since working and driving evolved out of the hunting activities of our ancient ancestors, cars have names such things as "Ramblers", "Land Rovers", and "Trail Blazers". Other cars have animal names such as "Mustangs", "Cougars", and "Impalas" that are a reminder of our distant link to the animal kingdom.

Cars also send a message about the owner such as, "I'm rich, I'm powerful, and I'm successful," or "I'm a family person". Most of all, automobiles represent the freedom and independence of most Americans. Just try taking their car from them!

Chapter 39

Speech Characteristics

"Inflection is the body language of speech."

Communications are verbal, nonverbal, electronic, manual, digital, analogue, wireless, and so on. Each kind is different with its own characteristics. Limiting communication to just one mode not only will be doomed to failure, but also will say very little about the "emotional" and "attitudinal" aspects of its content. It is estimated that verbal communications represent only ten percent of a person's "subjective perception" of other people. See Appendix "D".

Verbal communications, the experts argue, are rarely ideal and many people tend to hear only what they want to. They point out that oral communication is subject to improvement in two ways: One is the simple expedient of matching people with similar backgrounds such as matching salespersons with customers from a similar time, place, and background. The second way is to stress the vocal quality or the speech characteristics people use when communicating with each other. As stated before, it is not what people say, but how they say it that is important.

The body language of speech, or paralanguage, consists of voice quality, cadences, contours, pitches, tones, inflections, paces, dialects, snorts, hesitations, and accents. Each one reveals an aspect of how people feel about what they are saying.

Oral communication is heavily dependent upon highly personalized codes of meaning inherent in our choice of words and structural context. Representational mental concepts, relational coding, and inferencing are predicates to the shaping of these complex meanings. We are communicating nonverbally even if we say nothing, but when we do speak, we use a variety of communication skills to get out the "on" message instead of the "off" message".

In the personal context, people generally talk about things with which they have some ego involvement. If their body language suggests that they are reluctant to say anything, they are not ego involved or they feel diminished by their involvement. As a result, their message depends on utility maximization or preformed ideas about what is best for them.

Technology is the soul of communication. It speeds up the pace of life and eases people's jobs in many ways, but it also is demanding and time-consuming. For example, technology provides a constant flood of information, but realizing its benefits generally requires knowledge and understanding.

Understanding communication involves a few basics. In the broadest possible sense, every communication relationship involves a source or "sender", a channel or "medium" through which the information travels, and the "receiver". Two lesser variables are the message and the context of the communication.

The sources or "senders" who send the message are better equipped to deliver more powerful and credible messages if they have some expertise, trustworthiness, attractiveness, and likeableness. Messages travel through the internal biases of the sender and the receiver, which act as filters. That is, the sender and receiver process all messages through personal filters such as their emotional and attitudinal frame of mind.

A rule of thumb is that the higher a person's ego involvement, the lower his latitude of acceptance of new information becomes, and the lower his ego involvement the wider his range of acceptance becomes. As a result, people often hear and see only what they want to. A striking example is the price range of property. Outside of their preconceived price range, it is hard to get through to people.

People receive and process messages they hear and see in or two ways: by *periphery route* processing that depends on certain non-message peripherals such as the credentials and similarities of the messenger, or by *central route* processing that occurs when we accept as true the direct, unvarnished base line facts. Imagine in the first example a speech given by former President John F. Kennedy on car safety, and in the second example a technical car safety article in "Consumer Reports".

Channels are the mediums for sending messages, while message components are the kinds of information sent. For example, the less informed we are about a subject, or the more frightened, then the more emotional body language influences us.

> Getting to the bottom line is reductive logic.

Communicating clearly involves much more than the mere words people use. For instance, concurrent vocal quality and speech ability also make a huge difference in the impact and meaning of verbal communications. They enable people to nail down the content, truthfulness, and feelings of the message sender.

In sizing someone up, people take in account those vocal clues that help them connect their life experiences with the words and expressions the other person uses. Thus, most human communication is composed of several components all put together.

As said before, we all share some similarities despite our uniqueness. The good news is that conformity is not all bad, since interpersonal communication flows most effectively when people are in synchronization with each other. The upshot is that we usually persuade other people only if we talk their language. In business, the arts, education, and other endeavors effective communications are vital to establishing an atmosphere of trust and confidence, which are the social lubricants that make working together possible.

During interaction with others, it makes sense to adjust our communication style to be more "outcome determinative" by matching the style of others as much as possible in a short time frame. By matching and mirroring verbal and nonverbal body language in a respectful way, we quickly gain better rapport and enhance relationships no matter where we happen to be at the time.

Self-directed, indiscriminate copying and mimicry are offensive activities to most people, but crossover mirroring such as matching a person's arm movements with another small arm gesture is hardly noticeable. Always stay alert to the body language of other people in order to sharpen your own posture, body movements, and speaking style.

No one will argue with the concept that oral communication is more effective if we make listeners more receptive to our message. For instance, saying something positive makes listeners more receptive than if we talk trash. Communication experts have proven most of us only half listen with our minds already made up. Since many people tend to hear what they want to and not necessarily what someone is saying, it is always a good idea to get verbal promises and oral agreements in writing. Never make a business agreement over the telephone.

Speaking Styles

Some people are verbose and bombastic when speaking and others are devoid of anything interesting to say. Vocabulary is an indication of people's education, place of residence, and ethnic background, and speaking style is a good indication of their expertise, credibility, and trustworthiness.

Former President Reagan, for example, tried to give his speeches in a "homey", warm, and simple way that intentionally did not sound too intellectual. He began by prefacing many of his remarks with "Well . . ." It was his speechwriter, Peggy Noonan, that made him sound lovable and down-to-earth. For example, who can forget President Reagan's most famous line, "Mr. Gorbachev, tear down your wall".

The first thing that occurs to me when I encounter a person who talks too much is that this person does not have anyone to talk to because he or she is so verbose. Over-talk is a linguistic tool that helps free the speaker from inner anxieties such as loneliness. Intensifiers like those used by Ed Sullivan in his "really, really good" monologues are low voltage in power speaking, and colloquial barbarisms like "It's

| Fluency trumps disfluency |

like, you know, sooooo whatever," and "Wazzup dawg" rapidly become over-used linguistic crutches.

Language purists consider the words "like" and "way" to be low power fillers or discourse particles similar to "um" and "well". Words like this are bad because they often change the meaning of a sentence. For example, "like" is a hedge when the speaker is not positive about the accuracy of what he is going to say such as "It's like three or four miles away." The words "like" and "way" often preface exaggerations such as "It is way too far." Words such as, "I guess that . . ." or "I'm not sure, but . . .", and modifiers such as "rather" and "quite" are weasel words showing a lack of conviction.

Halting speech is low power communication that is indicative of insecurity, nervousness, excitability, biological, or medical problems. A person searching for the right words probably is not sure of what he wants to say. I believe that unless you are able to articulate it, you do not understand it yourself. People who use the word "awesome" and other worn out clichés are lazy because clichés are a way not to think about answers.

Talking Loud and Fast

Is a loud mouth a little bit tipsy, frustrated, or legitimately trying to make a point? Usually the louder people talk, the more insecure they are. Robust talk can also mean the speaker comes from a big family, or is immature, or is feeling discursive after the second bottle of Chardonnay. The trick is to distinguish temporary emotional states from consistent character traits. A valuable relationship skill is to be able to recognize deviations as well as normal patterns of speech under temporary as well as permanent circumstances.

A deviation occurs when a normally quiet and passive person suddenly speaks more assertively with higher volume and excitability. In addition, if a man suddenly lowers his voice, it probably means he is audibly trying to hide something and is saying by implication, "What else do you want me to tell you?" If a person's voice is rising along with his adrenalin, he is on the verge of trying to intimidate or dominate a listener by "over speaking".

Everyone has run across a fast-talking con man like the "Music Man" of River City, Iowa. We listen while he talks a good show, but inevitably he leaves us wondering, "What did he say?" Fast talk is a way to gloss over unpleasant facts. However, the real reason most of us instinctively do not fully trust fast-talkers is because our parents warned us against them. Clearly, the association between rapid speech and untruthfulness exists. However, this is just one possibility since some garrulous fast-talkers hail from regions of the country where fast talk is the norm.

On the other hand, fast talk is not always bad because speaking rapidly conveys a sense of urgency and sometimes is able to get us out of a predicament. For instance, changing the tone and speed of our voice is a way to terminate a telephone conversation quickly. By speeding up the pace, we are saying we are becoming impatient and the conversation needs to be over.

Some people intentionally talk faster because they enjoy hearing themselves talk and do not need to understand what they are saying as long as it "sounds" good, and at other times, they are impatient, uneasy, or restless. Consequently to determine the motives of fast-talkers, always take into consideration the context, pacing, consistency, and context of their speech.

The pitch in communication is the fundamental frequency level of sounds made by the normal human voice. People speak in a calm lower pitched voice for the most power, or they speak in a shrill, high-toned pitch that ranks lower in social power. The more excited, scared, or agitated people get, the higher the pitch of their voice gets, which is clear clue to their state of mind.

It is relatively easy to determine a person's emotional state by noting other body language clues accompanying changes in pitch. For example, people who are peeved or serious about something will intentionally lower their voice and slow down their pace while saying something such as, "I'm going to spell-it-out for you". This has greater impact and social traction than a high-pitched admonition from Barney Fife.

The tone of a person's voice is a good indicator of his emotions. Intonation affects the meaning of what we say by stressing different syllables or words. American speaking styles do not use intonation as heavily as some languages; nevertheless, most Americans are able to change the tone of their conversational voice in different ways by using verbal body language. An illustration of this point is how easily people put off unwanted advances by the tone of their voice and the emphasis they put on words like "if" and "but".

Similarly, some people stress syllables by phonetically stretching them out in a lyrical scooping way, or produce combination tones like a "difference" tone, a "summation" tone, and a "descending" tone in one sentence. Unemotional speech is as flat as your spare tire when you need it, and suggests that you are uninterested in the substance and content of what you are saying, or that you have no feelings about what someone is saying, or that you harbor some resentment about the conversation.

Try the following exercise as an illustration of the effect of stressing certain syllables: Frame a simple question three different ways to change its meaning. An auxiliary inversion is something similar to, "What *have* you done?" A tag question is "You've done it now, *haven't* you?" Unlike America, tag questions are a popular form of talking in the United Kingdom.. A rising-intonation contour question is something like "You have *done* what?"

Also, try saying a simple phrase such as, "Justice for all" in a flat pitch that sounds like a declarative, and then say it with a rising intonation contour stressing the word "all" at the end, which makes it sound like a question. Try this exercise using the phrase "Who Am I", or the amusing phrase "He's not just right", but practically any sentence will do.

If we confide good news to a friend, we naturally expect them to be happy about it, but if they respond with a flat and unemotional 'whatever', then we have a problem. Suddenly, we are unable to communicate because what we hear greatly affects our responses. To get to the crux of the problem, we need to take careful note of what we are hearing.

By paying close attention to paralanguage such as pitch, tonality, pausing, hesitations, hem hawing, and tag lines, we are able to read where a speaker is going with his train of thought, which is a valuable tool that enables us to anticipate his next move.

Nobody is interested in conversing with a person who has too much to say or rambles from one subject to another. Usually an extremely garrulous person is highly uninformed, insecure, afraid to look stupid, or is unprepared for the conversational message they need to send.

"Brevity is the soul of the law" is a well-known aphorism. Nonetheless, before modern litigation practices, many trial lawyers who were unprepared, or who had a bad factual case, were fond of saying, "If you have a good case let the facts speak for themselves, but if you don't have the facts pound the table and keep talking". Legal legends like Clarence Darrow, Temple Houston, Moman Pruit, and many other lesser-known barristers all had the ability to talk in court for hours, days, and even weeks at a time with no difficulty at all. A story is told about the man in the audience of one of Temple's speeches who said afterward, "I don't know what he said, but it shore (sic) lifted me outta my boots."

Not Saying Enough

What does it mean when people keep quiet when they need to be saying something? Does their silence mean they are trying to avoid or cover up something? People try to avoid stressful unpleasantness, emotionally difficult answers, and embarrassment by incomplete or sub vocal responses. All three are legitimate reasons for not talking in addition to other ego defenses as well.

People convey power and solidarity by their speech. Silence and not saying much are signs of exclusion from relationships and lack of power. They show weak solidarity and an acknowledgement of the supremacy of others. To be powerful, speech should be direct and expressive of the self. On the other hand, excessive speech usually is a sign of non-power commonly used by weak people.

Subservient people are poor communicators in either the verbal or nonverbal modes. In general, their speech is laden with self-abnegation and self-suppression. Their faces will be passive and their posture poor. They will be inattentive and unable to communicate much of anything. Their subconscious self may manifest other signs of non-status too.

For non-responsive people, it is a good idea to avoid asking questions that call for a simple "yes" or "no" answer and ask open-ended questions that lead to the areas you want to explore. Occasionally, some things are so personal or private that it is best to leave them alone. On the other hand, the sine qua non of all psychological questions designed to open doors is, "How do you feel about that."

Aside from the "did not, did too" conversations of children, a short conversation from an adult could be a sign of antisocial personality disorder or that he or she is self-conscious. In addition, it could indicate a conversation is scripted like that of a customer service representative at an insurance company. Someone who is forgetful or who uses few words to economize his speech, will converse in short, clipped sentences.

The task is to determine the difference between a short answer that is intentional and one that is non-intentional. Sometimes, when a pause precedes a short answer, it is a signal for more information before answering in full.

Conversational detouring is answering a direct question with a question. This frustrating practice avoids having to commit to an incriminating answer. My wife uses this maneuver to avoid a proper answer to a question of mine, and to put me on the defensive. Usually, this pre-emptive strike takes the form of a recrimination to deflect criticism such as answering a question with, a question such as, "Well, what about you", and "Haven't you ever done that?"

By and large, a person who does not say much, noticeably hesitates, or detours is naturally shy, pensive, or introverted. To find out if he is shy, or intentionally censoring himself to hold back, or if something more sinister is going down, we need to uncover more clues by asking probative open-ended questions such as, "Is there something else you want to add?"

Although I do not condone it, repeating a question begins to have some repetition value after awhile. At times, repetition works on people whose body language signals a clear reluctance to answer. Some people scoff and sneer at everything with a sort of fidgeting and uneasy behavior, and while their snarling speech clips say they "wouldn't dare attempt an answer" to a particular question, they actually do have some ideas on the subject. In reality, the front people exhibit to the outer-world is not always their true feeling about their capabilities. They are being intentionally modest, but inside they believe they are more than what other people see, much more.

For example, the seminal philosophy of Plato stresses that earthly things are only copies of greater unchanging absolutes. The transcendental doctrine of the nineteenth-century American writers, Henry David Thoreau and Ralph Waldo Emerson espouses the idea that knowledge must extend beyond the limits of experience, and renaissance philosophy, brought back to life in the 20th century, defends human dignity and worth. In other words, no one thinks they are value free.

Whining and Complaining

Nobody likes the distinct voice of a whiner or complainer. For one thing, people cannot always tell whether whiners want a solution or just sympathy. People who raise money for charitable causes know not to beg or whine to get donations. Lawyers know not to beg or whine to a jury about their client's case, or the jury will hold it against them.

In my experience, the litigants who get the largest trial awards are victims of obvious "Oh my God" injuries, but still do not overly complain. Instead, they convey an attitude to the jury of "I'm going to make it", with a little help. In a few cases, complaining has a "squeaky wheel gets the grease" value if it is not overdone, which is often the case.

Ironically, chronic whiners and complainers have difficulty with relationships, but still need others around them. They complain and whine ad nauseam as a technique to manipulate those around them without forceful words. For example, I had a client who told me his father-in-law adopted a system of chronic nagging, complaining, and criticizing as a way to put everyone in his family on a guilt trip. He complained that no one ever came to see him. He whined about his family putting him on a shelf, and so on, repeatedly without offering any proof.

In reality, his family saw him on a regular basis. One family member or another called him every day, but when he did not get his way all the time, he resorted to negativity on an aggravatingly personal level, which in turn caused his family to respond negatively. Not surprisingly, children are highly adept at using this technique, often going from one family member to another until they succeed in complaining to the right person.

Overall, chronic whiners tend to be infantile despite their age, and will exhibit correspondingly childish behavior. They simply withdraw, pout, and feel sorry for themselves in a cathartic effort to get others to feel sorry for them. Chronic whiners and complainers will use the same aggravating strategy repeatedly until they finally discredit themselves. Going to the well too often dries it up.

Sadly, whiners and complainers are never happy. Perpetually unhappy, whiners and complainers seem to feel the world owes them something instead of a single authentic complaint that is provable. It is a difficult trait to overcome because whiners are reluctant to admit they have this problem, and at times, it actually works for them and makes them feel a little better.

If people only complain sparingly, it is okay. When they regularly complain about their needs, however, they become neurotic, and it makes little difference whether their needs are gratified or frustrated. Actually, these people are looking for something else besides gratification, so the rest of us just have to deal with it.

Self-Editing

As said before, not many of us are capable of communicating pure objective facts, because we are ordinary people with no normative expectation of having to render an objective account of events or ourselves later on. Accordingly, people have the natural tendency to "level" out the objective facts by smoothing over unpleasant topics and glossing over the details of abnormal situations and irregularities. People also use novelties and not quite true pontifications to avoid the appearance of ignorance. Jurors are notorious for making up things for the sake of appearances.

Self-edited versions of events end up in memory as more homogenous, less incongruous, and more palatable than what actually happened. A reverse cognitive process in the world of verbal body language is "sharpening", which is overemphasizing certain details in order to counter monotonous factual thinking and avoid the pitfalls of stereotyping.

People have ingeniously developed many ways to circumvent the objective radar screen when it comes to unpleasant subjects such as their shortcomings, personal problems, and mistakes. In the long run, the correct facts and the true meaning of events often do not surface, but become hidden, masked, or opaque at best. This is another reason body language is such a valuable interpretative tool.

Control is a major component of social power and a pervasive characteristic of human coexistence that weighs heavily in our lives; therefore, it is a good bet that with few exceptions people who overtly attempt to control a conversation have a hidden agenda. By trying to control a conversation, people have a feeling of mastery over the situation.

Not many people are willing to debate issues without some kind of confrontational agenda that involves self-editing. For instance, people who chatter like magpies talking too loud and too much about themselves have an attention-seeking agenda in the same way name-droppers seek self-importance by leading people to believe that they know important people when they probably don't.

Stammering and Sub-vocalization

Not only is expressing ourselves well through fluent speech a daily challenge, but also discovering the exact meaning of someone else's speech. For instance, stuttering is a disfluency that affects three million people in the United States. Stuttering typically includes involuntary hesitations in the flow of speech, stammering, and repetition, which hinders normal communication. Strangely, however, stammering tends to improve or disappear when sufferers sing or speak in unison even though it is counter intuitive. The operative word is "involuntary", since voluntary disfluency unbelievably is a learned mannerism to suit a speaker's style.

Slow speech, muted speech, and other sub-vocalizations outside of our normative expectations are not necessarily congenital speech flaws. For one thing, people who are unable to articulate something quick enough, loud enough, or concise enough does not mean they are lazy, mentally slow, or uncomprehending. People who talk slower than the occasion calls for may be in a mood of reflective lassitude, or more likely, they are from an area of the country where slower speech is the norm.

Language is seldom static but is constantly changing from generation to generation. Regional dialect is part of a folk language that blankets the country like a patchwork quilt, and as a result, we are able to get an idea of where people come from by the way they talk. For example, "dese," "dem," and "dose" point to New York City.

Sub-vocalization has many causes such as fatigue, illness, and personal grief to name a few. At times, there is an intentional desire to be inaudible such as someone trying to mimic a Hollywood actor like Marlon Brando, because people like the powerful contrast of a big, strong figure who talks softly. In many instances, people intentionally lower their voices to barely audible when they have to admit something potentially embarrassing.

Even under normal circumstances, in the pronunciation of a few letters of our alphabet the consonantal sound needs an *–ee* or an *–ay* sound attached to it to make it readily audible. In addition, another difficulty exists in the similarity of certain consonantal sounds such as D, P, B, and so on. Consequently, muted speech is subject to interpretation in the context in which it occurs.

Mumbling and Other Disfluencies

Mumbling is a common disfluency that results from inarticulation or muted speech. Typically, a mumbler mutes his speech so much that it is inaudible to the untrained ear, which includes most everybody. Since people cannot hear what a mumbler is saying, the natural inclination is to ask them to speak up, but lamentably a non-elective mumbler is incapable of clear speech for very long.

Elective mumblers who are fully capable of speaking up will cover their mouth with something, or have a mouthful of food as they are talking, and the worst we are able to say about them is they are impolite, but if they avert their gaze and look away they are attempting to gloss over an uncomfortable message. Ordinarily, to get the last word in or equivocate most of us try mumbling something as we turn or walk away. Therefore, if this happens to you, it is your cue to say, "Wait a minute, let's start over".

People who ramble are usually unaware of the difficulty others have in understanding them. Rambling has a variety of causes but is most likely due to lack of focus and clarity of purpose because of common problems such as confusion or arousal agents that make people's speech discursive and desultory.

Normally we do not hear a person's breathing, so when breathing is audible there is a reason. Specifically, a person with noticeable breathing is often expressing sexual interest or physical arousal, which usually occurs with other obvious clues such as the use of licentious idioms and obscenities.

On the other hand, a breather may have problems breathing due to emphysema, chronic bronchitis, or worse, but a noticeable cough or wheezing is usually present. If we rule out sexual arousal and physical complications, which are obvious in other ways, then heavy breathing is most likely the result of an emotional state. For example, noticeable breathing such as a sudden gulp of air typically means a person is surprised or startled at something they see or hear.

Pausing, hemming, and hawing are ways to drag out a conversation while thinking about what to say next. Good speakers will avoid such conversational negatives by better preparation.

Choice of Words

In *Alice's Adventures in Wonderland and Through the Looking Glass (1871),* Louis Carroll gave the world a famous literary allusion when he had Humpty Dumpty declare, "When I use a word, it means just what I choose it to mean-neither more or less". People, like Humpy Dumpty, use words that suit them. If they want to call a horse a cow-that is okay-but only as long as other people share the same meaning.

The world famous philosopher and linguistic scholar, Ludvig Wittgenstein, hypothesized that words are tools. Words are flat or dull, the same as a tool, and they are employable in such a variety of ways that their intended meaning exists in their usage, and many words have more than one meaning depending on the literal or loose context of their usage. Body language is much the same way.

Although words convey ideas and body language conveys feelings, word choices and body language intertwine so much that the easiest way to think about the connection is to treat words as having their own body language in the way that they are used.

If you control your language, you can control the ideas that people have about the world. Words have the power to evoke images, sounds, and feelings the same as nonverbal communications. For example, certain words such as "un-American", "radical", reactionary", "subversive", and "agitator" are loaded with emotional appeal that evokes negative associations. Other words appeal to the senses like "tick-tock," "thunder," "ice-cold," "gritty," "spicy," and "fragrant," Omnibus words are used for large entities such as institutions and religion. Examples are "Feds", "Ma Bell", and "they".

Sometimes, words start a relationship and words break them up. Words provoke fights and put us in good or bad moods. Words convince others through good imagery and dissuade us through bad imagery. The mystery of how much body language a particular word has both emotionally and attitudinally depends on how it is used and what users agree that the word means. For example, the word "goodbye" is a simple farewell, a threat, or a command depending on how, when, and where people choose to use it.

A pastor I know once told me that he was so busy he was unable to get everything done. He said he did not know how to say "no" to anyone. I advised him to try telling people "maybe", because in my house the term "maybe" means "no!" That is to say, the ability to turn down something flat includes the contingency "maybe" that never occurs, but does not hurt so much. In addition, he might try, "I'm not in position to", which also means No! At any rate, I believe it is a good thing to do, because a counterwill is essential to longevity and a healthy personality.

At the most fundamental level, words are shared communications about life's experiences. Yet, we do not all see the same things or have the same life experiences; consequently, many words have novel meanings as referents depending on the point of view of the speaker. When a choice in words has a novel meaning known only to the speaker, then we must look for other clues as to meaning.

Words have more body language muscle and people are likely to pay more attention to the specific words in a sentence if they are part of a personal criticism or insult. Word choices like everything else, are more difficult to understand if they relate to negative ideas and events, if they are in the passive voice, and if they are ambiguous. See Appendix "A".

Slangdom

Slang, regional dialect, patois, and jargon make up the kingdom of Slangdom. This kingdom is alive with active words that have a lot of freedom, emotion, and dimension. They are "working" words that get down to business quickly and are rarely flat or slow getting to the point, thus speeding up communication between people. For good measure, they also define a community of users and exclude outsiders, thus help-ing people to identify with each other and bond together. The provenance of slang lies in the many subcultures that thrive within a nation's main culture. Besides making large groups of simi-lar people feel like they are different from others, slang becomes the easy-to-understand language of "insid-ers" and leaders, while fostering people's sense of cohesion and integra-tion with each other.

> "What chew lookin' at? You lookin' at me? Forgettaboutit. Nuff said."
> Gangster idiom

People naturally want to sound and act like their peers in order to have something in common with them; consequently, they manipulate speech and body language to meet their needs. People are constantly trying to communicate the best and newest way they know by putting local color and vitality into their everyday speech. In this way and not through formal education that many people, if not the majority of us, learn all about nuances of love, death, sex, and violence.

Euphemisms

Have you ever gotten a memo that your job has been "outsourced" due to "downsizing"? Words such as these seem to have an industry-wide rationale behind them instead of saying the company finds it expedient to fire you. "Outsourcing", "outplacement", and "downsizing", do not sound as harsh as a Donald Trump style "you are fired". Since, words such as "outsourced" convey a meaning somewhere between the truth and outright deception, they fit in the euphemism category.

Euphemism is a Greek word for "sounding good speech", and is a linguistic airbrush people use to make the hard vicissitudes of life easier to accept, which in my opinion constitutes linguistic body language. Generally, there are two varieties of euphemism: The positive kind used to inflate or magnify reality such as a super title for a menial job and the negative kind that deflates and diminishes reality such as words that gloss over death, disease, and bodily functions.

Affected elegance is a form of verbal body language that is in wide use by people hoping to appear as members of polite society. In addition, from time to time, practically everyone will use euphemistic elegance to conceal things such as lying, dying, and buying. People also convey difficult requests, suggestions, and commands by putting them into the form of polite questions accompanied with a smile.

Since euphemisms give rise to vague assurances, they are highly popular in the domain of politicians, diplomats, lawyers, doctors, and government bureaucrats. Although not limited to these groups, people in such categories seem to have the greatest need to bombard others with euphemisms that present a better image or "spin" to things they are promoting. The use of euphemisms is particularly effective when cleverly joined with practiced nonverbal body language techniques that add an extra injection of vitality.

Linguistic fig leaves that evade or sanitize the truth are reprehensible. Labeling blatant cheating as mere "technical fouls" and excusing lying if it is "plausibly deniable" are examples. Normally, most of us do not have a problem with the use of euphemisms that soften the inward anxieties, conflicts, and problems we face, but when euphemisms become ambiguities that mask the truth, the arrow of goodness starts to point away.

When is it all right to use a euphemism is the sixty-four dollar question? Is it better to label a divorce as a "boundary shift", "acute admiration failure" or "intimacy break" instead of a devastating breakdown of a legal relationship? The answer depends on the context of use and intuition about the possible effects.

Overused catch phrases just like euphemisms hinder good communications. I do not think it is too cynical to say that phrases such as "no problem" and "it works for me" are annoying because they do not really say anything. Words such as "Duh" and "Not" are mildly sarcastic, and the phrase, "Been there, done that" seems a little self-righteous and egotistical. "Enjoy" and "no problem" are entreaties used by almost every service person in the country, and rank high on the list of overused things to say along with the ubiquitous "Have a really good day".

Verbal and nonverbal communications go hand in hand and together produce a kind of magical synergy. The words we use amplify or modify our body movements. In fact, human speech without corresponding body language is slippery, opaque, filtered, and difficult to understand. A lack of hand gestures when speaking is a sign of uncertainty, lack of feeling, and hesitation, or if the hands remain clenched at their sides, of a scripted performance.

Although there is no easy way to cushion the bumpy road of harsh reality, we are adept at devising words and phrases with special meanings and a body language of their own, which is good. It is only when euphemisms, acronyms, waffling, and "group speak" are intentionally deceptive that ordinary citizens and hapless consumers suffer their misuse.

Since language is forever changing and evolving, and because people have a knack for euphemisms, trickery, and even self-deception, the best practice is to pay close attention to people's intentional inflections and word choices when assessing their motives and intent. Bear in mind that some people are physically unable to speak correctly, which is different from verbal dishonesty.

Practical Pointers

Communicating is a daily challenge because human beings deploy a wide array of stylistic communication devices to express thought. Creative conversationalists are able to use oral gesturing skills to enhance raw realities, convey important feelings and attitudes, and avoid stereotyping.

People do not always say what they mean and mean what they say, which results in diffuseness, redundancies, and colorful idioms that makes their speech more dramatic than informative. For example, paralanguage, clever word choices, and catchy phrases are useful linguistic tools under appropriate circumstances, but on the other hand, they tend to permeate our intellectual processes, and give rise to self-deception, vague answers, lazy thinking, and subtle cover-ups.

Chapter 40

Negative Body Language

"Just say no"

No one is one-dimensional. People are not cardboard cutouts, and everyone has a positive and a negative side. Most of the time, people control their negative side, but sometimes they do not and they can be brutal. For some people, the hardest sacrifice of all is to let go of their negativity, which presents a moral dilemma.

Do we carry negative people out of control or abandon them? The answer is easier when the body language of bad behavior manifests itself as more of a chronic disorder that is treatable than a random whimsy. What are the emblems of bad behavior?

Clear-cut monsters and lesser evils are easily recognizable by their body language. No horrendous dark forces, conspiracies run amok, or vampires can evade notice for long in the world of body language. When bad behavior disguises itself as goodness people need to be concerned.

Incongruent behavior resulting from people saying one thing, but doing something else is not good. An example is the mother who verbally scolds her child, but at the same time holds her arms out and smiles in a loving way.

Behavior that seems out of place consists of things such as in-your-face finger pointing, hand wringing, fist clenching, and other grandiose or daring gestures while trying to appear composed. Other examples of incongruent body language are gestures like defiantly placing the hands on the hips, looking at the floor, swaying, foot tapping, and lip smacking when we try being something other than our real selves.

Resistance is typically a negative behavior. Instead of cooperating when it is best for both moral and salutary reasons, we become defensive, guarded, surly, and touchy. If we get angry, we become hostile, argumentative, and belligerent. We get ourselves into trouble by raising our voices because loudness translates into rudeness.

If our temper gets the best of us, it is wise to make a quick exit instead of "venting" it. Always avoid building ourselves up at the expense of others, and give people the benefit of the doubt. Hovering around people is also a negative act since it risks invading their personal space as well as being an unnecessary annoyance.

To avoid social negativism, avoid pointing at body parts in a menacing manner such as running fingers across the throat. It is not funny. Do not speak to people in patronizing or scolding tones of voice, or demean people by mocking the way they walk or act due to physical impediments. Do not give fake names. Do not embarrass people with trendy, sassy words such as "Duh!" or "Hello" when they say something stupid.

With increased awareness, we are able to catch ourselves before we slip into negativity. Try to monitor your facial expressions better to make sure your face is congruent with what you are saying. Do not speak too loudly, too softly, too fast, or too slow. Never gloat about having a more fortunate life than someone else has.

When you best someone in a business or a social situation, always leave room for face-saving. Obviously people need to steer away from negative situations that are potentially stressful and bad for their health with no socially redeeming benefits.

Incongruent behavior contradicts our true intentions. Do not tell people that you intend to be upright, straightforward, and accessible, and then act sneaky, cagey, and suspicious. Often, behaving badly is nothing more than a bad habit, which people can change.

With proper awareness and concentration, people can reduce or eliminate obvious inconsistencies in their behavior and at the same time, strengthen the positive attributes of their behavior that have meaning or value that bears upon the conduct of life.

Aggression

Aggression comes to the forefront of news in times of war, and seems to be clear-cut, but what is it in terms of everyday life? Aggression is a general term used for a wide variety of acts involving the tendency to be hostile, self-assertive, and dominating. No one explanation fully unravels aggression, since it is the result of anger, frustration, inability to meet goals, the desire to fight or take flight, genetics, biochemistry, and learned behavior to name a few things. Usually, aggression is the manifestation of people's desire to push their interests at the expense of others, which invariably causes problems.

> Emotional problems are "internalized" and behavioral problems are "acted out".

Aggressive behavior is the subject of intense interest and considerable study, because no one knows for sure if it is inherently a part of our nature or if it is something we learn from observation of others. Often what goes around comes around. People's upbringing is a strong influence on how they treat others.

Some experts believe that children learn aggression from the observation of destructive behavioral patterns exhibited by their parents. Bullies typically project the emotional violence done to them onto others.

Destructive behavioral patterns emanate from a wide range of things such as over-parenting, fights between unhappily married couples, substance abuse, unrealistic expectations, and disenchantment with parental roles. In fact, there are a host of other things too numerous to list. That being the case, it is worthwhile to look at some popular theories.

Sigmund Freud theorized that all human beings have a primitive subconscious drive to be aggressive, but other eminent psychologists such as Adler regard aggression as a display of the will to power in the struggle against inferiority. Since aggressiveness is commonplace in the human and lower animal kingdom, I believe a good argument is that aggression is rooted in the primordial origins of existence, and due to adaptive biology, it is a part of the subconscious self.

Some people today, even though they consciously know better, are overly aggressive due to their instinct for self-preservation. The popular consensus, on the other hand, is that people learn aggressive behavior and its symptomatic body language. Learned behavior recurs when it is rewarded. In addition, hormone levels play a role.

I believe that aggression is a trait that derives from both our nature and our nurture. For one thing, we are able to teach people to be less aggressive. For another thing, not all aggression is inherently bad. A mother protecting her young is not a bad thing, and good intentions are an important extenuating circumstance in many instances of aggressive behavior.

Inasmuch as people are not aggressive all the time, body language clues offer valuable guidance about how and when people act aggressively. For example, people with an attitude are much more likely to be aggressive, violent, and substance abusers. It is unlikely that they are invading aliens trying to get inside us. On the other hand, some people show signs of being anti-social at times, but at other times, they are merely high strung and fussy, and on occasion, they become aggressive as a defensive tactic to protect themselves.

> In violence, we forget who we are.
> Mary McCarthy

The most common sign of aggression is the "readiness" gesture. The forward moving chin out and hands-on-hips pose of children and adults signals a readiness for action. It makes people seem larger and is more threatening if the aggressor unbuttons his coat, places his feet evenly apart, and clenches his fist. Other reliable signs of someone on the verge of becoming aggressive are a bulging red face, arms and hands up or crossed over the chest, finger pointing, tenseness, closed jaw, pinpoint pupils, and tight lips.

Sometimes, the faces of drug addicts have preternatural wrinkles, which add to their gaunt look. At other times, the face of aggression will have a hard, frozen look, coupled with a stiff body, and arms stiffly extended as an aggressor approaches ready to block any escape. Watch out if someone is visibly shaking, frequently repeating himself, and laughing when nothing is funny. If someone intentionally invades your space and sticks out their face or jaw daringly, retreat is your order of the moment.

Does biology play any role in aggression? Psycho-biologists say it does, although this claim is not conclusive. For the record, however, they theorize violence and aggression are the results of chemical imbalances from unusually high or low levels of blood sugar and certain other chemicals they have identified. Genetics could also play a role.

Tests have shown that the two chemicals involving aggression are high levels of testosterone and an adrenal hormone, cortisone, the "fight or flight" chemical. The release of body chemicals produces a state of excitement and arousal that amplify aggressive tendencies. It is a proven fact that people, who engage in exercise, vigorous work, or something similar, experience the heartbeat and respiration rate increases of an arousal state.

When people are in an arousal state, and are imprinting or fixated upon someone else, they are exhibiting early stage aggressive behavior. Even sexual arousal and high temperatures on a hot day have an effect on aggressive behavior.

Torrid temperatures are only half of what we feel as heat. Humidity and sweat also push us into the swelter zone; therefore, avoid passionate causes on hot and humid days. In the old days, jury trials recessed during the hot summer months for good reason.

Most teenagers spend their time discussing their latest crush, playing video games, studying, and learning how to drive. However, a worrisome form of defensive aggression occurs when teenagers wear all black and claim they are something akin to people from the netherworld while staying in their rooms listening to alternative music and surfing the internet.

Defensive aggression, according to many social cognitive psychologists, is a result of adolescents trying to come to terms with who they are while modeling their behavior from others they see and read about.

Experts posit that skinheads with their black boots, close-cropped hair, and special argot are exhibiting things learned from the aggression of others. Tattoos are visible covenants between individual members of larger groups. Perhaps, the key to understanding alternative lifestyles is recognizing that life is full of irreconcilable antagonisms, and some people are fascinated with the danger in it.

> Aggression is just another word for low self-restraint.

At any rate, even though not firmly established, many embattled parents think that at least some of the violence they see in their kids comes from the violent body language in video games, movies, television, and even comic books.

In our messy macro world, does viewing violent body language in the media lead impressionable people to believe aggression is socially acceptable? Are the images and themes of many movies, televised wrestling matches, gladiator games, reality shows, and even some popular sports shows the wrong ones?

To a degree, I believe repeated exposure to violent body language in the media reduces our normal inhibitions against behaving aggressively and desensitizes us to violence. For example, violent behavior on the movie screen teaches some susceptible people the kinetics of violent and aggressive body language. Whether or not this is true, it appears to be a good idea to monitor the behavior of impressionable people who seem to dress inappropriately, pride themselves in sinister body language behavior, over focus on media violence, and play violent, hyper-reality games for entertainment.

Apparently, the ideal of grace under pressure that Ernest Hemingway wrote about in the twentieth century has been replaced in the twenty-first century by nonspecific stupidity and conduct disorders that erupt under the slightest pressure of even the smallest minor events such as trying to park or driving in traffic.

Another theory cast in the same mold as the "aggression is learned" school of thought, is the notion that aggression is rewarding to the aggressor. A popular movie star likes to tell the story about the time he became angry with his director and knocked him out cold. He had to pay the director a large sum of money to settle a potential lawsuit, but afterwards the actor commented wryly, "It was worth every penny of it!"

Aggressive behavior is one of the ways to get satisfaction. In any event, when an angry, nervous, or finicky individual with an "attitude" displays his intent to satisfy a grudge, or even the score, the time has come to depart.

Aggressive behavior is rewarding if it reduces frustration. For example, we are frustrated if we cannot live up to our ego ideals; consequently, we either become angry with ourselves or displace our anger onto someone else by making accusations against them. A blamer always leaves himself out as a possible cause of a problem and goes straight for his target. Thus, anger displacement, acts of revenge, and blaming others all fall under the heading of "neurotic aggression".

Social provocation occurs when people think meeting aggression with aggression is all right as exemplified by the "hurt me and I'll hurt you" syndrome. Road rage occurs when we feel aggressive drivers have compromised our safety or time; however, responding is as dangerous as saturated animal fats. We are better off ignoring obscene gestures, tailgating, and harrowing road rage situations in the heat of the moment, and reporting them later when safe to do so.

How do we defeat aggression against us? To begin with, we need to recognize not only the causes, but also the psychodynamics of aggressive behavior in order to counteract it. As I said, before aggression occurs there will be certain "cues". Aggressive cues are stimuli we have learned to associate with aggression. For example, the sight of a weapon is an aggression cue, especially if it's a gun pointed right at you.

Research reveals people become much more aggressive after viewing a gun, even if it is unloaded and sitting on a shelf. A person carrying a knife is obviously aggressive, but if he holds it down trying to conceal it instead of brandishing it higher up on the vertical plane, where it is more visible, it is a dangerously aggressive cue.

We are in a bad patch when someone crouches down with feet firmly planted as we approach, or when a goal-directed person intentionally moves into our personal space. Both situations require great caution until we are able to move away.

If we know an aggressor well enough, then reinforcing good behavior, and punishing bad behavior helps because it takes out the reward component. Moral admonitions are not terribly effective, but sometimes we are able to use value clarification as a procedure with potential aggressors to encourage them to examine their actions.

Age-old wisdom about safety in numbers and forming friendships and alliances that are publicly visible to potential aggressors still has value and diminishes aggression against us. For example, a way to deal with aggressive co-workers is to recruit the help of fellow employees in a coalition to present a united front.

In order to hold a coalition together, however, it is advisable to offer to cooperate with each other in other ways as well. From the strategic point of view, helping co-workers with undesirable workplace chores promotes solidarity and reduces the desire of others for social dominance.

Practical Pointers

Everyone has distinctly negative moments and learned aggression seems to be increasing in today's society. Until people learn how to manage frustration and conduct disorders, the best defenses are recognizing negative clues and learning how to deal with them. Road rage is becoming a major problem, and neutral events like accidentally bumping into someone are hostile acts.

Some people are able to control much of their negativity, but that does not make them innocent. The best social policy is the use of manners and accepting responsibility for our actions instead of adding fuel to the fire.

Chapter 41

Mean Streets

"The face of evil is pretty ordinary."

Criminals, social misfits, degenerates, and violent types inhabit America with little or no outstanding commonality between them. Although criminals share some traits with each other, no one has been able to place all of the scorpions in one bottle. The reason is that violent people are ordinary looking people who are deceivers, pretenders, and manipulators by trade.

> The cardinal rule of the hustler is never stay in one place long.

Our task is to concretize disassociated criminal behavior, but since the most abhorrent terrorists, criminals, and other malefactors effortlessly blend into the crowd, keep few friends, and are careful to make no conspicuous mistakes, they are difficult to spot. That is why the knowledge of body language is an invaluable resource tool to help keep people safe from bad people.

Strip the thin veneer of civilization away and humans are capable of anything, which was evident after Hurricane Katrina. The social psychologists, Abraham Maslow and Carl Rogers, claim that people are not born inherently bad, but when fundamental needs are not fulfilled they will lie, cheat, steal, and kill before their victims have a chance to say "oops". According to this viewpoint, the pathology of evil stems from the thwarting of basic needs and not the natural state of humankind.

However, it is hard to tell if this theory is talking about morality or efficiency.

This theory is plausible to a fair extent, but it does not always fit some wanton killers and criminals who do not seem to have any apparent reason or discernible "need" to commit the crimes they do, Criminals are not ideologues, but opportunists who figure on gaining more than they have to lose. Most of the original causes for their behavior are left unresolved, and continue as long as no one catches the perpetrators.

Violent behavior rarely is the result of a single cause. Instead, criminality is rooted in an interrelated maze of complex factors such as biological anomalies, gender, genetics, environment, childhood upbringing, and experience, all of which severely hinders our systems of law enforcement and justice.

Abnormalities in the brain can lower the emotional controls that inhibit violent impulses. Other deficiencies are a low frustration threshold, poor socialization, and lack of compassion. Ironically, the cold, calculating criminals, terrorists, violent religious fanatics, and psychopaths

> One of the best places to hide is in the open.

that do bother to think their actions through apparently have normal brain patterns and body language even though they don't "roll that way".

No theory of criminality is absolute and effective in stopping crime much because of the confusion of concept with reality. The logic of law enforcement and our legal system hinges on casuistry and reason, but the reality is that the police and victims are not given time for a dispassionate analysis of a potential criminal's needs or other behavioral causes. This is why body language is so important, because it enables us to recognize giveaway clues in the early stages of criminal behavior.

The Invisible Underworld

Do all criminals have a certain look? Do they have menacing tattoos, earrings, and special clothes featuring gang colors? Does immorality and corruption mark people with any unique traits? Unfortunately, the answer is no. The worst criminals look uninspired and unspectacular with no physically unique characteristics in common. Sometimes villains have a touch of cruelty in their faces that shows up as lines around their mouth, but they are typically invisible.

The Rodney King trial illustrates the principal of "who do you fear the most". The police do not know who criminals are unless they happen to be in the national crime database. Historical attempts to stereotype crimes by facial types, cranium sizes, and so forth have all failed, and so law enforcement have developed behavioral profiles of who they fear the most, and Rodney King fit.

On the other hand, most black jurors fear the police, so it would seem that both have a bias, which is human nature. In addition, as much as society wishes it could recognize potentially lethal citizens, criminality is ambiguous because evil people sometimes do good things and good people do evil things.

Knowledge of body language is so important because evil does not have a special face and does not come at us as anthropomorphic monsters from the nether world like in a movie or childhood fantasy. In short, the most despicable criminals in the history of humankind have been ordinary looking people of no particular note, which makes them all but invisible.

Violent killers do not spend all their time murdering people, and when they are buying groceries and doing the laundry, they have benign appearances, unremarkable personalities, and unexceptional body language expressions that are fundamentally nondescript.

All kinds of people in diverse environments behave badly at times. Competition for limited resources and peer pressure often cause people to have a lack of remorse, underdeveloped super egos, and skewed morals.

> Don't follow evil and it won't follow you.

People not only lie to others, but deceive themselves as well, so instead of comprehending their sinister weaknesses they see themselves as essential and special people just doing their thing; consequently, lurking unseen in the background of their everyday routine are feelings of self-importance and arrogance. The body language behavior of anti-social people broadcasts that they are independent of society and are insensitive to the problems of others.

When asked about her concern for the poor and the starving populace of 18th century France, *The Rose of Versailles*, Josefa Johanna Von Hapsburg Lorraine officially known as Maria Antonia-Archiduchesse d' Autriche or simply Marie Antoinette, Queen of France, allegedly said circa 1795, "Let 'em eat cake". She went to the guillotine.

Anti-social feelings can be a recipe for a distinctive kind of malevolence in some people when they are fashioned from a disjunctive intertwining of moral ambiguity, vanity, and feelings of being a victim themselves. For another example, a CIA profiler said on CNN that the body language of millionaire Osama Bin Laden on one of his self-absorbed videotapes was jovial with an Arabic "good old boy" demeanor. The way he used his hands revealed that he had an active role in the tape's discussion, which was particularly chilling because his body language showed no remorse or respect for all the lives lost because of him.

Symptomatic body language clues are mischievousness, cruelty, abuse of animals, and dysfunctional traits such as shiftiness, trickiness, and lechery. Some criminologist's say that the reason many Americans are easy marks is the lack of proper role models and modern heroes coupled with the tendency to confuse cruelty with strength. Consequently, naive people misconstrue cruel, sadistic body language as characteristics of a strong person, whereas most diabolical killers are actually weak, insecure, and pathetic persons unnoticed in everyday life.

Since it is almost impossible for law-abiding people to identify potential thieves, rapists, drug abusers, robbers, killers and other hardened criminals, the best de facto practice is to take sensible precautions.

It is not perfect advice, but do not live or play in high crime zones such as shopping districts, areas with high rates of poverty, and major transportation routes. Do not flirt with danger. Do not push the envelope of safety. Never go anywhere alone, and do not meet, pick up, or deal with strangers for any reason at any time, even if they ram your car or get in your house.

Above all, do not attract a criminal's attention. The trick is to direct their attention to something else besides you. Do not let strangers focus on you by eye contact, open body language, or any other means. Instead of looking like an easy target, endeavor to not draw a criminal's attention. Keep moving. If you are going to be a target, it is best to be a moving one. Try not to look weak or easy, and do not look like someone that fulfills a criminal's needs. Never let anyone dehumanize you, so do not voluntarily get into any closed container like the trunk of a car.

Abraham Lincoln said, "Eternal vigilance is the price of liberty." We must be vigilant and aware of our surroundings at all times in order to notice the clues of criminal behavior and govern our behavior accordingly. For example, one clue is the remorseless mistreatment of animals, which correlates with the mistreatment of human beings.

Isolation is a need-based clue strongly correlated with anti-social behavior. Domestic squabbles, shouting matches, and macho behavior with alcohol are all clues correlated with relationships in which people need to take out their anger on someone or something.

In many instances, thieves target expensive looking cars, jewelry, and electronics they see or find out about as they cruise streets and public areas such as parks, stores, and shopping centers. Roving gangs of predators and individual muggers are able to tell which people are the best targets by the way they look, move, and act.

Some criminals are able to identify the body language of people who have trouble in their lives and therefore make easy prey. For example people who walk slowly with their head down and shoulders slumped, while acting scared are vulnerable to becoming victims. Elderly people who are barely able to get around and people who look "nerdy", weak, dependant, and defenseless become targets because crooks prefer to take the path of least resistance and pick on easy marks.

Career criminals go for vulnerable people such as women, children, and visitors from out-of-town. People in these groups are weaker and easier to victimize, and in the case of tourists, are less likely to take the time to summon the police, much less be prosecution witnesses at a trial several months or years down the road.

It is counter-intuitive, but the more ordinary a crime is, the more difficult it is to catch the perpetrator. Average people do not want to think that criminals look like them, but the troubling truth is that lawbreakers are nondescript with average body language and ordinary reasons for much of their behavior. This is one reason clever trial lawyers are able to switch the cards and put the victims on trial instead of their clients. Their strategy takes the emphasis off the circumstantial evidence of their client's motivation, opportunity, and means, and places it on characterization of the victim as someone who was abusive and had it coming.

Pick a Con, Any Con

The con artist will spring from a large segment of the population that is composed of unsavory characters, misfits, and sociopaths who cannot make an honest living, but who usually fall short of the violent hard-core criminals and degenerates that infest our society.

Flimflam artists come from everywhere. However, they are typically people who prey on others by capitalizing on their own glibness, lack of remorse, overreaching bravado, and ability to stay highly mobile.

Diabolical bunco artists will affect body language that appears to be polite, helpful, and sharing by offering to pass on some good fortune to victims under the guise of mutual benefit, but in reality victims get nothing of value, or something other than what they thought.

For their cunning schemes, con artists seek out lonely, isolated, and susceptible people whom they privately refer to as "greed heads". Such people are the victims of their own greed even when they know better

> The big print giveth, and the small print taketh way.

than to participate in such things as illegal chain letters and pyramid marketing schemes. People who fancy themselves smarter than they really are become the easiest victims.

Shameless disclaimers, small print, and phony warranties cost consumers millions every year, and there are thousands of "bait and switch" con games to take people's money. In creative adherence schemes, complacent victims do not lose all their money, but unwittingly obligate themselves to buy an inferior product or service at inflated prices way above fair market value, and the only way out is an overpriced "re-stocking fee" or stiff penalty. In these schemes, the big print "giveth" and the small print "taketh" away, so read the entire contractual agreement.

Friendly Persuasion

The fundamental techniques of persuasion are well-known legitimate selling methods that have been around for a long time. They are not dishonest or illegal unless used in bad faith by dishonest people. The four best-known techniques are as follows, in pertinent part:

1. *Foot-in-the-door:* This technique involves asking someone to agree to a small request first, then to a larger one later on. Agreeing to the first request makes it harder to resist the second one.

2. *Door-in-the-face:* The opposite of foot-in-the-door; this technique begins with a large request no one expects to be accepted followed by a smaller harder to turn down request.

3. *Low-balling:* This technique involves getting someone to agree to commitment first then adding disagreeable specifics later.

4. *Freebies:* In order to sell one thing, the seller includes something else "free of charge". The value-added package is in reality worth little or no more than the cost of the primary product.

> If it sounds too good to be true, it probably is.

Dishonesty is difficult to detect in an experienced con artist because they will have practiced enough to be good at what they do; they will be able to mask their true intentions by seeming to be perfectly normal, and they never stay in one place long. Besides, it does not take much talent to lie and deceive.

Certain gestures are dead give-a-ways when people act suspiciously, secretively, or dishonestly. For instance, superficial smiles are secretive attempts to hide true feelings. Touching the nose, covering the mouth, and peering over half rim glasses are suspicious sales gestures.

Be wary of rapid speech, exaggerations, big returns for small investments, and the "hot box" treatment. Pass up transactions you have to hurry into, as when a salesperson tells you, "This offer is only good for today", or when a Wall Street liftman masquerading as your friendly broker tells you, "You better buy now" and "This investment is good for the long term." Cut the deck a little bit deeper when dealing with these people, and ask what is the exit strategy and when.

As said before, the elderly are targets of choice because they are more likely to have money saved, and are less likely to take any punitive action. Home improvement, household goods, and car sales were the top three biggest consumer complaints in 2001.

In a fraudulent home repair scam, a con man seduces an older homeowner into repairing a roof, foundation, siding, or other problems for an exaggerated cost when repairs are not necessary. Sometimes the repairs are made and sometimes not. Victims who deposit good faith money with a shady contractor for so-called "building materials" never see him again, while at other times victims pay a diamond price for zircons.

Watch out for strangers, unknown contractors, and questionable characters who claim you need to do what they are proposing because it will help make the neighborhood better or solve a problem you do not see.

Typically, con artists will work a circuit of several states by driving around certain chosen areas and knocking on doors. People need to be leery of anyone they do not know who knocks on their doors offering home repair, tree trimming, and so forth.

Swindlers and grifters will peruse the "For Sale" ads in the local newspaper and pretend to be potential buyers. Do not meet any stranger at your home by yourself. If you must sell something, use a public location and take someone with you. Unaccompanied females should never agree to meet someone they do not know, anytime, anywhere.

Most con artists have a criminal record, and although they do not mention this salient fact voluntarily, they rarely have a sense of community and connectedness. Thus, the best practice is to ask for references from reliable people in your community before committing to anything.

Terrorists

Terrorism is not new, but the threat of terrorism at levels higher than ever before is new to Americans, so we had better prepare ourselves. To this end, the FBI recently added the study of body language to the training of their new agents, which is the first major change in its training program in over fifty years.

Terrorism is the unabashed weapon of fear. It involves the use of extreme violence in surgical strikes against particular targets by small groups of religious, political, and nationalistic fanatics to gain publicity for their cause.

It sounds loopy, but terrorists uniformly believe their cause is just and moral for social, political, or religious reasons. They know extraordinary violence spreads their message because most media coverage indulges the public's appetite for sensationalism, thus terrorist groups are quick to claim responsibility for violent acts to get their message out. This is a kind of psychological warfare waged through the media.

Although most of the world views terrorists as cowards, fanatics, and maladapted miscreants operating on the fringes of civilized society, the terrorists see themselves as martyrs and heroes. They have been socialized to terror from childhood and want to achieve a collective identity in their social group.

Dr. Jerrold Post analyzes terrorism in his book about the minds of terrorists. He asserts that normality is the most common characteristic of terrorists. He believes that they are psychologically normal and are not depressed or emotionally disturbed. Those types are screened out, he says.

Terrorists always have mentors or backers that they want to impress because their mentors have brainwashed them with narratives of divine ascent, a sense of heroism, and the necessity to increase or maintain their group's self-esteem. As long as an act of terrorism provides small groups and individuals with minimal resources a means to get their message heard, terrorism will continue.

What does a terrorist look like? Since terrorists come from many different countries and cultural backgrounds, it is impossible to identify them from their race, national origin, or beliefs. Because racial and religious stereotyping are unconstitutional, we must study cultural intelligence, the techniques of behavioral profiling, scientific criminology, and other useful social science tools.

Since terrorists are a moving target, it is a good idea to get a look at the playing field. Terrorists dress casually in conservative clothes that do not attract attention. They remain anonymous by blending into the crowd. They may be discontented American citizens or German nationals like the Bader- Meinhoff gang, but most likely terrorists will have connections to those countries ex-President Bush called the "Axis of evil".

Most terrorists will speak poor English, using foreign idioms. They will keep cultural icons of the countries they identify with, and in private, they will behave pursuant to the cultural mannerisms of the countries where they were born.

They are most likely young men or women, who tend to be political, unmarried, and have few family responsibilities. Trained to be unassuming, they will stay within small independent "cells", so if one cell ceases to exist another will take its place. Although I am no authority, I have read that in certain parts of the Middle East so-called "Shaheeds" are terrorist heroes, and those linked to "Abu Nidell" are the most violent.

Terrorists have little respect for life and property, so their body language will not be that of timid innocence, but brash boldness and risk taking. Most terrorists will be technically competent and will follow established procedures. All except the leaders and financiers will come from a working class background, living and thinking in terms of the short haul, with the ability to tolerate "all or nothing" outcomes.

Terrorist cells will be in working-class neighborhoods, apartments, and no-frills tract housing. Members will eat and drink together, network on the internet, and watch team sports. Most of them will be shiftless. They will spend long hours burning daylight and eating pizza until they are ready to do their dirty work.

The recently established Office of Homeland Security is busy working on new security measures for our protection. What other options are available? People should choose carefully where they live, work, and spend their leisure time.

Next, people should set up small, safe territories that avoid sites of high population density. Playing it safe is better than ending up a hapless victim. Acquiring knowledge of body language will help people to identify potential criminals and terrorists up front, and thereby reduce their vulnerability. It is not enough that certain people look like terrorists. There is much to say about things that do not feel right, that get under our skin, or that get on our nerves.

Practical Pointers

A hard to understand but well-known component of bad behavior, is the mindless ecstasy that accompanies it. It is a natural inexplicable euphoria that some of history's super bad people have spoken of. In one form or another, it resembles the attraction of a huge fire.

Criminals try to blend into the crowd, which makes them hard to spot. Nevertheless, anyone can augment their information-gathering and decision-making skills by practicing selective exposure, people reading techniques, evaluation methods, and social awareness.

Clues that are hard to hide are the body language, attire, and use of space, of potential criminals, which speaks volumes about who they are, what they do in life, and what kind of personality they have. Acquiring these skills can help people get through the dangerous and precarious situations that confront them in daily life.

Chapter 42

Autocratic Behavior

"My way or the highway."

Egotists, authoritarians, and tyrants are three types of autocrat that are moving forces in the world opposite of altruism. Autocratic behavior is plain while altruism is mysterious. It is the irreconcilable antagonisms between them that make life unpleasant, enigmatic, and dangerous, yet full of hope. Viewed in terms of social psychology, it is all about the degree of control one has over others. Social control ranges from simple, casual relationships to the degree to which a person can compel another to act against his will. *Formal* authority carries with it "legal" power, but *social* authority is the degree to which a person can dispense rewards and punishments, and resist the control of others at the same time.

> "Power" is the fundamental concept of social science.
> Bertrand Russell

Controlling behavior such as rigid adherence to conventional values and severe punishment for deviation is the common denominator, but each type has unique body language characteristics. Not all of the causes of controlling behavior are manageable here, but in the cognitive sense, self-interest predominates.

Social power is the power to shape and control the behavior of others. It is not inherently bad in all situations. For example, the political world is the most obvious use of social power. but when it overrides all other concerns, it is a bad thing.

Since the first maxim of some people's controlling behavior is "Me first, everyone else next", I believe it serves a beneficial purpose to mention the most typical body language behavior of the three most common types of controlling personalities that readers will undoubtedly encounter in their lives.

Egotists

Cognitively, egotists have an overblown opinion of themselves. In order to safeguard their self-esteem they will undervalue the achievements of others while overvaluing their own. This is evident in aggressive social behavior like gossip, intolerance, and prejudice against outsiders who are not good enough for them. The foremost intention behind every act of egopathy is to belittle others so that the egomaniac, by comparison, looks better.

Ego food is the taste of fame and attaining all of the material emblems of the so-called good-life. Wallowing in self-absorption, some folks like to wear expensive clothing, buy fancy houses, and drive luxury cars. They are narcissistic with little sensitivity for other people. If things are not right for them, their ego safeguarding tendencies kick in and they will find many excuses.

Monomania begins as a naïve manifestation of an abstract childhood fantasy that results in susceptible people believing they are the center of the universe and that the world revolves around them. By carrying such an attitude into adulthood, egomaniacs become very immature with self-interest becoming the basis of all their behavior and projects in life, often leading to quixotic perfectionism such as extreme "clean vocabulary" rules.

Egoverts are self-centered and constantly striving for personal power and insouciant superiority over others instead of paying heed to the higher social interest of what is good for humankind. Their body language behavior manifests the notion that self-interest is the only proper concern. They routinely reject the notion that others may have any opposing value. In fact, many experts think the one outstanding factor underlying ego maladjustment is an underdeveloped social interest, which makes it easier for others to be "dehumanized".

Naturally, everyone strives for various levels of achievement such as a college diploma, individual perfection in some field, financial security, or local fame. The recognition of success is compensation for the occasional feelings of inferiority and weakness that normal people have from time to time.

Egotists, however, act out their lives with a body language of wacky superiority and fatuous justifications for what they do that is consistent with their idealized self no matter how overblown it is. For example, egomaniacs will constantly brag about their accomplishments whether real or imaginary. Typically, they will fill their external reality with the best cars and material things they can get their hands on. There is an amusing saying amongst lawyers that one can tell the size of a lawyer's ego by the size of his car and the cost of his briefcase. Folklore like this, however, applies to several professions where self-indulgent accessories are the norm.

Ego Defenses

Selfhood is so important that we have to defend it at all times. It is the part of us in contact with external reality, which can be severely harsh at times. As a result, we have developed personal strategies that protect us from embarrassing and discomforting anxiety, conflict, and shame. For some, the strategy is to deal with personal problems by taking modern anxiety and anti-depression drugs like beta-blockers and serotonin reuptake inhibitors that change brain chemistry in helpful ways.

> Avoiding "discomfort" is a national pastime.

Modern pharmacology helps reduce performance nightmares, while other non-drug approaches involve learning and using strategies that deal directly with the problem itself instead of the source. Some well-known personal strategies that protect the ego are the so-called *defense mechanisms*. A complete discussion of this area of psychology is beyond the scope of this book, however. For an admittedly oversimplified sample list of typical defense mechanisms, see Appendix "C".

How do self-centered people handle harsh criticism, for example? Most will not suffer along in hurt silence, but will erect a defensive palisade. For example, they will engage defensive, closed-off body language. Reacting defensively is not a cure but protects the ego, the "Self", from potential psychic harm. At one time or another, all of us will use some form of defensive mechanism to deal with ugly realities.

Some typical ego defenses involve the use of characteristic body language, which if consistent over time take on the dimensions of a strategy to protect the ego. For example, simple regression may be little more than the use of infantile props and child-like behavior, but over time it causes relentless immaturity on a pathological level. How often do you tell someone to "grow up?"

Egomaniacs are ubiquitous today and are easy to recognize; therefore, the best practice is to avoid them. For one reason, their personality is undesirable and something you do not want to mirror and match. Dozens of defense mechanisms also are less than wonderful in the long run. Some are normal ego protection, but are counterproductive over the long run. Trying to prevent forbidden impulses from coming out is a daunting task, because they get through in the form of "slips" and "forgetting".

Authoritarians

The authoritarian personality is a good example of the central trait approach to behavior. Studies about

> Authority is more like a club than a sharp knife.

strong willed people in power abound, and on a smaller scale, we have all known one or two authoritarians with their rigid body language, controlling attitudes, and driving need for supremacy over others. I have met a few authoritarians in the courtroom, such as tough prosecutors and judges.

Authoritarian leaders are in the military because there is no requirement that they consult with other members of the group in decision-making. Sympathy appeals do not work on them, and they will apply the rules and law rigorously. The body language and principal attributes of authoritarians that stand out are the following:

1. *Toughness*: Authoritarians are hard, stubborn people who savor power and domination over others. They maintain a hostile and cynical outlook towards people and things that they have convinced themselves are inferior and of no value. They are very critical of everyone else, and find little good in people. They like power over others so much that they automatically try to control everyone around them by exuding a tough exterior. They are tenacious in their activities and seldom demonstrate flexibility.

2. *Destructiveness*: They believe the only way to succeed is to destroy their opposition. Callous in their regard for others, they try to break people. They have a dominating speaking style even to the point of banging and throwing things.

3. *Conventionalism*: They are closed-minded with conventional attitudes and mainstream values. They do not think in the abstract, instead, they are unthinking and inflexible.

4. *Submissive*: They unapologetically submit to higher authority as well as advocate aggressive punishment for the non-obedient. They will demonstrate their respect for authority and obedience by often saying, yes sir, and will tend to divide people into in-groups and out-groups.

5. *Aggressiveness*: Sometimes they become violent with a razor-thin temper. They value stern discipline and will punish those who do not go along with them.

6. *Anti-introspectiveness*: Unquestioning of themselves, they question the motives of others instead. Cynicism and suspicion are hallmarks of their character. They glorify their toughness and deny any tenderness.

7. *Superstitious*: Superstitious and fatalistic they are prone to stereo-typing and prejudicial behavior with a belief in supernatural authority.

They adopt strict patterns of behavior and are prone to unyielding measures that leads them to a kind of fatalism.

8. *Projective:* They project their own faults onto others around them. Curiously, they see others doing what they have told themselves they would never do.

9. *Repressive:* Since many authoritarians are sexually repressed, they tend to displace their repressed impulses onto those around them, which lead to unreal fixations on the sexual idiosyncrasies of others.

10. *Dogmatic:* Authoritarians are not receptive to the way other people do things. Their body language is unvaried because they are hard-liners with rigid beliefs and closed minds. To them, status relationships are more important than individual rights.

Authoritarians often are the product of a parental style that is bossy, over-controlling, dominating, highly judgmental, and characterized by a kind of conditional love that siblings must earn. By adulthood, many authoritarians will become neat-as-a-pin perfectionists due to their strong need for love and recognition. Living up to the demands of authoritarians is almost impossible since they are hard to please and need to keep others on the defensive. They are more about competition, power, and micro-management than values. There are several types of authority, to wit: traditional authority, legal authority, expert authority, and a few others. The authoritarian personality also includes persons who seek obedience and acceptance of authority, and not just the people in authority.

Tyrants

Tyrants are nothing new. They have been around as long as humankind has. The quintessential twenty-first century tyrant, Saddam Hussein, now deceased, dressed and looked like a thug and mafia boss. He not only ruled Iraq ruthlessly, but also constantly threatened his neighbors. Naturally, he was the source of great unease and worry for many people. The same is true of other tyrants since the beginning of written history.

In Greek mythology, for example, Procrustes was an ancient gangster who grabbed hapless travelers and placed them on a bed. If their legs were too long for the bed, he cut them off; if they were too short, he stretched them out to fit the bed. He thereby forced everyone who came into his clutches to conform to his desires. Procrustes symbolizes the tyranny of someone who only tolerates the behavior and opinions of others after they meet his own standards.

The elusive terrorist, Osama Bin Laden, is the cause of grave distress among freedom-loving people worldwide because of his control over terrorist cells and his maniacal hatred for Western culture. His body language on TV is easy to read because he usually has a gun in his hand. Since not all tyrants and bosses are so obviously violent, however, and exist in all levels of society, it is a good idea to learn something about their body language.

Tyrants at home, at work, or in government are the result of a high-handed attitude that everyone needs to be obedient to some authority. The manifestation of such an attitude is so common that it is almost generic, and includes both the person in authority and the person who is subservient. Both persons cling to the weighty power of authority that dominates their entire lives.

Since World War II, literature is abundant about people who wielded great power. On a smaller personal scale, almost everyone has encountered a tyrant or two, because all people are passengers on the cosmic train, and tyrants attempt to control everyone around them by exuding a menacing exterior complete with threatening and demonstrative behavior such as banging and throwing things.

Tyrants also maintain a hostile and cynical outlook toward people and things they believe to be inferior and of no literal value. Briefly, they are hypercritical, strict, and oppressive toward people they meet.

Tyrannical people of both sexes tend to project their own repressed impulses to others around them, because they see others doing what they think no one else should do, which causes them to have an almost unreal concern with the behavior of out groups. As a result, tyrants are often jealous of others for no good reason.

Domineering types project the body language of confidence and an unquestioning belief in themselves that almost amounts to a swagger. On the other side of coin, they are suspicions of others, and maintain a closed-mind that is inaccessible to anything but their own conventional, unimaginative, and inflexible ideas. Socially, they demand blind obedience while status relationships are primary, and individual rights are lower on the totem pole.

The most evident aspect of a controlling personality is the outright manifestation of groundless stereotyping and quirky prejudicial behavior with a low tolerance for "do-gooders". Tyrants view with equanimity the fact that fear carries more weight than love.

Practical Pointers

Authoritarians and tyrants are controlling people who feel that power and dominance are the central dimensions of interpersonal relationships. They are not shy and are easy to spot. Many have learned their behavior from their parents, and unfortunately, the cycle repeats itself.

The danger for egotists is getting so involved with themselves that they fall into solipsism like Ernest Hemmingway, and end up like he did, because they also developed an exaggerated self-identity that their ego could not handle. Kurt Vonnegut wrote in *Mother Night* that we are what we pretend to be; consequently, people must be careful about what they pretend to be. Hemingway was depressed about losing everything in the Cuban revolution, but mainly he had lost his ability to write.

Chapter 43

Bipolar Disorders

"At times we are not who we think we are."

B ipolar disorder is a term we hear and read a lot about today. A few years ago, this affliction was unknown, but currently there are more than two million American adults that have this disorder. Striking shifts in mood, energy, and ability to function properly afflict these unfortunate people and results in such things as reality challenged views, surreal motivation, paranoid projections, and highly erratic up and down behavior.

Mature people have ups and downs, which is normal unless they develop more severe symptoms later on. Today, however, the symptoms of bipolar disorder are showing up in children at an alarming rate. Onset usually comes in the late teens, but increasingly it shows up in childhood.

No longer the almost exclusive province of hapless adults such as the over achievers whose moods run high and low, or the successful professional with a terrible drinking problem, bipolar disorder is not selective. Not surprisingly, studies show that the illness affects children and teenagers in different ways than adults. Their biphasic symptoms last longer and they go back and forth between hyperactivity and lethargy more quickly.

Researchers believe that bipolar disorder is due to a chemical imbalance in the brain. Genetics may also play a role, so if you have a close relative with bipolar disorder, or severe depression, it increases your chances of becoming bipolar.

The three common forms of bipolar disorder are Bipolar-I, Bipolar-II, and Cyclothymia, which cover different parts of the mood scale. Adults go through mood swings over several weeks or months alternating between manic highs and periods of great enthusiasm and activity to rock bottom lows. Their body language is impulsive and aggressive when manic with increased energy and unrealistic beliefs in themselves. Clues are excessive spending, talkativeness, overconfidence, and little inhibition. When depressed, their body language is slow and sluggish with no snap due to extreme pessimism, apathy, and low self-confidence.

Children are different and jump back and forth between mood states several times a day. They wake up sullen and cranky, but by afternoon, they resist any effort to settle them down. They throw a loud fit if they do not get their way. In general, autistic children are too fractious to do well in school.

Bipolar children crave attention, but are naive about life. They do not have an understanding of human frailties, and as a result, they are unmoved by appeals to emotion and sympathy.

Autism

Autistic people are exploding in numbers. Although there is no ready explanation, stress is one cause of the onset of the disorder. As many as 300,000 children and one million adults suffer from some autistic symptoms today. What is it and what are the signs of the so-called "nerd syndrome"?

Autism is the tendency to become unrealistically absorbed in oneself. When a person sees things in terms of fantasies and dreams instead of in terms of a reality shared by others, it becomes pathological. The problem develops when a person's internal state is not consistent with reality. For example, infantile autism is a pathological condition marked by social withdrawal, little interest in

> Self-absorption leads to autism.

others, communication problems, learning disabilities, and lack of focus.

In a less serious kind of autism, some people construct their own little world with a tendency toward internalizing their thoughts, feelings, and desires, but do not allow it to become pathological. As a point of fact, people have a right to be preoccupied with their fantasies and gain pleasure from them as long as they are not excessively divergent from the reality shared by their peers.

Autistic Clues

Infantile autism is a serious disorder. Milder forms are a disorder known as Asperger's syndrome. Signs of serious autism include a major loss of oral and nonverbal language skills, attention deficit disorder, complete indifference, scant eye contact, hypersensitivity, repetitive body movements, fixations, and temper tantrums. Due to genetics and anomalous brain activity, victims cannot process information normally.

Two of the biggest problems of children suffering from Asperger's syndrome are the inability to read social clues very well and form close relationships with others. They have difficulty controlling eccentric behavior and are subject to an indifferent attitude and obsessive focus on just one thing at a time. By age six or seven, children with Asperger's have trouble reading facial expressions and communicating through body language. They will also demonstrate awkward motor skills and repetitive, monotonous speech patterns.

Adult sufferers will be abnormally subjective, aloof, and self-centered with little empathy for others. Devoting themselves to working or intense hobbies, they will be introverts that forgo both friendships and family, except many of them will be devoted to their mothers. If married they will work long hours at the office instead of going home. They will not travel much and will be self-absorbed in personal hobbies and activities.

Practical Pointers

Mildly autistic persons have few interpersonal and social skills. Self-restraint and a sense of order and perfection dominate their behavior, which make them crazy when others do not follow suit. Mild cases are actually much more difficult to detect than serious cases due to the lack of clues.

The good news is that these disorders are treatable with maintenance medication and therapy since there is no real cure yet. The bad news is that most afflicted people do not wish to stay on maintenance pills for the rest of their life.

Chapter 44

What's In A Name

"Names can be heavy burdens to carry."

Names have a body language of their own in the sense that people sometimes behave in accordance with the meaning of their given name. Parents strive to give their babies impressive names with which to begin life. A striking name is a sort of lucky charm that stays with its owner until the end. It is a precious possession, a forerunner of fame, an entry into politics, a password to family, and an open sesame to society. Consider the moniker, J. Pierpont Morgan. Would he have been so illustrious a person in the public eye if he had gone by John P. Morgan?

Why does the Pope change his name upon confirmation to something that sounds better and more holy like Pope Pious XIII instead of Bill or Bob? Truthfully, the armor of a Godly name is helpful in the struggle against wickedness and sin.

A terribly bad name dampens the spirit like a wet blanket. Think about carrying around millstones like Ebenezer, Drusilla, and Elvira. Elmer, Gomer, and Henryetta make people think you are uneducated. Some names are old-fashioned like Patience and Fanny. Moss-grown names such as Eunice, Hanna, and Marcella are out of fashion and almost completely forgotten. Mabel and Inez seem domestic and plain.

Names such as Trevor Charrington-Symth and Carlos Gonzales

are clues to nationality, while names like Cletus, Otis, and Bobby Joe conjure up a rural, backwoods image.

Sobriquets are nicknames that serve us much like body language in that they characterize certain personality traits or indicate tendencies. They are remarkably accurate and functional. Nicknames proliferate in the world of professional sports, since you are nobody without one.

Sobriquets also indicate a person's social and economic status. A person may start out as a dignified Andrew III and end up as Bubba. A couple of creative nicknames from the past are "Vinegar Joe" Stillwell who was the general in charge of the Burma campaign in WW II, and "Refrigerator" Perry formerly of the NFL Chicago Bears. It is not a stretch to imagine the personality of General Stilwell or the physical size of Mr. Perry.

Practical Pointers

Wise mothers would do well to give unpromising infants grand names to act as an incentive to greater achievements and as antidotes against future ridicule, while infants with great promise should not have to wrestle with dumb names that tag them the rest of their lives.

Conclusion

We like to say that looks, money, and power don't mean much, because it is what is on the inside of people that counts. However, we get an entirely different message from the media and their peers. For example, popular reality TV shows such as the "survivor" shows and those of men and women tying to marry rich spouses are all about money and power.

Another TV show has a group of losers competing for the affections of some pretty girl in the midst of a few good-looking men brought in by the producers to give the typical losers some competition. Do looks matter that much, and why is Hollywood preoccupied with sex and violence? The answer is that dramatic hour-long artificialities dealing with the law, medicine, sex, money, power, and violence are what sell.

Life seems to be random because we never know what or when something unexpected will happen. However, for people who want good things to happen to them, then being in the right place at the right time is important. For bad things, the best defense is to be prepared with coping and reframing skills.

People do not have to be so " down" in their lives that they have to resort to ridiculous forms of phony media escapism for entertainment. Life does not have to be so bad or boring that people cannot survive without such things as explicit sex and gratuitous violence. The solution lies in more social awareness and contact with each other through both verbal and nonverbal communications.

Language in all its forms is synonymous with consciousness. It defines who we are and who we aspire to be. It defines our thoughts and feelings, and is truly the limits of our world as Wittgenstein observed.

However, the revealed purposes of human activity come from what people do and not what they say. Body language, in particular, is real and constitutes a major part of the human communications system. It is the language of emphasis and dramatically affects interpersonal relations.

Despite the hard work of hundreds of psychologists, psychiatrists, and social scientists, there is no single unified theory of behavior..Single clues and absolute formulas that determine how different people will behave in different situations are yet to emerge. On the other hand, body language that is widely used over a long period tends to be highly consistent, and is reliable enough to predict future behavior.

Meanwhile, experts in many fields continue the search for a unified theory of behavior, and more is yet to come. Although, the experts are still debating whether human behavior is the result of people's nature, nurture, or something else does not mean that body language has no credibility.

Do people carry too much emotional baggage for us to get inside their head? I do not think so. Scientists are gradually unraveling the entire human genome that will give us a genetic blueprint showing which genes are responsible for human behavior. At the same time, social cognitive researchers continue to learn more about the powerful effects of environment, and the effect that people have on each other.

For the time being, there are three excellent reasons why body language is credible and reliable. First, the *convergent validation* of multiple clues is a good way to deal with the realities of body language skills. If several pieces of quality information converge on a common conclusion on a consistent basis, then it is highly reliable.

Secondly, if two or more things are strongly related, then within reason we can use *correlation theory* to predict behavior. Thirdly, if the body language interpretations of others agree with your own conclusions, and they too predict future behavior, then they have *consensus validity*. These three reasons alone, although there may be more, are sufficient body language indicators in almost all cases.

Appendix "A"

Word Choices

"Cracking the code"

The words and phrases people choose in verbal communications have special meanings that are not apparent at face value, but have meaning for the hearer who codes them into meaningful form. Speakers are trying to convey something about themselves by their word choices as well as hard information. In my opinion this process falls into the body language category. Since word choices are highly context dependent and largely subjective, it follows that not everyone will give the same meaning to a particular word or phrase, especially out-groups. Unless people agree upon the meaning of code words and phrases, they will make no sense. The simplified examples that follow come from my experiences with people in a courtroom.

<u>Usage</u>	<u>Speaker really means</u>
1. I want to hear all	My mind is made up, but…
2. Yes, but…	I want to agree/I am not sure.
3. Ok, Ok	I get it/Whatever you say.
4. Right, right	Move on. I give up.
5. I agree with…	I am a follower.
6. Really	I did not know/Is that true?
7. Not, really	I am not sure/I do not want to say.
8. Handle	I think I can do it.
9. Want	I am object oriented.
10. See	I am a visual person.

11. Hear	I am an audio person.
12. Do	Just do it/Show me how.
13. Mature	He/she is very old.
14. Athletic	She has no figure.
15. Fun	It was less than wonderful.
16. Think	I am a thinking person.
17. Figure	I am a technical person.
18. Mean	What do you mean/ I am insulted.
19. Hurt	I am a feeling person.
20. Believe	I am not certain.
21. Comfortable	I am ok with that/Yes.
22. Position	I am not able to/No.
23. Maybe	No.

Appendix "B"

Occupational Clues

"We are what we do."

People who work in certain occupations develop a personality and corresponding body language that fits with the kind of work they perform. If they stay with a particular avocation, they adopt much of the dress, posture, lingo, and behavior for that line of work. In fact, people feel pressured to conform to the particular ways and means of doing things when the majority of persons in their occupation do it that way. Thus, it is possible to predict certain kinds of generalized body language behavior from a person's occupation, or on the other hand, the kind of occupation for which a particular person is suited. The following types of behavior loosely fit the following occupations:

Results Oriented	**Ritualistic With Rules**	**Independent**
Lawyers	Wedding planners	Artists
Surgeons	Accountants	Farmers
Producers	Nurses	Barbers
Advertisers	Banking	Truckers
Construction	Clergy	Cab drivers
Counselors	Government	Outside sales
Brokers	Judges	Solo attorneys
Managers	Law enforcement	Insurance
Chefs	Assemblers	Craftsmen

Team Results	**Immediate Results**	**Bookwork**
Union person	Firefighters	Teachers

Sports	Mechanics	Clerks
Real Estate Office	Cooks	Librarians
Army/Navy	Retailers	Researchers
Hospital workers	Contractors	Planners
Manufacturers	Security	Secretaries
Charities	Rescue services	Historians
Musicians	Pollsters	Statisticians
Policemen	Repair people	Auditors

Appendix "C"

Ego Defenses

"The best offense is a good defense"

People everywhere have personal strategies to protect themselves from embarrassing moments, discomforting anxiety, conflicts, rejections, and so on. These hypothesized strategies are defensive behavioral mechanisms that help people maintain social equilibrium, safeguard their egos, and help present themselves better. Ego defenses are largely nonverbal behavior, but can be verbal and partly nonverbal, so I will briefly mention a few illustrations in a lighthearted fashion that reflect the spirit of some of the best-known defense mechanisms:

Repression: "Mad, me, I don't know what you are talking about."
Bragging: "I can't get mad. I'm too good for that."
Gossip: "Did you hear somewhere that I was mad."
Humor: "I'm as mad as a hot bull in a pepper patch.
Ingratiation: "I'll do anything for you not to get mad at me."
Denial: "No way I'm mad. I've don't know what you mean."
Displacement: "I'm not mad at you. I'm mad at your family."
Exaggeration: "I never get mad. It takes a week to get me mad."
Intellectualization: "Yes, I'm mad, but that is normal at my age."
Isolation: "Stay away from me. I don't need to get mad."
Projection: "I'm not mad. You're the one that's mad."
Reaction Formation: "I'm not mad. I love you and want you."
Recrimination: "Don't accuse me of getting mad. What about you?"
Regression: "My binky keeps me from getting mad."
Repetition: "I'm not mad. I am never mad. I'm so not mad."

Reversal: "I'm not mad at you. You're mad at me!"
Sarcasm: "Yeah, right, like you never get mad."
Self-critical: "I get so mad at myself. I hate myself for it."
Sublimation: "I'm too busy working to get mad,"
Undoing: "I was mad, but I worked it off".
Volunteering: "I'd like to tell the world how mad I am."
Withdrawal: "I'm leaving and staying out of it."
Rationalization: "I'm mad, because it is the right thing to do".
Narcissist: "I'm not mad. I love myself to much for that."
Leveling: "Everybody calm down. Nobody is getting mad here."
Jealousy: "I wish I could be mad like you."
Selective exposure: "I'm not listening. I said I won't be mad."
Sour grapes: "It doesn't do any good to get mad at you."

Appendix "D"

Verbal "Tells"

"Statements that give us away"

Verbal "Tells" are indicative of what a person's attitude, feelings, and thoughts might be at a particular moment. The following "tells" are simplified for brevity, and should not be considered as conclusive.

General Statements	Indication
1. "I've been screwed from the git-go."	Self-pity.
2. "I'm no trouble to anyone."	Conformist.
3. "I've been setup."	Paranoia.
4. "I couldn't have done that?"	Embarrassment.
5. "I've heard that before."	Unwilling to reason.
6. "Who am I?"	Identity Problem.
7. "That's not a problem."	Denial of problem.
8. "I didn't know that."	Denial of information.
9. "There's no hurry."	Denial of urgency
10. " Someone is singing in the attic."	Hallucination.
11. "I'm outta control."	Impulsive.
12. "I'm learning to live with it."	Chronic pain.
13. "Look out."	On edge.
14. "I'm just going through the motions."	Insincere.
15. "There's never enough time."	Type A personality.
16. "That's not good enough."	Stickler for details.
17. "I just need three days."	Procrastinator.
18. "I just can't cope."	Non adaptable.
19. "I couldn't care less."	Depressed.
20. "What am I doing here?"	Disoriented

CPSIA information can be obtained at www.ICGtesting.com
Printed in the USA
BVOW032144101212

307840BV00001B/81/P